HAYNES  Honda

CIVIC

The definitive guide to **modifying**

by **Bob Jex** & **Em Willmott**

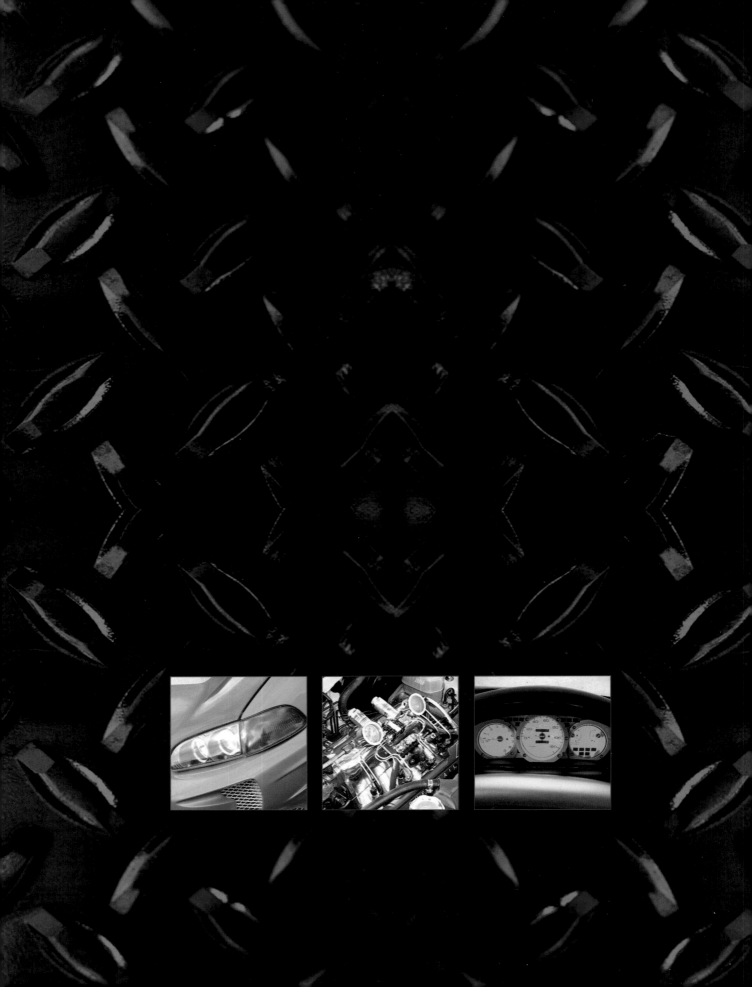

HAYNES MAX POWER Honda

CIVIC

The definitive guide to modifying
by Bob Jex & Em Willmott

Haynes Publishing

ISBN 1 84425 078 4

Printed by **J H Haynes & Co Ltd,**
Sparkford, Yeovil, Somerset BA22 7JJ, UK.

Tel: 01963 442030 Fax: 01963 440001
Int. tel: +44 1963 442030 Fax: +44 1963 440001
E-mail: sales@haynes.co.uk
Web site: www.haynes.co.uk

Haynes North America, Inc
861 Lawrence Drive, Newbury Park, California 91320, USA

Editions Haynes
4, Rue de l'Abreuvoir
92415 COURBEVOIE CEDEX, France

Haynes Publishing Nordiska AB
Box 1504, 751 45 UPPSALA, Sweden

It wasn't my idea guv'nor!

1 Advice on safety procedures and precautions is contained throughout this manual, and more specifically on page 178. You are strongly recommended to note these comments, and to pay close attention to any instructions that may be given by the parts supplier.

2 J H Haynes recommends that vehicle customisation should only be undertaken by individuals with experience of vehicle mechanics; if you are unsure as to how to go about the customisation, advice should be sought from a competent and experienced individual. Any queries regarding customisation should be addressed to the product manufacturer concerned, and not to J H Haynes, nor the vehicle manufacturer.

3 The instructions in this manual are followed at the risk of the reader who remains fully and solely responsible for the safety, roadworthiness and legality of his/her vehicle. Thus J H Haynes are giving only non-specific advice in this respect.

4 When modifying a car it is important to bear in mind the legal responsibilities placed on the owners, driver and modifiers of cars, including, but not limited to, the Road Traffic Act 1988. IN PARTICULAR, IT IS AN OFFENCE TO DRIVE ON A PUBLIC ROAD A VEHICLE WHICH IS NOT INSURED OR WHICH DOES NOT COMPLY WITH THE CONSTRUCTION AND USE REGULATIONS, OR WHICH IS DANGEROUS AND MAY CAUSE INJURY TO ANY PERSON, OR WHICH DOES NOT HOLD A CURRENT MOT CERTIFICATE OR DISPLAY A VALID TAX DISC.

5 The safety of any alteration and its compliance with construction and use regulations should be checked before a modified vehicle is sold as it may be an offence to sell a vehicle which is not roadworthy.

6 Any advice provided is correct to the best of our knowledge at the time of publication, but the reader should pay particular attention to any changes of specification to the vehicles, or parts, which can occur without notice.

7 Alterations to vehicles should be disclosed to insurers and licensing authorities, and legal advice taken from the police, vehicle testing centres, or appropriate regulatory bodies.

8 The vehicle has been chosen for this project as it is one of those most widely customised by its owners, and readers should not assume that the vehicle manufacturers have given their approval to the modifications.

9 Neither J H Haynes nor the manufacturers give any warranty as to the safety of a vehicle after alterations, such as those contained in this book, have been made. J H Haynes will not accept liability for any economic loss, damage to property or death and personal injury arising from use of this manual other than in respect of injury or death resulting directly from J H Haynes' negligence.

Contents

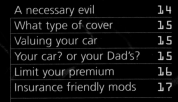

Security

04

Body styling

05

Lights & bulbs

06

Wheels & tyres

07

11

ICE

12

Engines

13

Exhausts

14

Reference

Haynes
Max Power

What's that then?

Haynes Publishing have, for more than forty
years, been helping people keep their cars on the
roads in countries all over the world by
publishing maintenance manuals. Chances are
you've either got one of them yourself or you
know somebody who has.

00
36

*"Lights & bulbs"
includes fitting
high-power blue
headlight bulbs,
side repeaters,
etc.*

Before

After

Remember what it feels like on your birthday, or at Christmas, when you're faced by a pile of pressies? So do we, that gnawing feeling in your gut, what's in them? What did I get? Take that feeling and multiply it by twelve, that's how we felt when we started this project. When we decided that it was time to try something new, we couldn't wait. Because the same theories apply to modifying your car as servicing it, we reckoned we'd better get on and do it ourselves. We don't pay other people to do it for us, and we get the same dodgy instructions with kit as everybody else.

So if you've ever wondered how to fit a universal door mirror properly, smooth a tailgate or just bolt a seat in, this book is for you.

We've picked up a skip full of tips along the way, and they're all here for you to use. We haven't tried to set any trends, but we've covered every possible process we think you'll need. So where we've tinted a front door window, the same rules apply to a rear one, job done.

If you look in the magazines and want some of that, join us, 'cos so do we, and we'll show you how to get it.

Keeping it real

Modifying a car is not without its problems in the 'real world', as opposed to the seemingly fantasy world of the glossy mags. For instance, it's pretty silly to spend hours fitting illegal window tints or smoked lights if you get pulled the first time you're out

afterwards. Of course, you can get pulled for all sorts of reasons (and just driving a modified car is reason enough sometimes), but keeping the car actually legal is one of the 'hidden' challenges with modifying. Throughout the book, our tips should give all the help you need to at least appear to be on the right side of the law. The annual MOT test is another favourite time for your mods to get panned, and again, we aim to give you all the help necessary to ensure at least that what you've changed doesn't lead to a fail.

Security is another major issue with a tweaked motor, and the perils of insurance cannot be taken lightly, either. We aim to give down-to-earth advice to help you keep the car in the first place, and to help you in not upsetting your insurers too much if the worst happens.

A word about fashion

In producing this book, we're aware that fashions change. What we show being fitted to our car might well be hideously out of date in 6 months time, or might not be your thing in the first place! Also, some of the stuff we've acquired from our various suppliers may no longer be available by the time you read this. We hope that, despite this, our approach of showing you step-by-step how to fit the various parts will mean that, even if the parts change slightly, the procedures we show for fitting will still be valid.

Our main project car was a 1.5 LSi Coupé, 1994 L reg.

"Wheels & tyres" takes a detailed look at all the options.

"Body styling" shows you how to fit universal mirrors to full body kits.

"Interiors" includes seats, painting trim, gear knobs and loads more.

One for the
boy ricers

Jap cars - velly reliable, loved by the over-60s and driving schools, plasticky interiors and slightly dull styling. Okay, so you wouldn't accuse a Skyline, Evo or Scooby of any such things, but a Honda Civic? Guilty, I do believe. So how come the Civic's one of the hardest Maxed cars you'll see at your average cruise - where did that come from? Well, you could say it's an American import. The huge street racer Civic scene in the US (now made famous by a certain recent film) has slowly filtered across the pond, and now more British boy racers than ever want affordable fast, furious rides. Big up to the banzai beauty.

Honda have long been masters at making engines, and the EG Civic's no exception, bringing the famous VTEC technology to a mass-market motor for the first time. Even the non-VTEC engines sing their heads off - it's just that slightly more happens when you

try it in a VTEC. Typically triggering at around 5500 rpm (when more boring engines sound like they're about to blow up), the variable valve timing technology gives the engine an extra kick, and produces an excellent go-for-it roar as well. Who needs a turbo? This is a car not to be messed with off the lights. With engine tuning about the hottest topic on any Civic chat forum, and plenty of tuning goodies (which actually work) from Japan and the US, 200 brake from a Civic VTi is a real possibility - and that's before turning to NOS.

Before we get too carried away here, let's remind ourselves that a Civic's typical first owner might well qualify for the state pension, which partly explains the (let's face it) pretty bland looks in its shopping-trolley clothing. But give it a serious makeover with any of the Jap-inspired bodykits available from US suppliers, and no apologies are needed - like chunky chocolate bars, a war-painted Civic's not for girls. Just remember to take off the mudflaps.

There's no getting away from the fact that Hondas cost - big-time. A first-timer's car, this is not - with VTEC insurance starting at Group 14, and expensive spares/servicing, this is normally a second or third car for most people. Still, that underlying Honda build quality makes it a car worth investing your hard-earned in - and one big laff is that modifying parts often cost far less than the stock items! With the newer EK Civic well-established on the scene as well, and the newest Type-R already laying down a marker of serious intent, will Civic be more than passing trend? You bet!

Buyer's guide

What to buy

So - is it going to be a Hatch, or a Coupe? Unfortunately, there's lots of Civic 4-door Saloons in the UK, and they're not usually a modifier's first choice - if it doesn't say in the advert which it is, ask. Even so, there's plenty of 4-door bodykits out there, so there's still a glimmer of hope for a sweet-looking ride, even with rear doors.

Then there's the slightly wacky CRX Del Sol, which is a bit of an acquired taste, and doesn't have much room for your mates (or for an impressive ICE install). But it does offer wind-in-the-hair fun, especially in VTi form, with a crowd-pleasing trick electric roof. The Coupes are unusual in that they were born in the USA, rather than Japan, and they usually only come in 1.5 litre form (but with multi-point injection, the Coupe engine is worth another 11 bhp over the same engine in the Hatch). Other than that, the Hatch or Coupe choice is purely down to personal taste - either one can look really tasty after some cash has been splashed.

Civics are all about performance, and Honda parts are expensive if you crash it, so it should come as no surprise that insurance is going to be just a tad pricey. If you want a 'proper' VTEC Civic (and who wouldn't?), you're looking at a minimum of Group 14, rising to 16 for the 158 bhp VTi. Ouch - especially if you're the 'wrong' side of 21. Let's break down what you get for your money.

For Civic looks with smaller bills, try the 1.3 models (the DX and the later Bali). With a 74 bhp 16-valve engine, these are still nippier than your average Nova, and insurance starts at Group 9 - just lose the giveaway badging to avoid embarassment. The 1.3 models have carburettor fuelling (no induction kits) and the DX is the only Civic without power steering (heavy, if you're thinking of fitting 17s).

If cheap insurance is important, the best compromise has to be the 89 bhp 1.5 LSi Hatch, with decent levels of kit, half-sensible performance and Group 12 premiums. Beware the 1.5 Coupe, however - you might think it would be in the same group as the 1.5 Hatch, having almost the same engine - but the insurers rate the Coupe a Group 14 car. Why? Well, the Hatch has 89 bhp from its dual-point injection engine, while the Coupe makes 100 bhp from its multi-point injected motor. Two groups extra for 11 horses - someone's having a laff. If you must have a Coupe, make it an LSi rather than the basic 1.5i - if you're paying extra for that insurance, you might as well

have electric windows, sunroof and mirrors to show for it. Coupe SE models are also packing air con - worth looking out for.

The first of the VTECs is the oddball 1.5 VEi model. Nothing strange about the looks - it's the same visually as any other Civic 3-door - but what's under the bonnet is less impressive for the modifier. While other Hondas use the VTEC system to make more power at the top end, the VEi is tuned for economy. Performance is no worse than the normal 1.5, just disappointing for a VTEC Honda - and insurance is Group 13. As with the 1.3 models, best to lose the VEi badges quickly if you don't want to look like a pensioner.

Packing 123 bhp from its 1.6 single-cam VTEC engine, the Civic ESi looks like value in Group 14, especially with 'luxury' touches like rear headrests, and ABS from 1994 onwards. When you consider an XR2i's in the same insurance group, the screaming Honda looks even better value! Just so you know, this is the hottest Civic you can get with an automatic box. As an option, you understand. Well, some old dears find a gearstick a bit too much…

The daddy of the range, with the most tuneable engine, is the VTi. Almost Golf-esque in having a very understated exterior, but it'll be a good Golf that can keep up with one of these, driven hard. The twin-cam VTEC engine screams round to 8000 rpm, producing 158 bhp on the way (which is close enough to 100 bhp per litre as makes no difference). No wonder owners of lesser Civics all dream of a B16A engine transplant. The VTi is already a modern classic, in EG form - the later EK version (1996-on) had the same engine, but put on weight. In exchange for your Group 16 premiums, you get all-round disc brakes with ABS, 15-inch alloys (space-saver spare), two rear spoilers and unique front seats. Must be all about the engine, then.

No Jap car buyer's guide would be complete without mentioning the imports and specials. The Civic's got a huge following in Ireland (which seems to be the land of the imported Jap machine), where demand to own the 'ultimate' Civic has resulted in several SiR/SiR II models coming over. The SiR badge will be familiar to *Gran Turismo* fans - what it means in real life is a tweaked B16A engine with 170 bhp at 7800 rpm, typically-trick Jap-special wheels, badges, body features and extra kit. What your insurance company will make of it is anyone's guess (get a quote first), and sourcing SiR parts from Japan could be expensive, time-consuming, or impossible - best to buy one from an imports specialist, for guaranteed back-up.

Don't buy a **dog**

Honda - surely the pinnacle of mass-market Japanese reliability and quality, yes?

So nothing ever goes wrong? Er, no, not quite - but they're way better than average. As we keep saying, most Hondas will be bought new by the older section of the population, and if you can find one that's had one careful, elderly lady owner from new, you're doing well - providing she kept it serviced. Regular servicing on any Civic is essential, and especially important on a VTEC, which demands six-monthly services and decent oil - beware any Civic without a service history, or any owner who's vague about maintenance (checking the oil level between services is just as important).

So what goes wrong? Well, be very wary of any Civic which seems reluctant to start, or which stalls frequently (chances are, it's not your bad driving that's causing it). Civics (along with several other Hondas of the same age) suffer problems with distributors, ignition modules, injection relays, and even the ignition switch, all of which can result in a completely dead engine, or puzzling intermittent engine cut-outs. Parts are very expensive, even secondhand, and they all seem to suffer. Worth asking if any ignition components have ever been replaced - if not, and the car's up on the miles, be prepared for a large bill sometime soon.

All Civics have a camshaft drivebelt (cambelt, or timing belt) which is made of reinforced rubber. The belt deteriorates with age, and for safety's sake, a new one should be fitted every 3 years or 36000 miles, especially if the engine gets a regular caning. If the belt snaps, the engine could be wrecked. Finished. Ruined. Knackered. It's not too bad a DIY job if you're confident under the hood, or budget for a garage bill around the £80 mark.

Other underbonnet problems you might run into include oxygen sensor failure (get the exhaust emissions checked at an MoT centre), clutch master cylinder leaks (poor clutch operation), and piston ring wear (especially on abused high-revving VTi models, which may show a smoky exhaust - get the compressions checked).

Rust isn't a big problem, but you do sometimes get signs in the lower half of the tailgate on Hatch models, and some rusting around the front and rear arches. Any serious rust quite possibly indicates badly-repaired accident damage, so make your excuses and leave.

Inside, look for worn carpets/seats, and check the front seats for excessive movement, caused by worn seat sliders. Electric windows should be checked a few times, as the driver's one (the most used) sometimes sticks - if the problem's not dealt with properly, the motor can burn out (expensive). On Hatch models, the strut mountings for the glass section of the two-piece tailgate can break. Do all the rear lights work? Civics sometimes develop a strange appetite for rear light bulbs.

The hotter models can go through front tyres, discs and pads in a big hurry. Worn tyres are obvious, but see if you can peer through the front wheel for a look at the discs - heavy grooving, or a big wear lip on the edge, and it could be a big bill. If the owner's not been too careful about hitting kerbs when parking, this won't just have killed the wheels - the suspension bushes could be feeling some pain too (check for strange clonks through the steering over bumps).

General stuff

Usually, it's far better to buy your Civic privately, as long as you know what you're doing. Dealers charge over the odds for Hondas, and sometimes all you'll get for the extra money is a full valet and some degree of comeback if the car's a dog. Buying privately, you get to meet the owner, gaining you valuable clues about how the car's been treated. But - like we said before - don't discount the value of buying an imported Civic from a Jap import specialist, and remember that a problem Civic could prove expensive to fix - good dealer backup could be worth shelling out extra for.

Everyone's nervous when buying a car, but don't ignore your 'gut feelings' when you first see the car, or meet its owner. Also, don't make the mistake of deciding to buy the car *before you've even seen it* - too many people make up their minds before setting out, and blindly ignore all the warning signs. Remember, there *are* other cars, and you *can* walk away! Think of a good excuse before you set out.

Take someone who 'knows a bit about cars' along with you - preferably, try and find someone who's either got a Civic, or who's had one in the past.

Never buy a car in the dark, or when it's raining. If you do have to view any car in these conditions, agree not to hand over any major money until you've seen it in daylight, and when the paintwork's dry (dull, faded paint, or metallic paint that's lost its lacquer, will appear to be shiny in the rain).

Check that the mileages and dates shown on the receipts and MoTs follow a pattern indicating normal use, with no gaps in the dates, and no sudden drop in the mileage between MoTs (which might suggest the mileage has been 'clocked'). If you are presented with a sheaf of paperwork, it's worth going through it - maybe the car's had a history of problems, or maybe it's just had some nice expensive new parts fitted (like a clutch, starter motor or alternator, for instance).

Tricks 'n' tips

Tyres can be a giveaway to a car maintained on a shoestring - four different makes of tyre, especially cheap brands, can indicate a penny-pinching attitude which won't have done the rest of the car any favours.

Check the chassis number (VIN number) and engine number on the registration document and on the car. Any sign of welding near one of these numbers should be treated with suspicion - to disguise the real number, a thief will run a line of weld over the old number, grind it flat, then

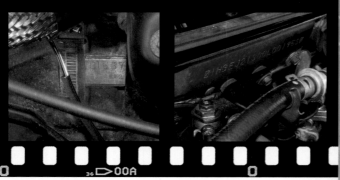

The engine number is stamped into the front of the engine block . . .

. . . and the VIN is stamped into the bulkhead.

Full service history (fsh)

Is there any service history? If so, this is good, but study the service book carefully:

a *Which garage has done the servicing? Is it a proper dealer, or a backstreet bodger? Do you know the garage, and if so, would you use it?*

b *Do the mileages show a nice even progression, or are there huge gaps? Check the dates too.*

c *Does it look as if the stamps are authentic? Do the oldest ones look old, or could this 'service history' have been created last week, to make the car look good?*

d *When was the last service, and what exactly was carried out? When was the cambelt last changed? Has the owner got receipts for any of this servicing work?*

One sign of a genuine car is a good batch of old MOTs, and as many receipts as possible - even if they're for fairly irrelevant things like tyres.

stamp in a new number. Other scams include cutting the section of bodywork with the numbers on from another car, then cutting and welding this section into place. The VIN number appears on a plate on the front crossmember, sometimes at the back of the engine compartment, or on the driver's door frame (seen with the door open). If there's any sign this plate has been tampered with, walk away - the car could be a 'ringer' (a stolen car with a fake I.D.).

The engine number position varies by model, but it's stamped into the front of the engine block, at the transmission end - shouldn't be difficult to spot. If the number's been removed, or if there's anything suspicious about it, you could be buying trouble.

Check the registration document very carefully - all the details should match the car. If buying privately, make sure that it's definitely the owner's name and address printed on it - if not, be very careful! If buying from a dealer, note the name and address, and try to contact the previous owner to confirm mileage, etc, before handing over more than a deposit. Unless the car's very old, it shouldn't have had too many previous owners - if it's into double figures, it may mean the car is trouble, so checking its owner history is more important.

While the trim on a Civic is quite durable, it should still be obvious whether the car's been abused over a long period, or whether the mileage showing is genuine or not (shiny steering wheels and floppy window winder/sunroof handles are a good place to start checking if you're suspicious). Okay, so you may be planning to junk most of the interior at some point, but why should you pay over the odds for a tat car which the owner hasn't given a stuff about?

Although you may feel a bit stupid doing it, check simple things too, like making sure the windows and sunroof open and shut, and that all the doors and tailgate can be locked (if a lock's been replaced, ask why). Check all the basic electrical equipment too, as far as possible - lights, front and rear wipers, heated rear window, heater fan; it's amazing how often these things are taken for granted by buyers! If your chosen Civic already has alloys fitted, does it have locking wheel bolts? Where's the key? What about the code and removal tools for the stereo?

Is the catalytic converter ('cat') working? This is a wickedly expensive part to replace - the best way to ensure at least one year's grace is to only buy a car with a full MoT (the cat is checked during the emissions test). Many Civic modifiers remove the cat altogether (by fitting a de-cat pipe), which is great for performance, but means the car's illegal to use on the road.

Sports models

Has it been treated well, or thrashed to death? We wouldn't pay top dollar for any hot Civic without seeing evidence of careful maintenance, because any car will stand a good ranting much better if it's been properly serviced. Even a fully-stamped service book only tells half the story, though. Does the owner look bright enough to even know what a dipstick is, never mind how to check the oil level between services? Most Civics are owned by enthusiasts, which is a start.

Remember that there's even more to look out for than on a lesser model. If the car's temptingly cheap (and even if it's not), never take anything just at face value - check everything you can about the car yourself. Getting your hands on a really good hot Civic is not a simple task - dodgy dealers (and owners!) know there's a market for repaired write-offs and stolen cars ('ringers'), and gullible private punters get ripped every day.

More so than any other model, check for signs of accident damage, especially at the front end. Ask if it's ever been in a shunt - if the seller says no, but there's paint overspray under the bonnet, what's going on? Also check for paint overspray on the window rubbers, light units and bumpers/trim. With the bonnet open, check that the headlight rear shells are the same colour - mis-matched or new-looking ones merit an explanation from the seller.

Does the front number plate carry details of the supplying garage, like the back one? If not, why has a new plate been fitted?

Check the glass (and even the head and tail lights) for etched-in registration numbers - are they all the same, and does it match the car's actual registration? A windscreen could've been replaced for any number of innocent reasons, but new side glass indicates a break-in at least - is the car a 'stolen/recovered' (joyridden) example? Find the chassis and engine numbers, as described earlier in this Section, and satisfy yourself that they are genuine - check them against the 'logbook' (registration document). An HPI check (or similar) could be well worthwhile, but even this won't tell you everything. If you're at all suspicious, or if the answers to your questions don't ring true, walk away. Make any excuse you like.

It's still worth a bit of discount if an approved (Thatcham Cat 1 or 2) alarm or immobiliser is fitted. Make sure that any aftermarket kit actually works, that it looks properly installed, with no stray wires hanging out, and that you get the Thatcham certificate or other paperwork to go with it. If possible, it's worth finding out exactly how it's been wired in - if it goes wrong later, you could be stranded with no chance of disabling the system to get you home.

Model history

Note: *Like many small-car ranges in recent years, there's been a number of 'special edition' Civic models offered. Don't pay over the odds for a special edition, unless it's genuinely got some extra kit you're interested in having.*

November 1991 (J reg) - Civic EG range introduced. Japanese-built front-wheel-drive 3-door Hatchback or 4-door Saloon. New 16-valve engines - 1.3, 1.5 and 1.6 SOHC, and 1.6 DOHC (VTi model). 1.3 DX has tints, catalyst carburettor engine. 1.5 LSi has fuel injection, power steering, electric windows/sunroof, central locking. 1.5 VEi has VTEC-E 'economy' engine, driver's airbag. 1.6 ESi has VTEC engine, 14-inch alloys, electric mirrors, rear headrests, driver's airbag. 1.6 VTI has VTEC engine, twin rear spoilers, 15-inch alloys, ABS disc brakes.

November 1993 (L reg) - 1.3 Bali first introduced, replacing DX. Power steering, centre console, Bali graphics. Tahitian Green or Milano Red.

January 1994 (L reg) - Minor revisions - all models gain RDS radio/cassette, Hatch has separate handle for tailgate glass, new front seat folding mechanism. ESi models now have ABS disc brakes.

February 1994 (L reg) - 2-door Coupe models introduced. Built in Honda's USA plant, only available with 1.5 SOHC engine. 1.5i has tints, central locking, electric aerial, power steering. LSi model adds electric windows/sunroof/mirrors. 1.3 DX Hatchback reintroduced.

April 1994 (L reg) - 1.5 Bel Air Hatch and Saloon introduced - spec as LSi, but with air conditioning. Coupe SE (special edition) also has air conditioning.

December 1994 (M reg) - 1.3 Glacier special edition introduced. Driver's airbag, alloys, tints, in white only.

June 1995 (M reg) - Driver's airbag now standard on all models, passenger airbag standard on ESi and VTi. 1.3 Marlin Hatch special edition introduced, with electric sunroof. 1.5i Coupe Ltd edition introduced, with alloys and 3-spoke leather steering wheel.

March 1996 (N reg) - All models discontinued, replaced by EK Civic.

Performance figures

	0-60 (sec)	Top speed (mph)
1.3 DX / Bali	11.2	99
1.5 LSi Hatch	10.7	108
1.5 LSi Coupe	9.8	118
1.5 VEi	10.0	113
1.6 ESi	8.7	122
1.6 VTi	7.4	133

Insurance
A necessary evil

Ah, insurance - loads of money, and all you get is a piece of paper you're not supposed to use! Of course, you must have insurance - you're illegal on the road without it, and you won't be able to get the car taxed, either. If you're ever caught driving without insurance, you'll have great trouble ever getting insurance again - insurance companies regard this offence nearly as seriously as drink-driving, so don't do it!

The way insurance companies work out premiums and assess risks is a mystery to most of us. In general, the smaller the engine you have in your Civic, the less you'll pay. However, if one company's had a lot of claims on Civics in the past, the VTi factor might 'unfairly' influence the premiums of lesser Civics, too (this is why it's important to shop around). An 'insurance-friendly' LSi 3-door should be a good bet for a sensible premium, but remember that insurance companies aren't stupid - if you swap in that B16 engine and turn your LSi into a VTi-alike, they may well 'load' the premium to VTi level (and that's Group 16). Insurance is a game you can't win, but you must play.

If your annual premium seems like the national debt of a small African country (and whose isn't!), always ring as many brokers and get as many quotes as you possibly can. Yes, there's loads better ways to spend an evening/afternoon than answering the same twenty questions over and over again, but you never know what the next quote will be. A few extra minutes spent on the phone (or on the 'net) once a year may result in an extra few hundred quid in your back pocket. Well, you live in hope don't you!

With modified cars, insurance becomes even more of a problem. By putting on all the alloys, trick body kits, nice interiors, big ICE, you're making the car much more of a target for thieves (yes, ok, we know you know this). The point is, the insurance companies know this too, and they don't want to be paying out for the car, plus all the money you've spent on it, should it go missing. There is a temptation 'not to tell the insurance' about the mods you've made. Let's deal with this right now. Our experience has been that,

Tricks 'n' tips

When ringing for quotes, watch your language. Arguing with the bloke/girl on the other end will always get you a higher quote, even if it makes you feel better. Also, don't say anything if you get put on hold. Some companies will put you on speaker - if you're trying to pull a fast one and they then catch you giggling or bragging to your mates, it's game over.

while it can be painful, honesty is best. Generally, the insurance company line is: "...thanks for telling us - we won't put the car 'up a group' (ie charge you more), but we also won't cover the extra cost of your alloy wheels/body kit/tasty seats in the event of any claim...". This is fair enough - in other words, if your car goes missing, you get paid out, based on a standard car, minus all the goodies. If you particularly want all the extras covered, you might have a long hard search - most companies only offer 'modified for standard' policies. There are specialist insurers who are more friendly towards fully-loaded cars, but even they won't actually cover the cost of replacement goodies.

What type of cover, Sir?

For most of us, cost means there's only one option - TPF&T (third party, fire and theft). Fully-comp insurance is an unattainable dream for most people until they reach the 'magic' age of 25, but what's the real story?

Third Party only

The most basic cover you can get. Basically covers you for damage to other people's cars or property, and for personal injury claims. Virtually no cover for your own stuff, beyond what you get if you take the optional 'legal protection' cover.

Third Party, Fire and Theft

As above, with cover for fire and theft, of course! Better, but not much better. This is really only cover in the event of a 'total loss', if your car goes missing or goes up in smoke. Still no cover for your car if you stack it into a tree, or if someone breaks in and pinches your stereo (check your policy small-print).

Fully-comprehensive

In theory at least, covers you for any loss or damage. Will cover the cost of repairing or replacing your car, often with discounted windscreen cover and other benefits. If you lose control of the car on an icy road (arguably, not your fault) you get paid. If someone pinches your wheels and drops the car on the floor, you get paid - at least for the damage done to the underside, and for standard wheels and tyres. Most policies include provision of a hire car after a shunt, which is pretty useful. Some offer cheap breakdown cover packages in with the main policy. With a fully-comp policy, you can 'protect' your no-claims bonus for a small fee so you don't automatically lose all those hard-earned years' worth of discount if you prang it (generally, you can only do this on fully-comp).

All this extra cover costs, obviously, but how much? You might be surprised what the actual difference is. Think about it, anyway - it's got to be worth a couple of hundred quid more to go fully-comp, if your car's worth into four figures, surely?

Valuing your car

When your insurance pays out in the event of a total loss or write-off, they base their offer on the current market value of an identical standard model to yours (less your excess). The only way you'll get more than the average amount is to prove your Civic is in above-average nick (with photos?) or that the mileage was especially low for the year.

With this in mind, don't bother over-valuing your Civic in the hope you'll get more in the event of a claim - you won't! The only way to do this is to seek out an 'agreed-value' deal, which you can usually only get on classic-car policies (with these, the car's value is agreed in advance between you, not worked out later by the company with you having no say in it). By over-valuing your Civic, you could be increasing your premium without gaining any benefit - sound smart to you?

Equally though, don't under-value, in the hope you'll get a reduction in premium. You won't, and if there's a total loss claim, you won't get any more than your under-valued amount, no matter how loudly you complain.

Work on what you paid for the car, backed up with the sort of prices you see for similar cars in the ads (or use a secondhand car price guide). Add no more than 10% for the sake of optimism, and that's it.

Your car? Or your Dad's?

Insurance really costs when you're the wrong side of 25. Ever been tempted to tell your insurance that your full-on sorted Civic belongs to your Dad (old insurance-friendly person), then get him to insure it, with you as a named driver? Oh dear. This idea (known as 'fronting') is so old, it's grown a long white beard. And it sucks, too. First of all, insurance companies aren't stupid. They know your Dad (or your Mum, or old Uncle Bert) isn't likely to be running around in a kid's pocket-rocket, and they treat any 'named driver' application with great suspicion. Even if they do take your money, don't imagine they've been suckered. In the event of a claim, they'll look into everything very carefully, and will ask lots of awkward questions. If you get caught out in the lie, they've taken your money, and you've got no insurance - who's been suckered now?

This dubious practice also does you no favours in future years. All the time you're living the lie, you're not building up any no-claims bonus of your own - you're just delaying the pain 'til later, and without having real cover in the meantime.

'Legit' ways to limit your premium

If you do enough ringing around for quotes, you'll soon learn what the 'right answers' to some of the questions are - even if you can't actually give them (don't tell lies to your insurance company). Mind you, with a little thought, you can start to play their game and win - try these:

Volunteer to increase your excess. The 'excess' is put there to stop people claiming for piddling little amounts - when they pay out, it's always the repair/replacement cost MINUS whatever the 'excess' is. So, for instance, if you've got a £200 theft excess, it means you'll automatically get £200 less than the agreed value of your car, should it be stolen. Most policies have 'compulsory' excess amounts, which you can do nothing about. By increasing excesses voluntarily, you're limiting the amount you'll get still further. Insurance companies like this, and should reduce your premium in return - but this only goes so far, so ask what the effect of different voluntary excesses will be. Don't increase your excess too far, or you'll get paid nowt if you claim!

Limit your mileage. Most companies offer a small discount if you only cover a small annual mileage. To get any meaningful reduction, the mileage has to be a lot less than 10,000 per year. Few companies, though, ever ask what the car's current mileage is - so how are they gonna know if you've gone over your self-imposed limit?

Make yourself the only driver. Pretty self-explanatory. The more people who drive your car, the greater the risk to the company, and a car's owner will always drive more carefully (it's their money that bought it) than any named driver. If you've built up 2 years' worth of no-claims, but your partner hasn't, putting them on your insurance will bump it up, due to their relative inexperience.

Get a garage - and use it. Where you park can have a big effect on your premium. Parking it on the street is the worst. Park off the road (on a driveway) when you're at home. The best thing is to have a garage of your own (don't pretend you use your Dad's garage) - see if you can rent one locally, even if it means walking a few hundred yards. If you're a student living away from home, tell your company where the car will be parked during term-time - if you're at Uni in London, this is a bigger risk than living at home 'in the country', and vice-versa.

Fit an approved alarm or immobiliser. See if you can get a list from your company of all their approved security devices, and fit whatever you can afford. Not all companies approve the same kit, so it might even be worth contacting more than one company for advice. Any device with a Thatcham or Sold Secure rating should be recognised. In some cases, the discounts offered are not that great any more - but an alarm is still a nice way to get peace of mind.

Build up your no-claims bonus. You'll only do this by owning and insuring a car in your own name, and then not making any claims. Simple really. One rather immoral (but not actually illegal) dodge is to buy an old banger, insure it cheap, then never drive it. You'll need to keep it fully road-legal (with tax, MOT) if you park it on the road. For every year you do this, you'll build up another year of NCB.

Hang onto your no-claims bonus. Obviously, the less you claim, the less your insurance will cost. If something happens to your car, don't be in too big a hurry to make a claim before you've thought it all through. How much will it cost to fix? How much is your excess? How much will your renewal premium be, next year? If you have a big enough accident which you're sure isn't your fault, ring your company, but make it quite clear you're NOT claiming yet - just informing them of the accident. It should be down to the other driver's insurance to pay. You don't always lose all your no-claims, either, even if it was your fault - depends how many years you've built up. Once you've got a few years, ask whether you can 'protect' your no-claims.

Avoid speed cameras and The Law. Yes, okay, easier said than done! But anything less than a clean licence is not good from the insurance perspective. One SP30 won't hurt much, but the second strike will, so take it easy. Don't get caught on traffic-light cameras, either - just one is a major no-no.

Insurance-friendly mods?

Insurers don't like any changes from standard, but some things you'll do are worse from their viewpoint than others. The guidelines below are just that - for guidance. No two companies will have the same outlook, and your own circumstances will play a big part too.

Golden Rule Number One: Before you spend huge money modifying the car, ring your insurance, and ask them how it will affect things.

Golden Rule Number Two: If in doubt, declare everything. Insurance companies are legally entitled to dispute any claim if the car is found to be non-standard in any way.

Body mods – Even a tiny rear spoiler could be classed as a 'bodykit' (yes, it's daft, but that's how it is). Anything which alters the exterior appearance should be declared. As long as the mods don't include a radical full-on bodykit, the jump in premium should be fairly small. Any genuine Honda add-ons (VTi 3-door rear lower spoiler) might not cost at all - bonus.

Brakes – The companies view brake mods as tampering with safety-related kit, and modifying the brakes implies that you drive fast and hard. You might get away with standard-sized grooved/drilled discs and pads, but fitting bigger discs and replacement calipers will prove expensive.

Engine mods – 'Mild' mods such as induction kits and exhausts don't give much more power, so don't generally hurt. But 'chipping' your Civic will lead to drastic rises in premiums, or a complete refusal of cover. With complete engine transplants, you'll be required to give an engineer's report, and to get your wad out.

Interior mods – Don't assume that tarting up the inside won't interest the insurance company. By making any part of the car more attractive, you're also attracting the crims. Cars get trashed for parts, as often as not - and your racing seats and sexy steering wheel could be worth major money. Still, the effect on premiums shouldn't be too great, especially if you've got an alarm/immobiliser.

Lights – Change the car's appearance, and are safety-related. You'll probably get asked for lots of details, but as long as you've kept it sensible (and legal, as far as possible), the effect on your wallet shouldn't be too harsh.

Security – Make sure you mention all security stuff - alarms, immobilisers (including mechanical devices), locking wheel nuts, large Alsatian in the back seat… But - don't over-sell the car. Tell the truth, in other words. If you've got a steering wheel lock, do you always fit it? If you didn't when your car went missing, you're in trouble. Don't say you've got a Cat 1 alarm if it really came from Argos, and don't tell them you garage the car at night if it's stuck out in the road.

Suspension – Changes the car's appearance, and is safety-related. Some enlightened companies once took the view that modded suspension helps the car corner better, so it's safer. Drops of only 30 to 40 mm shouldn't mean bigger premiums.

Wheels – Very appearance-altering, and very nickable. At least show some responsibility by fitting some locking nuts/bolts and an approved alarm/immobiliser. Quite likely to attract a low-to-moderate rise in premium, which still won't cover your wheels properly - you could arrange separate cover for your wheels, then at least you'll get paid. Some companies may ask for a photo of the car with the wheels on.

And finally - a new nightmare

Not telling the insurance the whole truth gets a little tricky when you make a claim. If the insurance assessor comes to check your bent/burnt/stolen-and-recovered 'standard' Civic, and finds he's looking at a vehicle fitted with trick alloys/bodykit/radical interior, he's not going to turn a blind eye. Has the car got an MoT? Oh, and did you declare those points on your licence? No? You're then very much at the mercy of your insurer, especially if they can prove any mods contributed to the claim. At best, you'll have a long-drawn-out battle with your insurer to get a part-payout, and at worst they'll just refuse to get involved at all.

One more thing - *be careful what you hit*. If your insurance is declared void, they won't pay out for the repairs to the other car you smacked into, or for the lamp-post you knock down (several hundred quid, actually). And then there's the personal injury claims - if your insurance company disowns you, it'll be you who has to foot the bill. Even sprains and bruises can warrant claims, and more serious injuries can result in claims running into lots of zeroes! Without insurance cover, **you'll** have to pay. Probably for a long, long time. Think about it, and we won't see you in court.

Security

Lock me or lose me

It's a sad fact, but making your car attractive to the opposite sex also tends to attract attention of a less-welcome kind, from less-than-human pond life.

04

Avoiding trouble

Now come on - you're modifying your car to look cool and to be seen in. Not a problem - but be careful where you choose to show your car off, and who to. Be especially discreet, the nearer you get to home - *turn your system down* before you turn into your road, for instance, or you'll draw unwelcome attention to where that car with the loud stereo's parked at night.

Without being too paranoid, watch for anyone following you home. At night, if the car behind switches its lights off, be worried. If you suspect this is happening, do not drive home - choose well-lit public places until they give up. Believe us - it happens.

If you're going out, think about where you're parking - well-lit and well-populated is good.

Thieves hate light being on them, so don't make it easy by parking somewhere dark - think about this if you park up in daylight, knowing you won't be back 'til late.

Hands up, who doesn't lock their car when they get petrol? Your insurance company has a term for this, and it's 'contributory negligence'. In English, this means you won't get a penny if your car goes missing when you haven't locked it.

If you're lucky enough to have a garage, use it. On up-and-over garage doors, fit extra security like a padlock and ground anchor.

A clever thief will watch your movements and habits over several days before trying your car. Has it got an alarm, and do you always set it? Do you only fit your steering wheel lock when you feel like it? Do you always park in the same place, and is the car hidden from the house or from the road? Don't make his life easier. Ask yourself how you'd nick your car…

A word about your stereo

From the moment you bolt on those nice alloys, it's taken as read that you've also got stereo gear that's worth nicking - and the thieves know it. All the discreet installation in the world isn't going to deter them from finding out what's inside that nice motor.

Please don't advertise your love of ICE around your car. Your nice stereo gear will fit other cars too, and can be ripped out in nothing flat. You may be very proud of your ICE install, but nothing is more of an 'invite' than a huge ICE sticker or sunstrip. If you've fitted one just to look cool, replace it now with something less provocative - seriously. Your set might not actually be very expensive, but you could still lose a side window for advertising something better.

You'll have got a CD player, obviously, but don't leave discs or empty CD cases lying around inside the car. A nice pair of 6x9s in full view on the back shelf is an invite to having your rear window smashed - stealth shelf, anyone? When you're fitting your system, give some thought to the clues you could accidentally leave in plain view. Oxygen-free speaker cable is great stuff, but it's also a bit bright against dark carpets, and is all the clue necessary that you're serious about your tunes. Hide amps and CD changers under your front seats.

Most modern sets are face-off or MASK, so if they've got security features like this, use them - take your faceplate off when you leave the car, and take it with you rather than leaving it in the door pocket or glovebox (the first places a thief will look).

Things that go beep in the night

Unless your insurance company demands it up front, fitting an alarm is something generally done as an after-thought. We know alarms aren't exactly sexy, but don't skimp - an alarm may never be put to the test, but if it is, you'll be glad you spent wisely…

The simplest first step to car security is to fake it. Tacky *'This car is fitted with an alarm'* stickers won't fool anyone, but if you want cheap, just fit a flashing LED. We know it's not the real thing, but everyone else will think you've got a posh alarm. An LED is cheap to buy and easy to fit, and can be rigged to a discreet switch inside the car.

Don't overlook the value of so-called 'manual' immobilisers, such as steering wheel locking bars and gear-to-handbrake lever locks. These can be a worthwhile deterrent - a thief not specifically after your car may move on to an easier target. Some of the items offered may be 'Sold Secure' or Thatcham Cat 3, accolades well worth checking out, since it means they've withstood a full-on brute force attack for a useful length of time.

The only way to combat the more determined thief is to go for a well-specified and intelligently-installed alarm. Immobilisers alone have their place, but sadly, even a pro-fitted immobiliser on its own won't stop someone pinching your wheels, or having it away with the stereo gear. Neither, incidentally, will a cheap alarm - you have to know how the thieves operate to stand any chance defeating them. Any alarm you fit yourself probably won't gain you any insurance discount, but it will give you peace of mind, and DIY means you can do a real trick installation, to make it very hard work for the gyppos.

Finally, one other scam which you might fall victim to. If you find your alarm is suddenly going off a lot at night, when previously it had been well-behaved, don't ignore the problem. It's an old trick for a thief to deliberately set off your alarm several times, each time hiding round the corner when you come out to investigate, then to wait until the fifth or sixth time when you don't reset it (in disgust), leaving him a clear run. If your alarm does keep false-alarming

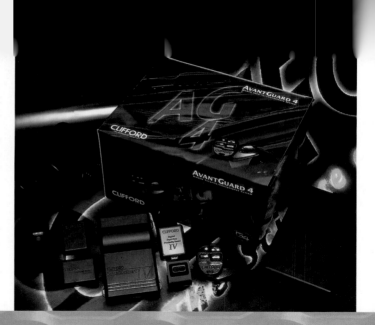

without outside assistance, find out the cause quickly, or your neighbours will quickly become 'deaf' to it.

Thatcham categories and meanings:

1 Cat 1. For alarms and electronic immobilisers.

2 Cat 2. For electronic immobilisers only.

3 Cat 2-1. Electronic immobilisers which can be upgraded to Cat 1 alarms later.

4 Cat 3. Mechanical immobilisers, eg snap-off steering wheels, locking wheel bolts, window film, steering wheel locks/covers.

5 Q-class. Tracking devices.

Other alarm features

Two-stage anti-shock - means that the alarm shouldn't go off, just because the neighbour's cat jumps on your car roof, or because Little Johnny punts his football into your car. Alarm will only sound after a major shock, or after repeated shocks are detected.

Anti-tilt - detects any attempt to lift or jack up the car, preventing any attempt to pinch alloys. Very unpopular with thieves, as it makes the alarm very sensitive (much more so than anti-shock). Alarm may sound if car is parked outside in stormy conditions (but not if your suspension's rock-hard!).

Anti-hijack - immobiliser with built-in delay. If your motor gets hi-jacked, the neanderthals responsible will only get so far down the road before the engine cuts out.

Rolling code - reduces the chance of your alarm remote control signal from being 'grabbed' by special electronic equipment.

Total closure - module which connects to electric windows/sunroof and central locking, which closes all items when alarm is set. Alarms like this often have other nifty features such as remote boot opening.

Pager control - yes, really - your alarm can be set to send a message to your pager (why not your mobile?) if your car gets tampered with.

Current-sensing disable - very useful feature on some cars which have a cooling fan which can cut in after the ignition is switched off. Without this feature, your alarm will be triggered every time you leave it parked after a long run - very annoying.

Volumetric-sensing disable - allows you to manually disable the interior ultrasonics, leaving the rest of the alarm features active. Useful if you want to leave the sunroof open in hot weather - if a fly gets in the car, the alarm would otherwise be going off constantly.

Talking alarms - no, please, please no. Very annoying, and all that'll happen is you'll attract crowds of kids daring each other to set it off again. Unfortunately, these are becoming more popular, with some offering the facility to record your own message!

The knowledge

What people often fail to realise (at least, until it happens to them) is the level of violence and destruction which thieves will employ to get your stuff - this goes way beyond breaking a window.

It comes as a major shock to most people when they discover the serious kinds of tools (weapons) at many professional thieves' disposal, and how brutally your lovingly-polished car will be attacked. Many people think, for instance, that it's their whole car they're after, whereas it's really only the parts they want, and they don't care how they get them (this means that these parts are still attractive, even when fitted to a basic car which has yet to be fully modded). Obviously, taking the whole car then gives the option of hiding it to strip at leisure, but it won't always be the option chosen, and you could wake up one morning to a well-mangled wreck outside.

Attack 1 The first option to any thief is to smash glass - typically, the toughened-glass side windows, which will shatter, unlike the windscreen. Unfortunately for the thief, this makes a loud noise (not good), but is a quick and easy way in. The reason for taking this approach is that a basic car alarm will only go off if the doors are opened (voltage-drop alarm) - provided the doors aren't opened, the alarm won't go off.

Response 1 A more sophisticated alarm will feature shock sensing (which will be set off by the impact on the glass), and better still, ultrasonic sensing, which will be triggered by the brick coming in through the broken window.

Response 2 This kind of attack can also be stopped by applying security film to the inside of the glass, which holds it all together and prevents easy entry.

Attack 2 An alternative to smashing the glass is to pry open the door using a crowbar - this attack involves literally folding open the door's window frame by prising from the top corner. The glass will still shatter, but as long as the door stays shut, a voltage-drop alarm won't be triggered.

Response This method might not be defeated by a shock-sensing alarm, but an ultrasonic unit would pick it up.

Incidentally, another bonus with ultrasonic alarms is that the sensors are visible from outside - and act as a deterrent.

Attack 3 The next line of attack is to disable the alarm. The commonest way to kill the alarm is either to cut the wiring to the alarm itself, or to disconnect the battery, 'safely' hidden away under the bonnet. And just how strong is a bonnet? Not strong enough to resist being crowbarred open, which is exactly what happens.

Response 1 If your alarm has extra pin-switches, be sure to fit one to the bonnet, and fit it in the bonnet channel next to the battery, so that it'll set off the alarm if the bonnet is prised up. Also make sure that the wire to the pin-switch cannot be cut easily though a partly-open bonnet.

Response 2 Make sure that the alarm module is well-hidden, and cannot be got at from underneath the car.

Response 3 Make the alarm power supply connection somewhere less obvious than directly at the battery terminal - any thief who knows his stuff will immediately cut any 'spare' red wires at the battery. Try taking power from the fusebox, or if you must source it under the bonnet, trace the large red battery lead to the starter motor connections, and tap into the power there.

Response 4 Always disguise the new alarm wiring, by using black insulating tape to wrap it to the existing wiring loom. Tidying up in this way also helps to ensure the wires can't get trapped, cut, melted, or accidentally ripped out - any of which could leave you with an alarm siren which won't switch off, or an immobiliser you can't disable.

Response 5 An alarm which has a 'battery back-up' facility is a real kiss of death to the average thief's chances. Even if he's successfully crowbarred your bonnet and snipped the battery connections, the alarm will still go off, powered by a separate battery of its own. A Cat 1 alarm has to have battery back-up.

Fitting a basic **LED**

All you need for this is a permanent live feed, an earth, a switch if you want to be able to turn it on/off, and the flashing LED itself (very cheap, from any car accessory shop).

An LED draws very little current, so you'll be quite safe tapping into almost any live feed you fancy. If you've wired in your ICE, take a live feed from the permanent (radio memory supply) wire at the back of your head unit, or have a delve into the back of the fusebox with your test light. An earth can easily be tapped again from your head unit, or you can make one almost anywhere on the metal body of the car, by drilling a small hole, fitting a self-tapping screw, then wrapping the bared end of wire around and tightening it.

The best and easiest place to mount an LED is into one of the many blank switches the makers seem to love fitting. The blank switch is easily pried out, and a hole can then be drilled to take the LED (which usually comes in a separate little holder). Feed the LED wiring down behind the dashboard to where you've tapped your live and earth, taking care not to trap it anywhere, nor to accidentally wrap it around any moving parts.

Connect your live to the LED red wire, then rig your earth to one side of the switch, and connect the LED black wire to the other switch terminal. You should now have a switchable LED! Tidy up the wiring, and mount the switch somewhere discreet, but where you can still get at it. Switch on when you leave the car, and it looks as if you've got some sort of alarm - better than nothing!

Wiring
basics

With your wires identified, how to tap into them? Before we even get that far, is that wire you're planning on playing with live?

Switch off the ignition at least - and ideally disconnect the battery before you do anything else. On cars with airbags, don't go tapping into any of the airbag wiring, which is usually bright yellow. With that cleared up, how were you planning on joining the old and new wires together?

Here's our advice:

Soldering - avoids cutting through your chosen wire - strip away a short section of insulation, wrap your new wire around the bared section, then apply solder to secure it. If you're a bit new to soldering, practice on a few offcuts of wire first - it ain't rocket science! Re-insulate the soldered connection afterwards, with tape or heatshrink tube.

Bullet connectors - cut and strip the end of your chosen wire, wrap your new one to it, push both into one half of the bullet. Connect the other end of your victim wire to the other bullet, and connect together. Always use the 'female' half on any live feed - it'll be safer if you disconnect it than a male bullet, which could touch bare metal and send your motor up in smoke.

Block connectors - so easy to use. Just remember that the wires can come adrift if the screws aren't really tight, and don't get too ambitious about how many wires you can stuff in one hole (block connectors, like bullets, are available in several sizes). Steer clear of connectors like the one below - they're convenient, but they can give rise to problems.

With any of these options, always insulate around your connection - especially when soldering, or you'll be leaving bare metal exposed. Remember that you'll probably be shoving all the wires up into the dark recesses of the under-dash area - by the time the wires are nice and kinked/squashed together, that tiny bit of protruding wire might just touch that bit of metal bodywork, and that'll be a fire...

Fitting an auxiliary fusebox

You'll need plenty of fused live feeds from the battery during the modifying process, for stereo gear, neons, starter buttons - and alarms, and it's always a pain working out where to tap into one. If you make up your own little fusebox, mounted somewhere easy to get at, you'll never have this problem again - and it's easy enough to do.

The first job is to run a main supply cable from the battery positive terminal, to inside the car - but don't connect the wire up to the battery terminal just yet. Make sure that the main cable is man enough for all the loads you're likely to put on it - starting with eight-gauge wire (available from all good ICE suppliers) will mean you're never short of current.

Make a note of which fuse is for which circuit, and carry the paper around in the glovebox (along with some spare fuses). If a fuse ever blows, you won't end up with your head stuck under the dash, trying to remember where you tapped in, and where the fuse is. You'll just pull the cover off, and replace the fuse. Who would've thought electrical safety could be so cool?

01 First job is to find a suitable place to locate the fusebox. We've chosen the floor area under the passenger seat to locate ours - easily accessible in the event a blown fuse, and out of the way. Place the boxes on a flat area of floor, and in such a way that the forward/backward movement of the seat is not affected. Next, create paper templates of the two boxes, and transfer them to card.

02 Place the card template in position and cut out the shape. Then repeat process for other box - ensure at least a four-inch gap between the two boxes, to allow some wire-connection room.

07 Push the grommet back into place. Might be a good idea to treat it to some silicone sealant, to keep the elements out - after all, if you get water trickling down that new wire, where's it going to end up? Oops.

08 Next job is to connect the cable to the positive terminal of the battery using a ring terminal. Make sure you do a decent job here - there could be a load of accessories depending on it. Take care once that lead goes onto the battery, too - the business end inside the car will be live.

09 Inside the car again, and pick up the cable we threaded through the bulkhead. To tidily route the wire to the junction box, the sill trim and carpet will have to be pulled up and out of the way. Fortunately, this is easy on the Civic - prise the sill trim up, and remove two seat belt rail retaining bolts.

10 With the carpet lifted up, thread the cable down the car. For a neat job, hold the wire in place with some tape.

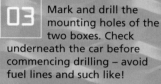

03 Mark and drill the mounting holes of the two boxes. Check underneath the car before commencing drilling – avoid fuel lines and such like!

04 Hold the boxes in place using self-tapping screws. If you're really lucky, you might find those same screws could be used as earth points, giving you ready-made lives and earths in the same place - how clever is that?

05 To the engine bay now, to find a path for the wire to travel from the battery through the bulkhead, down the car into the fusebox. As luck would have it – a perfectly-situated grommet underneath the battery!

06 Make a slit in the grommet and thread your wire through the slit (the cable must be at least eight-gauge if lots of loads are going on it). It's a good idea at this point to make sure you have a long enough cable to reach down to the fusebox under the seat as well as extending up to the battery - don't cut the wire from the reel until you're sure.

11 We could've joined the single live feed to the six wires of the fusebox, using a large bullet connector, or a terminal block. Both of these options are a little dodgy, so we bought a junction box from the same place as our fusebox. Pop open the junction box to see the two nut-and-bolt connection terminals - it's a much simpler and safer solution. Crimp a ring terminal to the end of the cable, and fix to the left terminal of junction box.

12 Next cut six lengths of wire (long enough to reach fusebox), and solder all six wires to a ring terminal. To protect the wires we added some heat shrink as well - no such thing as too much electrical safety. Then fix the ring connector to the right-hand terminal of the junction box.

13 Crimp connectors onto the ends of each of the six wires, and slot them into place on the fusebox. Then as and when you need a live feed, you can take a feed wire from whatever you're fitting and connect it to one of the fusebox terminals – simple-as.

14 Oh, and don't forget to add the correct fuse – otherwise your efforts were in vain! You might need some guesswork as to the right fuse rating for some accessories, but don't just go for the biggest fuse you can every time. Remember to pop the fusebox cover back on, too.

Alarm fitting

Our Civic actually had a pretty decent alarm on it already, so we decided not to mess with it. And that, in a way, is your first lesson in alarms - if you're thinking of fitting one to a car that's already got one, be prepared for some nasty surprises when you dive behind the dash. How the heck have they wired this in? Will chopping that wire mean the car won't start? If it looks a mess behind there, it's best to leave it - and then hope it never goes wrong, or you'll have to suss it all out anyway.

If your Civic's still a virgin in the aftermarket alarm sense, things are a bit easier. Here's a few tips to successful alarm fitting which we've picked up on our other project cars.

Disconnect the battery negative lead, and move the lead away from the battery, or you'll be blowing fuses and your new alarm will go mental the minute it's rigged up. Decide where you're going to mount the alarm/siren. Choose somewhere not easily reached from underneath, for a start, and if you can, pick a location away from where you'll be topping up washers, oil or coolant - fluids and alarm modules don't mix.

Now there's wires to play with. Most of them should go thorough into the car, but not all - check your alarm's instructions. You've probably got a bonnet pin switch and an earth wire which can stay in the engine bay. The rest? Get out the electrical tape, and wrap that bunch of wires into a neat loom, to go inside. On our Civic, removing the battery and its tray gave us a handy grommet to work with. If you're making a hole of your own, rather than using a bulkhead grommet, dismantle some dash first, and feel inside for any obstructions. Don't forget to use a rubber grommet on any sharp-edged hole with a wire passing through.

The bonnet pin switch should be close to the battery, but it must hit a 'good' (flat) spot on the bonnet - getting this right can be tricky. Partly shut the bonnet, and peer through the gap, or

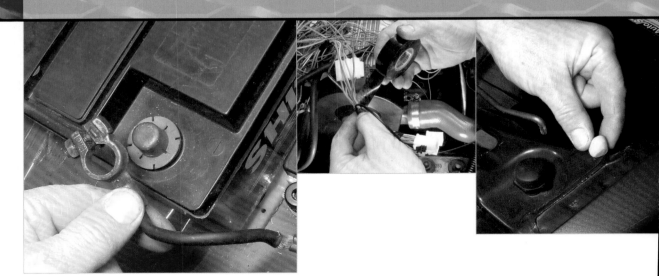

Tricks 'n' tips

Don't assume you'll automatically be able to close the bonnet fully, when you first fit your pin switch - the plunger might be too long, and you'll bust the switch if you force the bonnet shut. Also, check that the switch plunger can be pushed fully down, without catching on any other vital components. If the bonnet opens much before the switch works, you'll be giving access which the crims can exploit. Just trim off some of the plastic switch plunger until all's well - trimming the pin switch down will make it 'go off' sooner, but only take off a little plastic at a time, then re-test. If you go too far when trimming down a pin switch, you can sometimes rescue the situation by screwing a little self-tapping screw into the top of the plunger. You can then 'adjust' the length of the plunger at will. The proper answer, though, is to buy a new switch.

experiment by placing a lump of Blu-tac on the bonnet, then close it and see where the lump sticks.

Tapping into the car's wiring - always makes the less-experienced Maxer a tad nervous. Will I mess up something else by chopping in my alarm wires? The trick we use is not to cut through any of the standard wiring if we can help it. Instead, once you've identified the wire you need to join onto (like an ignition live, say), just

carefully strip off a little of the plastic insulation so part of the wire's bare, then wrap the bared end of your new wire around it, and secure with a little solder (finish off with a little insulating tape). That way, whatever circuit you've tapped into should still work afterwards. Arm yourself with the Haynes manual wiring diagrams to help track down those pesky wires.

The only other bit to worry about is drilling a hole somewhere on your dash for the alarm LED. The best place for one of these is in a blank switch (there usually is one, even on a top-spec Civic) - the blank can be prised out, making feeding the LED wire up through a bit easier, and it'll be in a good prominent place on the dash, so the pikeys can't miss it.

So come on - does it work? Most alarms require you to 'programme in' the remotes before they'll work. Test all the alarm features in turn, remembering to allow enough time for the alarm to arm itself (usually about 30 seconds). When you test it for the first time, don't forget to either shut the bonnet completely, or do like us, and hold the bonnet pin switch down. Our way, you can pull out the alarm fuses and shut it up, if something goes wrong!

Set the anti-shock sensitivity with a thought to where you live and park - will it be set off every night by the neighbour's cat, or by kids playing football? Finally, and most important of all - next time you park up, remember to set it!

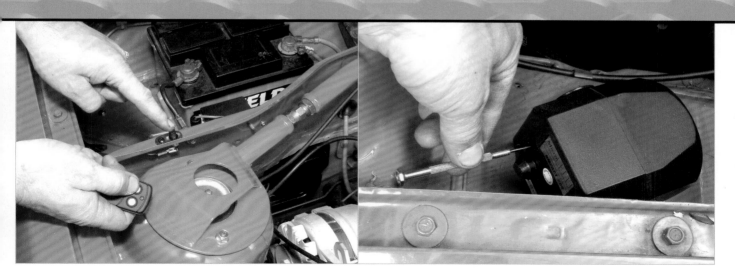

Body styling

If you're planning a major body job, you've probably already got some good ideas about how you want your Civic to look, from *'Max Power'* or *'Revs'*, or maybe from a friend's car. While it can be good to have a target car to aim for, if you're just starting out on the road towards a fully-loaded car, you probably don't want (or can't quite afford) to go 'all the way' all at once.

If you're new to the world of modifying, it's a good idea to start with smaller jobs, and work up to the full body kit gradually, as your skills increase; spending loads on a body kit is a pretty lame idea if you then make a mess of fitting it! There's plenty of small ways to improve the look of your Civic, which don't cost much, and which are simple enough to fit; start with some of these before you go too mad!

One golden rule with any body mods is to plan what you're going to do, and don't rush it. It's better that the car looks a bit stupid for a week (because you couldn't get something finished) than to rush a job and have the car look stupid forever. Do half the job properly instead of messing up all of it. Try and think the jobs through - plan each stage. Have you got all the tools, screws or whatever before you start, or will you have to break off halfway through? If you get stuck, is there someone you can get to help, or have they gone off for the weekend? Above all, if something goes wrong - don't panic - a calm approach will prove to be a huge bonus (that job doesn't have to be done today, does it?).

If a piece of trim won't come off, don't force it. If something feels like it's going to break, it probably will - stop and consider whether to go on and break it, or try another approach. Especially on an older car, things either never come off as easily as you think, or else have already been off so many times that they either break or won't fit back on properly. While we'd all like to do a perfect job every time, working on an older car will, sooner or later, teach you the fine art of 'bodging' (finding valid alternative ways of fixing things!). Don't assume that you'll have to bodge something back on, every time - if a trim clip breaks when you take something off, it might be easier and cheaper than you think to simply go to your Honda dealer, and buy a new clip (remember, even Honda mechanics break things from time to time, so they will keep these things in stock!).

Water features

This is all about giving you a couple of highly-visible features up front. Forget Charlie Dimmock. Do not even think Charlie Dimmock. Washer jet lights are now almost expected at a cruise, and it's such a simple feature to fit, it's nearly a crime not to. Course, our friendly fellas in blue uniforms don't see it quite that way - showing anything other than a white light up front is illegal, and plenty of people get stopped for it. The best answer? Fit them by all means, but rig them into a well-placed switch for emergencies.

Removing the boring standard washer jets is easy, and will take no time at all. On the underside of the bonnet, unclip **01** the pipe that leads from the washer bottle to the jets.

Then remove the existing washer jets by pressing the retaining lugs in, and lifting the jet out. Try not to break **02** them - you might be refitting them one day.

Slide the rubber base gasket up the wire and onto the bottom of the new washer jet. If you don't fit this, your bonnet will **03** leak water - possibly straight onto the plug leads.

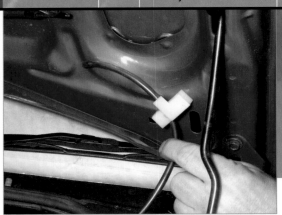

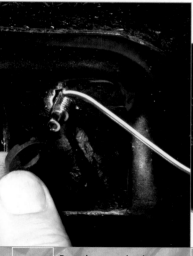

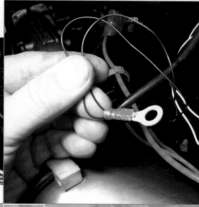

04 Pop the new jet into the bonnet and slide the rubber washer up the wire. The rubber washer has a small recess cut out to stop the retaining nut crushing the wire. Don't be alarmed to see that our bonnet has changed colour – we've just fitted a carbon fibre bonnet!

05 Add the metal washer and retaining nut and tighten. With the old washer pipe refitted, the end result should look something like this.

06 This next bit is really fiddly, so take your time. The wires from the jets need to be routed into the engine bay, where they will be passed through the bulkhead to the switch on the dash. Use a length of welding wire and attach the end of each wire to it, then pull them through behind the bonnet beams. Using cable-ties attach the two wires to the existing washer pipe until you reach the battery.

07 Each jet has a black and a white wire - according to the instructions, the blacks are earths. Using a ring terminal, connect the two black wires together, then fit them to a convenient earth point (should be lots available under the bonnet, or make your own by drilling a hole in the metalwork).

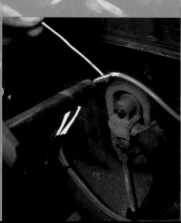

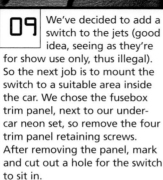

08 Now to the two white wires (the live feeds). At this point, we have to add a length of our own wire, as the wire supplied is not long enough to get it to its final resting place inside the car. Solder the two white wires to the new wire, remembering to insulate the joint afterwards. Or you could use crimps.

09 We've decided to add a switch to the jets (good idea, seeing as they're for show use only, thus illegal). So the next job is to mount the switch to a suitable area inside the car. We chose the fusebox trim panel, next to our under-car neon set, so remove the four trim panel retaining screws. After removing the panel, mark and cut out a hole for the switch to sit in.

10 Feed the new wire through the bulkhead, under the dash and into the driver's footwell, where a female connector will join the wire to the back of the switch. The final stage of the wiring is to find yourself a live feed. We've taken one from our auxiliary fusebox (refer to security section) but a feed from the battery will be fine. Another female crimp will join our yellow live wire to the switch and complete the circuit.

11 That live feed should be fused, of course - that's easy for us to say, with our posh DIY fusebox. Use an in-line fuseholder instead if you have to. Put out the daylight, and enjoy the effects.

Mirror, mirror

Mirrors are another simple to fit, must-have accessory. The DTM or M3-style door mirrors are well established on the modified car circuit, but there are lots of variations of mirror styles and finishes, so finding some you like won't be hard.

If you want to be just a little different, try some 'California' mirrors. The trouble with being different is it's always more work - California mirrors are 'universal fit', meaning you have to make them fit your car. You bought a Civic 'cause it's a popular car, so why make life difficult? Buy some Civic mirrors (or at least some Civic mirror bases), and your new M3, Cup or Bomex mirrors could be fitted in minutes. Remember - 'universal' means 'won't fit any car easily' !

There's more to mirrors than just looks, though - some have toys attached. Like side repeater lights (in a Merc stylee) or thumb switches for releasing your de-locked, de-handled doors. We want some of that.

M3 repeater light mirrors

01 Removing the old mirror is easy, and takes just a few minutes. After prising off the interior trim panel using a screwdriver, disconnect the wiring plug. For those of you without electric mirrors as standard, there won't be a plug.

02 Remove the three bolts whilst supporting mirror with one hand so that it doesn't fall. With the aid of pliers, push the wiring plug (if you've got one) through the hole and lift the mirror away.

03 Check that the new mirrors fit by offering them into place. Our chosen mirrors from APC (American Products Company - available from MSI Online) are some of the best-fitting we've seen. If you're not so lucky and your mirror bases don't fit properly, this is the time to make them fit – this may mean attacking the bases with a Stanley knife or other suitable tools!

04 Feed the new wiring plug through the hole, then tighten the three mirror mounting bolts.

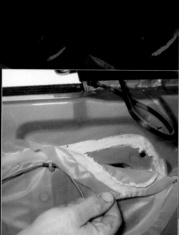   

05 The door card must now be removed (as described in 'interiors') - this only applies to mirrors that require some wiring changes. The lights in our mirrors have two functions - they act as a side repeater and a sidelight. Once the door card has been removed, peel back the plastic membrane.

First job with the door off is to pull the trunking from its hole and remove any insulation tape to reveal a nice big bunch of wires. To the left of the trunking, you can see a feed that branches off from the main trunking to the side repeaters – we can use this for the indicators in our mirrors – excellent.

06 Taking out the door speaker will give us more room to work inside the door. Before going any further, though, it's a good idea to disconnect the battery. Remove the four speaker mounting screws, and disconnect the wiring plug.

07 Time to mount the electronic black box supplied with the kit (we'll wire them up later). The boxes are supplied with double-sided tape to stick them in place, but screwing's better. Mark and drill a hole in a suitable flat surface to mount the box. Before drilling, check there's no wiring routed behind, and keep clear of the door check strap and window mechanisms. Mount the box using a self-tapping screw.

Identify the green/white wire that acts as the live feed to the side repeaters. Cut the wire (near the top of the trunking), and crimp a male bullet to each end. Next, select the yellow/white wire, and cut it. Tape one end of wire . . .

08 Connect the plug from the mirrors to the plug from the black box. Reconnect the battery, and put the window up again. At this point, to gain better access to the wires needed inside the plastic door trunking, we completely removed the door. We'd advise that you only do this if you have a mate handy to help you support/lift the doors, as they are blooming heavy! For door removal, see your Haynes manual.

. . . and crimp a male bullet connector to the other. Using a block connector, join the three wires together (2 x green/white, 1 x yellow/white wires). There's various ways, of course, that you could've chosen to join these wires, but you get the idea.

09

10 Disconnect the wiring plug from the existing side repeater light.

11

12

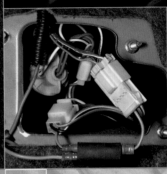

13 Similarly, locate and cut the black earth wire - add a male bullet to each end. Select the black/blue wire. You may find (like us) that there's two black/blue wires - if so, select the thinner of the two wires to use. Then… you guessed it – join them all together using a block connector.

14 That should be the indicators sorted, now onto the sidelights. The door trunking doesn't hold any wires that will give us a suitable feed to the sidelights - in fact, your easiest option is to tap into a wire from the headlights or rear lights! Feed a length of wire through inside the car - we're going for the rear lights, so a fair length of wire was needed.

15 Just to explain why we're tapping into the rear light wiring for some sidelights - when the sidelights are on, so are the tail lights (and the number plate light, come to that). After running our new wire to the back of the car (taped down, under the carpets), we removed the rear light inner cover and cut into the red/black wire - which our Haynes wiring diagram told us was the tail light feed.

16 With the wire cut, we used our bullet-and-block connector method to join in our new red wire, which of course feeds back to our front doors. The sidelight feed doesn't quite reach our mirrors yet though - somehow, we've got to get it out into the doors.

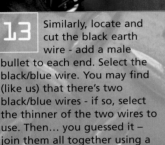

After consulting our Haynes wiring diagram (and doing a little checking with our test light), we found a blue/white wire in the door wiring loom which we could use to tap our new red wire onto, to **17** carry the feed through to the mirrors.

Lastly, refit the trunking and tape up the collection of wires. Once this has been done, reconnect the side **18** repeater plug and refit door.

Back to the black box we mounted earlier. Begin by cutting the black, blue and red wires from the box to a suitable length (so that the wires from the box can reach the wiring plug from the old mirrors). Tape the wires up to a couple of inches from the end to protect them, then **19** cut off the existing mirror wiring plug.

Route the new black box wires over the top of the door membrane to the old mirror wiring plug, and join the wires as shown in the accompanying table. Once this is done, the door trim panel can go back on, and you can check **20** out your sweet new mirrors.

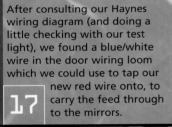

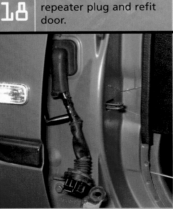

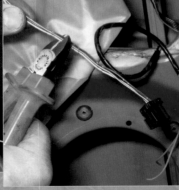

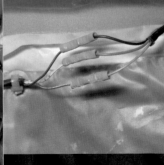

Old mirror plug	Black box wires
Black/blue	*Black*
Blue/white	*Red*
Yellow/white	*Blue*

Smoothly does it

If you've bought a basic Civic, it's understandable that you might not want to declare this fact loudly from the rear end of your car. Badges also clutter up the otherwise clean lines, and besides, you're trying to make your Civic look different, so why give them obvious clues like a badge?

Most Civics also come with admittedly-useful but actually quite ugly side rubbing strips of some sort - lose these, or at least colour-code, if you're at all serious about raising your game.

General bodywork smoothing (including de-seaming) takes time and skill, and is probably best done on a car which is then getting the full bodykit and wicked respray treatment. There's no doubt, however, that it really looks the business to have a fully-flushed tailgate/boot lid, or even to have those ugly roof gutters smoothed. Probably best to put the pros at a bodyshop to work on this. De-badging you can definitely do at home, so get to it.

De-stripping

Side rubbing strips. Good - they save your paint if Mr Numpty opens his rusty Metro door into your car. Bad - they look hideous. If looks are important, removal is easy.

Once the strips are off, you've got a problem - they leave deep recesses in the door and wings. So just fill them? Well, yes, but the doors may be a problem. The filler tends to break up and fall out at each end of the door's strip recess, unless you weld on a small plate across the ends. There may also be problems with the filled door edge catching on the similarly-filled edge on the front wing.

To make life easier, we put our capable team at Avon Customs on the job of removing and colour-coding our strips.

01 The strips are held on by several clips along the side of the car - these clips will probably break during the removal operations, leaving you a bit stuck. However, at least you can 'glue' the strips back on with proper bodyshop mastic. On the door sections, the front and rear ends of the strip have a nut. Which might come off okay (the front one's a pig to reach), or it might just shear off. Back to the mastic, then.

02 Once the strips have come off, the plastic clips that didn't break can be slid out sideways, and refitted to the car while the strips are being sprayed (if that's your plan too).

03 The strips require the use of a special primer before the 'real' paint can go on. But since this is just a clear coat, we thought we'd at least show you paint you can see. Here are our strips (and some other bits) after their base coat stage. The short sections of the strip are especially fiddly to paint. Use a thin piece of wood or wire to make up a holding tool, so you can pick these bits up easily while spraying.

Roof **gutters**

Something else the makers 'fit', to mess up the smooth lines of your car. Well, that's how it seems, anyway. So it's just like the side rubbing strips then - rip the plastic trims out, and fill in the channels? You just know there'll be more to it than that.

01 Okay, so removing the gutter trims is easy. Protecting the paint is compulsory, but removing the rear window glass isn't - it's just that our Civic's having a complete respray, that's all.

02 Out comes the strip, leaving the channel in the roof to deal with.

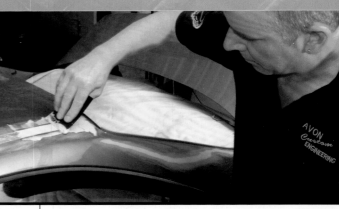

03 Although it seems like a simple job, it's one we were very glad to leave to the experts. Here's one we met earlier - it's Kevin roughing-up the roof channel for its first taste of filler.

04 For a deep channel like this, fibreglass-based filler (eg P40) is used first, to bring the level almost up to the roof line. Notice the two strips of masking tape down the sides of the channel - this filler's sticky stuff (one reason it gets used first), and it's hell to get off paintwork. Another trick of the trade, brought to you by Haynes.

05 Now we're back to 'normal' filler for the fiddly stuff. The problem with our Civic (and hopefully only the Coupe's affected like this) is that the roof profile changes quite a bit from one side of the roof channel to the other, meaning plenty of filler work was needed to make it look right - the final filler area came in beyond the sunroof!

De-badging

The Honda 'H' badges prise off pretty easily (don't wreck the paint doing it, though), but they leave holes behind. Virtually all the other badges they use just peel off - try softening the glue up with a heatgun first, which makes it more likely they'll come off in one piece. How do we deal with tiny but annoying holes? We have a plan.

Filling holes - a cunning plan

01 When it comes to car bodywork, every hole is not a goal. At least small holes can be filled without stretching your talent envelope too far. First, cover the area around your chosen hole (two holes, in this case) with masking tape - make sure you get a decent working area around the hole.

02 Now neatly cut out your holes in the tape.

03 Here's where we start to see the true cunning of this plan - mix up some Araldite (or similar glue for bonding metals), and apply a blob of it to a washer large enough to cover the hole, on the inside. Rich types among you may prefer to use a coin.

04 Stick the washer or coin on from inside, then stand around looking stupid, holding it in place while the glue dries.

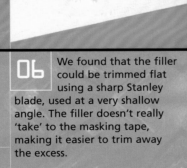
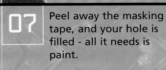

05 Mix up some filler, and apply to your hole - the masking tape prevents any getting on the paintwork. Apply more than one layer, and build the filler up evenly.

06 We found that the filler could be trimmed flat using a sharp Stanley blade, used at a very shallow angle. The filler doesn't really 'take' to the masking tape, making it easier to trim away the excess.

07 Peel away the masking tape, and your hole is filled - all it needs is paint.

08 If you haven't done such a great job, remember that you can improve things by applying layer after layer of paint (wait for each one to dry). When you've built the paint up proud of the hole, T-Cut it back smooth.

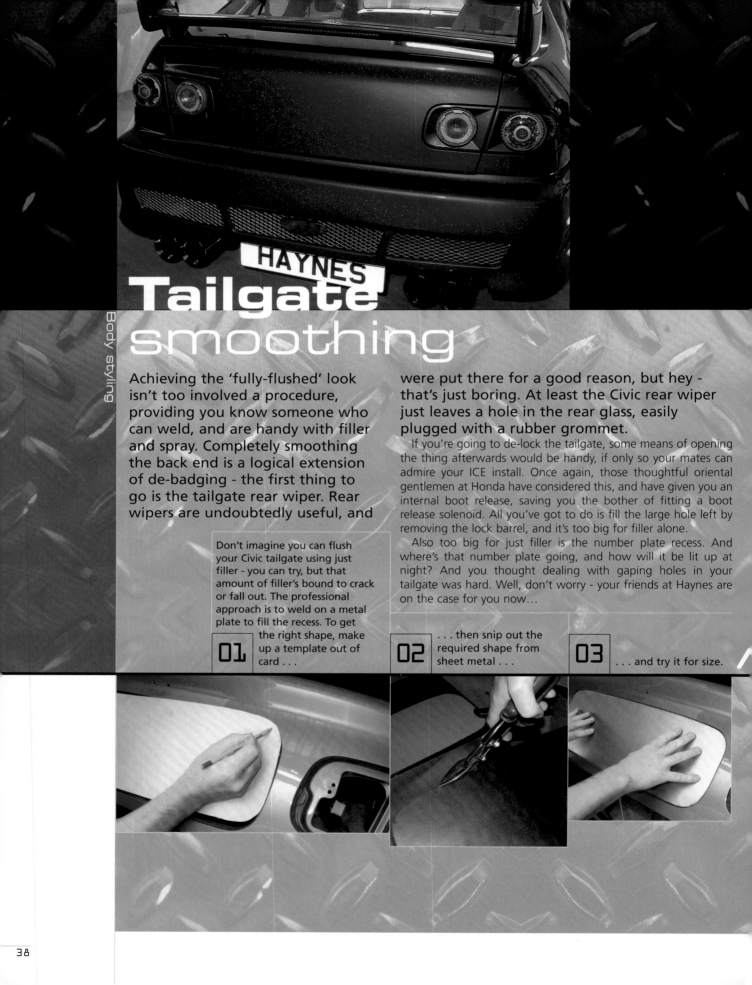

Tailgate
smoothing

Achieving the 'fully-flushed' look isn't too involved a procedure, providing you know someone who can weld, and are handy with filler and spray. Completely smoothing the back end is a logical extension of de-badging - the first thing to go is the tailgate rear wiper. Rear wipers are undoubtedly useful, and

were put there for a good reason, but hey - that's just boring. At least the Civic rear wiper just leaves a hole in the rear glass, easily plugged with a rubber grommet.

If you're going to de-lock the tailgate, some means of opening the thing afterwards would be handy, if only so your mates can admire your ICE install. Once again, those thoughtful oriental gentlemen at Honda have considered this, and have given you an internal boot release, saving you the bother of fitting a boot release solenoid. All you've got to do is fill the large hole left by removing the lock barrel, and it's too big for filler alone.

Also too big for just filler is the number plate recess. And where's that number plate going, and how will it be lit up at night? And you thought dealing with gaping holes in your tailgate was hard. Well, don't worry - your friends at Haynes are on the case for you...

Don't imagine you can flush your Civic tailgate using just filler - you can try, but that amount of filler's bound to crack or fall out. The professional approach is to weld on a metal plate to fill the recess. To get the right shape, make

01 up a template out of card . . .

02 . . . then snip out the required shape from sheet metal . . .

03 . . . and try it for size.

04 You can get away with just a few little tack-welds to secure the new metalwork, but if the metal isn't secured all the way round, it could flex, and the filler you'll put over the top could crack. Running a bead of weld round runs the risk of warping the tailgate, so the real trick here is to use the welder all round the edge, but only in short bursts.

05 All that should be needed now is a light skim of filler around the edges. This isn't really a two-man job, but you can never have too many Avon Customs men on the case…

06 After a quick rub-down (or even, several rubs-down, more filler, a guide coat, more rubbing-down and some primer) the back end's ready for paint.

Number plate mounting and lighting

Though you probably wouldn't think it, this is one of the most forgotten-about items - and it causes no end of problems. Try and think ahead when planning a boot-smooth, as an illegal number plate is a bit of a come-and-nick-me to you-know-who.

01 Yes, we know this isn't even a legal number plate - it's just for show. As you can see, our new rear bumper didn't give much scope for plate mounting, so we made two little brackets, and slung it underneath. Fortunately, it still shows up well enough not to attract the flashing-blue-light kind of attention.

02 Our lighting solution might not be strictly legal, but at least we tried, and again, this might be enough of a gesture to avoid getting pulled. A row of four white LEDs mounted above the plate will hopefully be bright enough to do the job. Wired, in case you wondered, from the existing number plate light circuit.

repeaters

If you've got Merc-style mirrors like us, those side repeaters are a bit redundant, suddenly. And since anything we don't need on the exterior gets binned, they're next. Removing the lights isn't a problem (see the lights section), but dealing with that hole just might be - small it is not.

01 A hole this size needs a metal strip welding-in for a sensible job. So guess what? Here we are, measuring up a metal strip.

02 Since the back of this particular hole's just a tad difficult to reach, we'll be welding from the front. Where the paint is. We can't expect weld to take on a painted surface, so the grinder's brought into play, to clean off the area.

03 Getting the plate into position means unclipping the wheel arch liner, then having a brave (and suitably-protected) assistant hold the plate in place while it's tacked. Even when all that's been done, the welder can only be used in very short bursts, otherwise the excess heat will distort the wing. Notice the brown paper used to protect the paint and side skirt from weld sparks. The pros think of everything.

04 After a quick skim of filler . . .

05 . . . and a rub-down, it's "what side repeater?".

Travelling incognito

If you is a gangsta wiv da Staines massive, blacking those windows is a must. Window tinting is also one of the best ways to disguise a naff standard interior, or a good way to hide a sorted interior (or ICE install) from the pikeys…

Tints look right with almost any car colour (limo-tint on a black Civic is virtually essential, while mirror film looks trick on a silver car), and with 'reflex film' available in various rainbow colours, there's something for everyone. Only downside is - not all tints are legal to be run on the road, and you'll be chancing it buying any advertised as 'for show cars only'. The boys in blue don't like to see tinted front windows (at cruises, it can be an instant pull), but just doing the rear windows looks a bit stupid. Tints don't suit everybody - if you're doing your car to pose around in (and why not?) it's hard enough to see you in there anyway, without blacking-out the windows!

Because window tinting involves sticking a layer of film to the inside of the glass, fitting tints might help to prevent a break-in, since your side windows won't shatter when hit. Car security firm Toad market an adhesive film specifically designed to prevent break-ins in this way, and even humble window-tinting kits are claimed to offer the same effect.

Generally, window tint comes on a roll, but you can sometimes buy pre-cut kits for popular cars. Buying a kit (if you can) sounds a better deal, but if you muck up fitting one section, you'll be buying another complete kit. With a roll of film, check how many windows you'll be able to do with it - one roll usually isn't enough for the whole car.

At this point, we'd better 'fess up and tell you that tinting will severely try your patience. If you're not a patient sort of person, this is one job which may well wind you up - you have been warned. Saying that, if you're calm and careful, and you follow the instructions to the letter, you could surprise yourself - our mechanic did, when we tried it for the first time and got a near-perfect result!

In brief, the process for tinting is to lay the film on the outside of the glass first, and cut it exactly to size. The protective layer is peeled off to expose the adhesive side, the film is transferred to the inside of the car (tricky) and then squeegeed into place (also tricky). All this must be done with scrupulous cleanliness, as any muck or stray bits of trimmed-off film will ruin the effect (tricky, if you're working outside). The other problem which won't surprise you is that getting rid of air bubbles and creases can take time. A long time. This is another test of patience, because if, as the instructions say, you've used plenty of spray, it will take a while to dry out and stick… just don't panic!

Legal eagle

The law on window tinting currently is that there must be no more than a 25% reduction in light transmission through windscreens, and a limit of 30% reduction on all other glass. How the heck do you measure light reduction? Also, many cars come with tinted glass as standard - so can you fit a tinting kit on top and still be legal? Hard to know what line to take, if you're stopped by Plod - try and choose a tinting kit which is EC-approved (ask before you buy, and if you think it could be a serious issue, get a letter from the company to support the legality of the kit, to use in your defence). Some forces now take this seriously enough to have portable test equipment they can use at the roadside - if your car fails, it's an on-the-spot fine.

Tinting windows

It's worth picking your day, and your working area, pretty carefully - on a windy day, there'll be more dust in the air, and it'll be a nightmare trying to stop the film flapping and folding onto itself while you're working.

Applying window tint is best done on a warm day (or in a warm garage - if there is such a thing), because the adhesive will begin to dry sooner. For fairly obvious reasons, don't try tinting when it's starting to get dark! It's a good idea to have a mate to help out with this job, but you might get fed up hearing 'you've missed another bubble' or 'you can still see that crease, y'know'.

01 Get the window being tinted clean - really clean - inside and out. Don't use glass cleaners (or any other product) containing ammonia or vinegar, since both will react with the film or its adhesive, and muck it up. Also clean the area around the window - it's too easy for stray dirt to attach itself to the film - and by the time you've noticed it, it could be too late. On door windows, wind them down slightly, to clean all of the top edge, then close them tight to fit the film.

02 Before you even unroll the film, take note - handle it carefully. If you crease it, you won't get the creases out - ever. First work out which way up the film is, by applying a small bit of really sticky tape to the front and back side - use the tape to pull the films apart, just at one corner.

03 Lay the film onto the glass, with the clear side facing you. Unroll the film, and cut it roughly to the size of the window (on a door window, leave plenty at the bottom edge for now). Some kits have a logo on the film, which seems daft - tinting's difficult enough, without having to get a logo straight! The only benefit of a logo is to establish which layer is the tint. Make life easier - lose the logo.

04 Spray the outside of the window with a weak soapy water solution (Folia Tec supply a small bottle of Joy fluid in their kit, but you could use a few drops of ordinary washing-up liquid). Get one of those plant sprayers you can buy cheap in any DIY store, if your kit doesn't contain a sprayer.

05 Lay the roughly-cut sheet of tint back onto the glass, and spray the outside of the film with soapy water . . .

06 . . . then use a squeegee to get out the air bubbles, sticking the film to the outside of the glass.

07 On a door window, trim the bottom edge to leave some excess to tuck down inside the door - this stops the film peeling off on the bottom rubber when you roll the window down!

08 Using a sharp knife (and taking care not to damage your paint or the window rubber), trim round the outside of the window. An unimportant piece of plastic (like an expired video club card) is brilliant for tucking the film into the edges to get the shape right, but don't trim the film right to the absolute edge - leave a small, even gap of just a few mill all round (this helps to get rid of excess water when you squeegee it on the inside - you'll see).

09 Now go inside, and prepare for receiving the tint. On fixed glass, waterproof the side trim panels in anticipation of the soapy water which will be used, by taping on some plastic sheet (otherwise, you'll have some very soggy panels. And seats. And carpets). Spray the inside of the glass with the soapy solution.

10 Back outside, it's time to separate the films. Use two pieces of sticky tape to pull the films slightly apart at one corner. As the films come apart, spray more solution onto the tinted piece underneath, to help it separate cleanly. Try not to lift the tint film too much off the glass when separating, as this increases the risk of creasing.

11 Have your willing helper on standby, to assist with transferring the film to the inside (a prime time for messing it all up). Peel the tint film off the glass, keeping it as flat as you can. Without letting it fold onto itself, move it inside the car and place it fairly accurately on the inside of the glass. The surface which was outside should now be on the inside of the glass (now that you've cut it, it will only fit one way!). Carefully slide the film into the corners, keeping it flat.

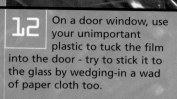

12 On a door window, use your unimportant plastic to tuck the film into the door - try to stick it to the glass by wedging-in a wad of paper cloth too.

13 Spray the film with the soapy water . . .

14 . . . then carefully start to squeegee it into place, working from top to bottom. We found that, to get into the corners, it was easier to unscrew the blade from the squeegee, and use that on its own for some of it.

15 You'll end up with a few strips at the bottom, which seemingly will not stick to the glass. Don't panic. First, soak up any excess water at the base of the film, with paper towels. Now using a hot-air gun to very gently warm the film should help to finish drying, and encourage the film to stick. Be careful squeegee-ing the film when it's dry - risk of damage. Don't lift the film off the glass - the adhesive will stick, given time. Persistence pays off.

Fitting a sunstrip

The modern sunstrip, first seen as a lovely green shadeband on Cortinas and Capris back in the 70s, usually bearing imaginative slogans such as 'DAVE AND SHARON'. Just goes to show that some things improve with age.

There are two options to make your car look (and maybe even feel) cooler:

a The sunvisor, a screen tint band inside the screen, which is usually a graduated-tint strip. As this fits inside, there's a problem straight away - the interior mirror. Your Civic mirror may be bonded to the screen, and it seriously gets in the way when trying to fit a wet and sticky (nice!) strip of plastic around it. Go for a sunstrip instead.

b The sunstrip, which is opaque vinyl, colour-matched to the car, fits to the outside of the screen. Much more Sir.

A really wide sunstrip imitates the 'roof chop' look seen on American hot rods, and colour-coded, they can look very effective from the front - plus, of course, you can use the space to advertise your preferred brand of ICE (no, no, NO! Not a good idea!). As it's fitted to the outside of the screen, the sunstrip has a good chance of seriously interfering with your wipers (or wiper, if you've been converted). If this happens to the point where the wipers can't clean the screen, Mr MOT might have a point if he fails your car... The wiper blades may need replacing more often, and the sunstrip itself might start peeling off - still want one? Well, you've got to, really.

01 This is only stuck to the outside, so only the outside of the screen needs cleaning - excellent! Do a good job of cleaning, though - any dirt stuck under the strip will ruin the effect.

02 With the help of an assistant (if you have one handy), lay the strip onto the car, and decide how far down the screen you're going to go. Legally-speaking, you shouldn't be lower than the wiper swept area - so how much of a 'badboy' are you? If you measure and mark the bottom of the strip with tape, you'll be sure to get it level, even if it's not legal.

Legal eagle

The rule for tinting or otherwise modifying the windscreen is that there must be no more than a 25% light reduction from standard. In theory, this means you can have a sunstrip which covers up to 25% of the screen area, but some MOT testers may see it differently. A sunstrip's got to come down the screen a fair way, to look any sense (otherwise, why bother?). You could argue that accurately measuring and calculating the windscreen area isn't actually that easy, if you get stopped, and anyway, a sunstrip also cuts out harmful glare! If you go so far down the screen that you can't see out, though - well, that's just stupid.

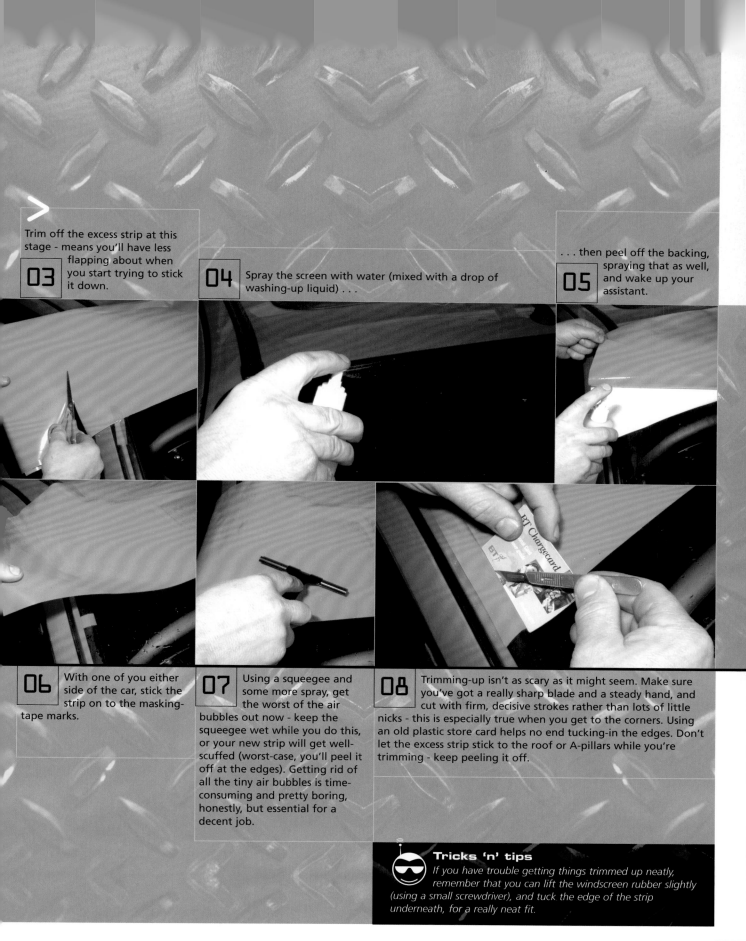

03 Trim off the excess strip at this stage - means you'll have less flapping about when you start trying to stick it down.

04 Spray the screen with water (mixed with a drop of washing-up liquid) . . .

05 . . . then peel off the backing, spraying that as well, and wake up your assistant.

06 With one of you either side of the car, stick the strip on to the masking-tape marks.

07 Using a squeegee and some more spray, get the worst of the air bubbles out now - keep the squeegee wet while you do this, or your new strip will get well-scuffed (worst-case, you'll peel it off at the edges). Getting rid of all the tiny air bubbles is time-consuming and pretty boring, honestly, but essential for a decent job.

08 Trimming-up isn't as scary as it might seem. Make sure you've got a really sharp blade and a steady hand, and cut with firm, decisive strokes rather than lots of little nicks - this is especially true when you get to the corners. Using an old plastic store card helps no end tucking-in the edges. Don't let the excess strip stick to the roof or A-pillars while you're trimming - keep peeling it off.

Tricks 'n' tips
If you have trouble getting things trimmed up neatly, remember that you can lift the windscreen rubber slightly (using a small screwdriver), and tuck the edge of the strip underneath, for a really neat fit.

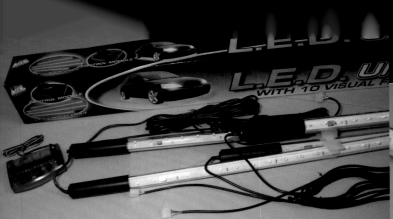

Glow for it

Ever since 'The Fast and the Furious' first glued us to our screens, every cruise-goer wants a cool neon glow under their car. Wanting's one thing - make it a reality, and you'll have to explain it to the Law. Under-car neons are totally illegal on the road, and rather an obvious 'come-and-nick-me' to Plod (who will then have a field day with any other semi-legal features on your Civic). So - you have been warned. But we know you still want them, anyway...

01 First job is getting the car airborne (see 'wheels 'n' tyres' for jacking info). Then unpack the kit, and check you've got everything you should have. When this has been done, we can start by adding the little plastic clips that hold the tubes to the car.

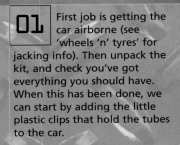

02 Positioning the tubes on the car isn't always easy, especially the back one, which interferes with the exhaust, usually. Beware of covering jacking points on the sills when fitting the side tubes, and of moving parts or extreme heat sources. When you're happy with the positioning, mark the clip holes with a pen or scribe, ready for drilling.

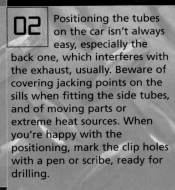

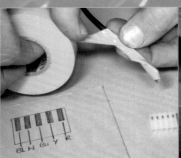

07 With the plugs temporarily removed, tape up the wires for feeding into the car - this makes the job easier, and protects the contacts.

08 Drill a hole in the floorpan to feed each cable up into the car. Yes, we know it's scary stuff. When drilling the holes for the side tubes, pull back the plastic sill trim and carpet, so you don't drill through them as well. Thread a grommet onto the wire and feed it into the car. Some neon kits operate at 6000 volts; we don't want those wires to rub through on a sharp-edged hole - not good - so use a grommet!

09 When the three remaining wires have entered the car, the plugs can be refitted. If you were careful prising out the wires, they should just clip back into their plugs (in the right place, preferably). Tidily route the wiring into the driver's footwell.

10 Choose a suitable spot for your control box - we went for the trim panel above the fusebox, which is held on by some very obvious screws at the corners. Our box not only had a large sticky pad on the back, but screws as well - so we used both.

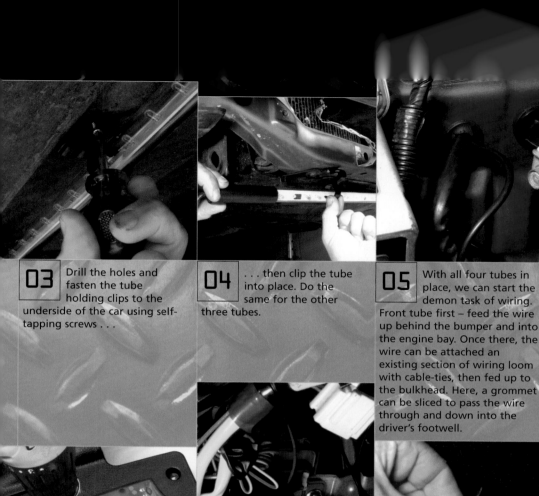

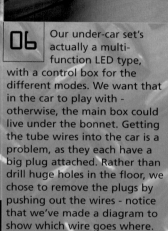

03 Drill the holes and fasten the tube holding clips to the underside of the car using self-tapping screws . . .

04 . . . then clip the tube into place. Do the same for the other three tubes.

05 With all four tubes in place, we can start the demon task of wiring. Front tube first – feed the wire up behind the bumper and into the engine bay. Once there, the wire can be attached an existing section of wiring loom with cable-ties, then fed up to the bulkhead. Here, a grommet can be sliced to pass the wire through and down into the driver's footwell.

06 Our under-car set's actually a multi-function LED type, with a control box for the different modes. We want that in the car to play with - otherwise, the main box could live under the bonnet. Getting the tube wires into the car is a problem, as they each have a big plug attached. Rather than drill huge holes in the floor, we chose to remove the plugs by pushing out the wires - notice that we've made a diagram to show which wire goes where.

11 Next, we want an access hole to feed the wiring through from behind the trim panel, before plugging into the control box. Not exactly the hardest thing we've ever done.

12 Now to wire the control box in. It's a simple enough job – a live and an earth is all we need. Using a ring terminal, connect the black wire onto a suitable earth point - our favourite is the mounting bolt to the right of the fusebox.

13 To get a live feed, you have several options. You can poke around behind the fusebox with a multimeter/test lamp and your Haynes wiring diagrams for an existing wire to join onto (tricky), or you can run one into the car from the battery (easy). For a really cool solution, fit an auxiliary fusebox like we have, and take a feed from that (see the security section). Use a suitable size fuse (at least 10 amps).

14 Feed the tube wires and their plugs in from behind through the hole in trim panel, and plug them into the control box. Tidy up the wires behind the trim panel, then refit the panel to the car. All done? Is it dark yet? Time to glow, baby glow!

This is not the section where we tell you how to respray your entire Civic in a weekend, using only spray cans, okay? Mission Impossible, we ain't. This bit's all about how to spray up your various plasticky bits before final fitting - bits such as door mirrors, light brows, spoilers, splitters - hell, even bumpers if you like. As we've no doubt said before, with anything new, fit your unpainted bits first. Make sure everything fits properly (shape and tidy up all parts as necessary), that all holes have been drilled, and all screws etc are doing their job. Then, and only when you're totally, completely happy with the fit - take them off, and get busy with the spray cans..

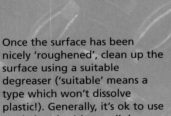

01 The first job is to mask off any areas you don't want painted. Do this right at the start, or you could be sorry; on these door mirrors, we decided to mask off just at the lip before the glass, to leave a black unpainted edge - if we hadn't masked it as the very first job, we would've roughed up all the shiny black plastic next, and wrecked the edge finish.

02 Remove any unwanted 'seams' in the plastic, using fine sandpaper or wet-and-dry. Some of these seams look pretty cool, others don't - you decide. Also worth tidying up any other areas you're not happy with, fit-wise, while you're at it.

Especially with 'shiny' plastic, you must rough-up the surface before spray will 'bite' to it, or - it'll flippin' flake off. Just take off the shine, no more. You can use fine wet-and-dry for this (used dry), but we prefer Scotchbrite. This stuff, which looks much like a scouring pad, is available from motor factors and bodyshops, in several grades - we used ultra-fine, which is grey. One advantage of Scotchbrite is that **03** it's a bit easier to work into awkward corners than paper.

Once the surface has been nicely 'roughened', clean up the surface using a suitable degreaser ('suitable' means a type which won't dissolve plastic!). Generally, it's ok to use methylated spirit or cellulose thinners (just don't inhale!), but **04** test it on a not-so-visible bit first, so you don't have a disaster.

Before you start spraying (if it's something smaller than a bumper) it's a good idea to try a work a screw into one of the mounting holes, to use as a **05** 'handle', so you can turn the item to spray all sides.

Another good trick is to use the screw to hang the item up on a piece of string or wire - then **06** you can spin the item round to get the spray into awkward areas.

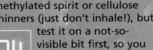

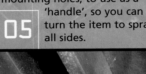

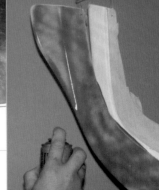

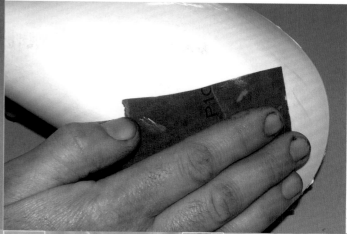

07 If you like a bit of wildlife in your paint, you can't beat the great outdoors. If it's at all windy, you'll end up with a really awful finish and overspray on everything (which can be a real bitch to get off). Even indoors, if it's damp weather, you'll have real problems trying to get a shine - some kind of heater is essential if it's cold and wet (but not one with a fan - stirring up the dust is the last thing you want).

08 If you're a bit new at spraying, or if you simply don't want to balls it up, practice your technique first (steady!). Working left-right, then right-left, press the nozzle so you start spraying just before you pass the item, and follow through just past it the other side. Keep the nozzle a constant distance from the item - not in a curved arc. Don't blast the paint on too thick, or you'll have a nasty case of the runs - hold the can about 6 inches away - you're not trying to paint the whole thing in one sweep.

09 Once you've got a patchy 'mist coat' on (which might not even cover the whole thing) - stop, and let it dry (primer dries pretty quickly). Continue building up thin coats until you've got full coverage, then let it dry for half an hour or more.

10 Using 1000- or 1200- grade wet-and-dry paper (used wet), very lightly sand the whole primered surface, to take out any minor imperfections (blobs, where the nozzle was spitting) in the primer. Try not to go through the primer to the plastic, but this doesn't matter too much in small areas.

11 Rinse off thoroughly, then dry the surfaces - let it stand for a while to make sure it's *completely* dry, before starting on the top coat.

12 Make sure once again that the surfaces are clean, with no bits left behind from the drying operations. As with the primer, work up from an initial thin mist coat, allowing time for each pass to dry. As you spray, you'll soon learn how to build a nice shine without runs - any 'dry' (dull) patches are usually due to overspray landing on still-wet shiny paint. Don't worry if you can't eliminate all of these - a light cutting polish will sort it out once the paint's hardened (after several hours).

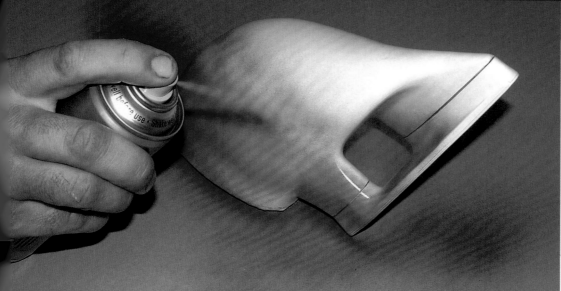

13 Especially with a colour like red (which is notorious for fading easily), it's a good idea to blow on a coat or two of clear lacquer over the top - this will also give you your shine, if you're stuck with a very 'dry' finish. It's best to apply lacquer before the final top coat is fully hardened. The spraying technique is identical, although pro sprayers say that lacquer should be applied pretty thick - just watch those runs! Lacquer also takes a good long while to dry - pick up your item too soon, for that unique fingerprint effect!

There's no way in

One way to tidy up the Civic lines is to do away with the door locks, and even the door handles - but be careful. Flushing the rear door handles (on 4-door models) is okay, legally/MOT-speaking, but removing the front door handles will land you in trouble, come MOT time.

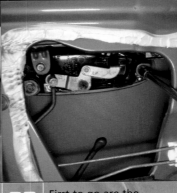

Construction & Use regs require your car to have an independent mechanical means of door opening from outside (so fire-fighters can get you out, if you stick your all-action Civic on its roof, or in a ditch...) If you must lose the front handles, find some trick mirrors which have door catches built-in, underneath.

01 By far the neatest way to de-lock any EG Civic is to replace the complete front door handles with rear-door ones from a 4-door. While you're at it, you could even colour-code them. Remove the door trim (as described in 'interiors'), then carefully slice through the mastic holding on the plastic membrane, and peel it back - don't be ignorant and just rip it.

02 First to go are the door handles themselves - undo the two bolts inside the door . . .

03 . . . then, to actually release the handles so you can remove them, we're into disconnecting their operating rods, which can be a bit of a pain - try not to bust any of the plastic bits when you prise them with your screwdriver. Unhook the lock barrel rod at the back (shouldn't need that again) . . .

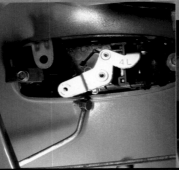

04 . . . and then the interior handle rod, whose plastic end fitting prises out of the operating arm on the handle. The lock barrel rod will be left flapping about inside, so if this bothers you, try unhooking it from the door lock (much dismantling might be needed). Otherwise, tape it up so's it can't rattle inside the door.

05 Our Civic rear door handles came from our friendly local dealer - but there's a problem. The mounting bolt holes don't line up, so the first job is to make up a small bracket (visible here on the left) so we can fit the handle to the door. You can also see the operating rod here - looks like it'll fit the new handle then?

06 Yes it does, but the new handle won't open the door. Why? The operating rod's working at the wrong angle, so another new bracket had to be made - this time from a DIY-store corner bracket. First, the original handle mounting lug had to be chopped . . .

07 . . . then the new bracket gets bolted to the handle's inner lever. The operating rod pushes through, and gets fixed to the bracket using the original plastic end fitting. Easy-to-do mods are for wimps.

Remote **locking**

So you can lock and unlock your freshly de-locked doors, you'll need to buy and fit a remote central locking kit, which you can get from several Max Power-advertised suppliers (our Microscan kit, supplied by Performance Products Ltd of Chester, is really an extension kit for our chosen alarm, but is pretty typical of what you'll get). If your Civic already has central locking, you're in luck - buy yourself a cheap car alarm, and a central locking interface.

Tricks 'n' tips
If your battery goes flat, you'll be locked out. We ran two thin wires from the battery terminals (with a 10-amp fuse in the live, and the ends insulated), and tucked them away for access from below in an emergency. By connecting a slave battery to these wires (do not try jump-starting), you'll put enough juice into the system to operate the locks, saving you a red face. Think it over.

Central locking **kit**

If your Civic doesn't have central locking as standard, don't despair - there's several kits out there to help you towards your goal. Our project Civic already had central locking and an alarm, so regrettably there are no Civic-specific photos to show you, but hopefully, the details below, together with your kit's instructions, will help you out.

Before you start fitting your new lock solenoids, it makes sense to test them. Connect them all together as described in your kit's instructions - with power connected to all the solenoids, pull up on the operating plunger of one, and all the rest should pop up too - clever, eh?

Decide where you're going to mount the lock control unit, then identify the various looms, and feed them out to the doors.

The new lock solenoids must be mounted so they work in the same *plane* as the door lock buttons. What this means is it's no good having the lock solenoid plungers moving horizontally, to work a button and rod which operates vertically! Make up the mounting brackets from the metal bits provided in the kit, and fit the solenoids loosely to the brackets, and to the doors.

The kit contains several items which look uncannily like bike spokes - these are your new lock operating rods, which have to be cut to length, then joined onto the old rods using screw clamps. It's best to join the old and new rods at a straight piece of the old rod, so feed the new rod in, and mark it for cutting.

Cut the new rod to the marked length, fit the cut rod to the solenoid, then slip the clamp onto it. Fit the solenoid onto its bracket, and offer the rod into place, to connect to the old rod. Join the new rod and old rod together, and fasten the clamp screws tight. If the clamp screws come loose, you're basically going to be locked out.

Now you can connect up the wires - the easy bit is joining up inside the door. Hopefully, your kit's instructions should be sufficient, but if not, you'll have to resort to the Haynes manual wiring diagrams.

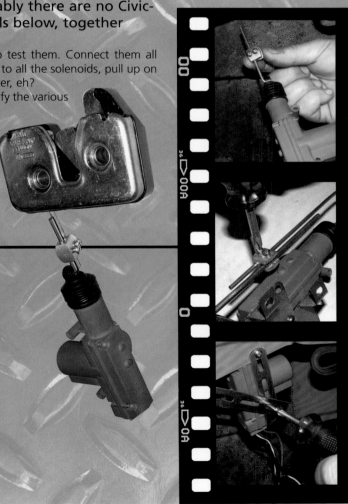

Don't mesh with me, boy

A meshed grille or bumper is just one way to demonstrate who's the daddy of the cruise, and it does a great job of dicing any small insects or rodents foolish enough to wander into the path of your motor. So if you're sick of scrubbing off insect entrails from your paint, and fancy getting even, read on…

Which style of mesh to choose? Classic diamond-shape, or round-hole? In our humble opinion, the round-hole mesh works best on modern roundy-shaped cars (like say, a Corsa) - for everything else, we'll settle for the original and best. But wait - the choice doesn't end with what shape you want. Mesh can now be had in various anodised colours too, to match or contrast with the rest of your chosen paint scheme.

01 Anyone can mesh a hole. Ab-so-lutely anyone - it's dead easy. First, measure your hole, then cut out a roughly-sized piece of mesh, leaving some over the sides to bend around the edges of your hole.

There's loads of ways to secure your mesh. One of the most permanent is to use small self-tapping screws, but this won't always be possible. Our hot-glue gun method worked a treat, as the glue flows into place. You can use mastic (quick-setting, exterior-use type) or even builder's 'no-nails' adhesive, but you squirt on a bead of the stuff, and then have to smooth it on by hand, to 'squidge' it over the mesh. Very meshy - sorry, messy.

02 Of course, holes usually have corners - and some of the sides you'll encounter aren't exactly straight. Make small cuts in the edge of the mesh at strategic points . . .

. . . and bending over the edges will be much easier. The main mesh panel will also stay flatter, and you'll be less stressed, too. **03**

04

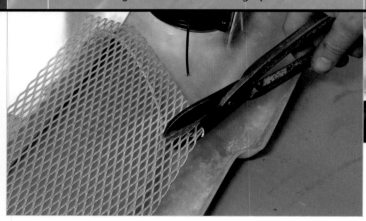

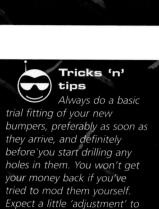

Tricks 'n' tips

Always do a basic trial fitting of your new bumpers, preferably as soon as they arrive, and definitely before you start drilling any holes in them. You won't get your money back if you've tried to mod them yourself. Expect a little 'adjustment' to be needed to make them fit, but bear in mind you might have been sent the wrong ones, before you go too far.

Bumpers 'n' bodykits

If you can't find a kit you like for a Civic, you're not trying. Providing you like the Jap-look, anyway. The Japanese might produce some pretty bland-looking standard shopping trolleys, but some of their bodykits are totally banzai-ori-mental.

In no particular order, names you might consider are Wings West, Bomex, Kingdom Developments, Sarona, Blitz, Erebuni, Kaminari, and Rawsushi (okay, so we made the last one up). The challenge between them seems to be who can make your Civic look the widest, with the greatest area of mesh up front.

One thing you should be concerned about is how well it's all going to fit. Even if you're giving the joy of fitting to a bodyshop, they'll still charge you more if your cheap duff kit takes a week longer to fit than expected. Ask around before splashing the cash. Our choice of a Wings West kit may not be the most original, but they're not popular for nothing, and the quality's right there.

Front bumper

01 Getting the old bumper off's not hard to do, but some of it's hard to show you. There's five screws along the top edge between the headlights, some of which might require unusual methods to persuade into turning . . .

02 . . . then there are two bolts in the centre of the bumper, underneath (ignore the row of bolts securing the black lower spoiler - these don't have to come out).

03 Finally, there's one screw each side, tucked inside the wheelarch liner (peel back the plastic liner to get to it).

>>

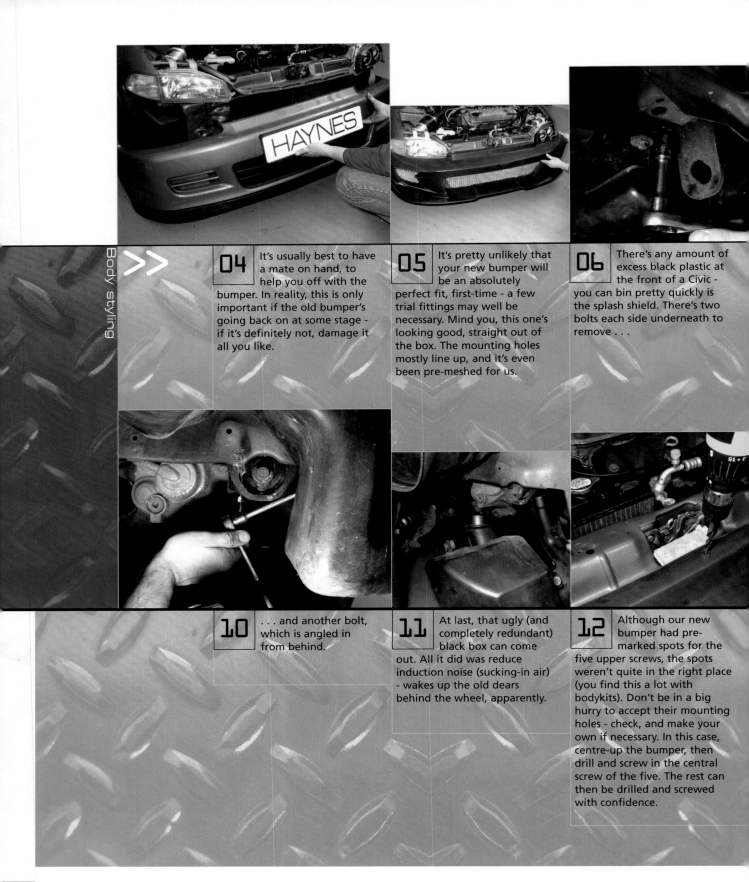

04 It's usually best to have a mate on hand, to help you off with the bumper. In reality, this is only important if the old bumper's going back on at some stage - if it's definitely not, damage it all you like.

05 It's pretty unlikely that your new bumper will be an absolutely perfect fit, first-time - a few trial fittings may well be necessary. Mind you, this one's looking good, straight out of the box. The mounting holes mostly line up, and it's even been pre-meshed for us.

06 There's any amount of excess black plastic at the front of a Civic - you can bin pretty quickly is the splash shield. There's two bolts each side underneath to remove . . .

10 . . . and another bolt, which is angled in from behind.

11 At last, that ugly (and completely redundant) black box can come out. All it did was reduce induction noise (sucking-in air) - wakes up the old dears behind the wheel, apparently.

12 Although our new bumper had pre-marked spots for the five upper screws, the spots weren't quite in the right place (you find this a lot with bodykits). Don't be in a big hurry to accept their mounting holes - check, and make your own if necessary. In this case, centre-up the bumper, then drill and screw in the central screw of the five. The rest can then be drilled and screwed with confidence.

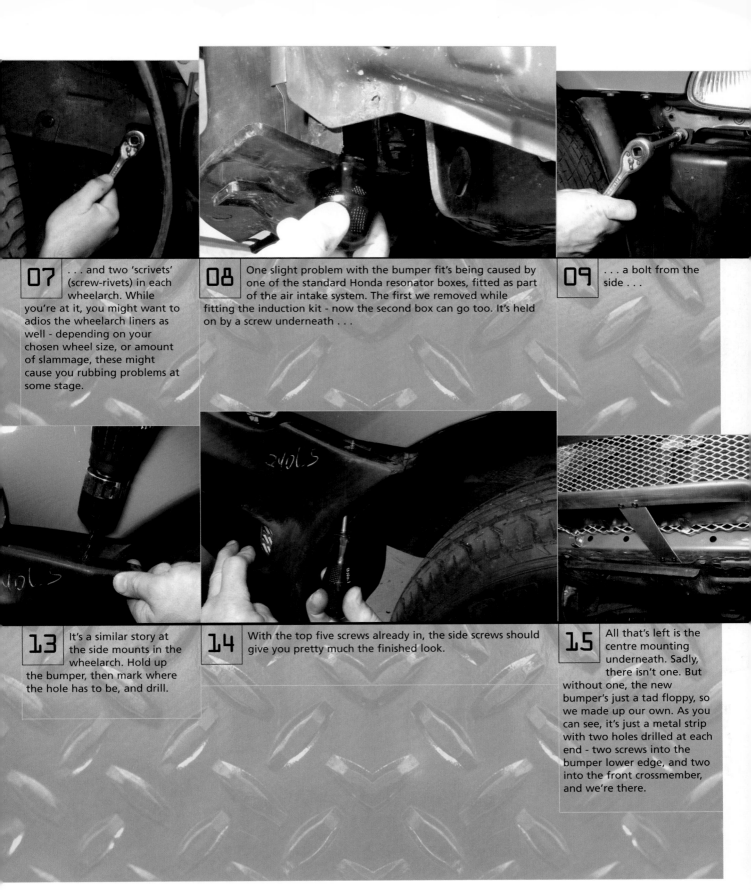

07 . . . and two 'scrivets' (screw-rivets) in each wheelarch. While you're at it, you might want to adios the wheelarch liners as well - depending on your chosen wheel size, or amount of slammage, these might cause you rubbing problems at some stage.

08 One slight problem with the bumper fit's being caused by one of the standard Honda resonator boxes, fitted as part of the air intake system. The first we removed while fitting the induction kit - now the second box can go too. It's held on by a screw underneath . . .

09 . . . a bolt from the side . . .

13 It's a similar story at the side mounts in the wheelarch. Hold up the bumper, then mark where the hole has to be, and drill.

14 With the top five screws already in, the side screws should give you pretty much the finished look.

15 All that's left is the centre mounting underneath. Sadly, there isn't one. But without one, the new bumper's just a tad floppy, so we made up our own. As you can see, it's just a metal strip with two holes drilled at each end - two screws into the bumper lower edge, and two into the front crossmember, and we're there.

Rear bumper

01 Taking off the back bumper's virtually the same deal as the front - there's five screws along the top edge . . .

02 . . . one more each side, inside the wheelarch . . .

03 . . . and two bolts in the centre, underneath.

04 Off comes the old bumper - or does it? What have we forgotten?

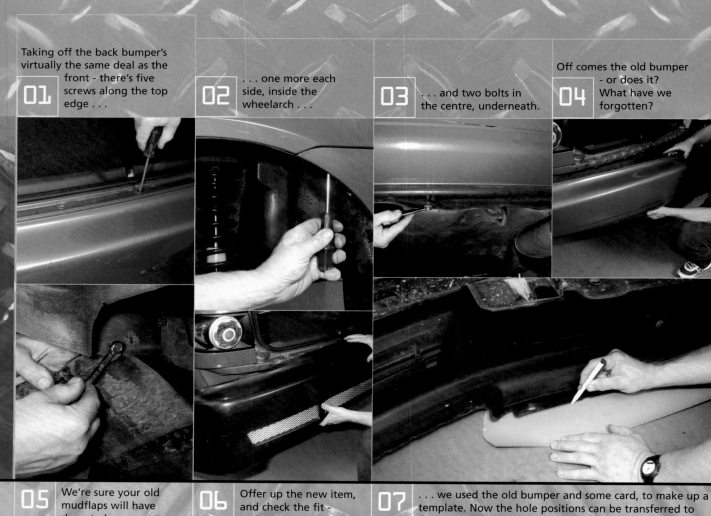

05 We're sure your old mudflaps will have departed as soon as you bought the car, but ours were still attached. The mudflap clamp bolts have to be removed, to release the bumper each side. So there you are - mudflaps look rubbish, stop you fitting bodykits.

06 Offer up the new item, and check the fit - looks good, but not all the holes line up, so . . .

07 . . . we used the old bumper and some card, to make up a template. Now the hole positions can be transferred to the new bumper - game on. Shame about those mudflaps, though. Not.

Side skirts

So what's the deal with side skirts, then? Well, they're an 'artificial' way of visually lowering the car, making it seem lower to the ground than it really is, and they also help to 'tie together' the front and rear sections of a full bodykit. This much we know from our magazines. But where did skirts really come from?

As with so much else in modifying, it's a racing-inspired thing. In the late 70s, the Lotus 'ground-effect' F1 cars ran very, very low (for the time) and had side skirts made of rubber (or bristles), to give a flexible seal against the track. With a clear downforce advantage, Lotus blew the opposition away.

So will fitting skirts to your Civic give you race-car levels of downforce, greatly increasing your overtaking chances at the next roundabout? You already know the answer, I'm afraid…

 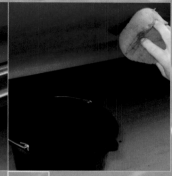

01 Removed your mudflaps? We know - you Civic never had flaps. Wouldn't know what they look like, even. Good. Now the first step is checking the fit of your new skirts, especially making sure the doors will actually close. Mark up any dodgy areas for trimming later. Are the plastic arch liners staying, or being ripped out? Decide before you trap them in place with the side skirts.

02 Give the sill and rear wing a good clean and de-grease, then do the same for the edges of the skirt - we want it to stick. Get some proper mastic designed for the job (try a bodyshop or car paint suppliers), and wear gloves, as it's hell to get off hands. Our skirt had its own sticky strips (no mastic required), which makes things less messy.

03 Especially with our 'one-shot' stick-on skirts, it's useful to give yourself a line to guide you when fitting (using mastic gives you flexibility to slide the skirt a little once it's on). Offer up the skirt, and mark round it with a crayon or non-permanent marker.

04 We're still not sticking it on yet. Now we need some screw holes at front and rear arch edges, and two or three along the underside, to really pin the skirt into place. Get a mate to hold the skirt in the right place while you drill.

05 With our skirt, finally fitting means getting it lined up with our guide marks, ripping off the backing tape, and pressing firmly to our super-clean paintwork. If your skirt's fitted using mastic, get the excess off quickly, and run your finger along the join between skirt and car, to give a neat finish.

06 Those screw holes we made earlier? Now need some screws. If you're using mastic, those (ugly?) screws could be removed once the mastic's cured - you could even fill the holes you made, prior to painting. With our sticky-tape skirt, we'll keep the screws, thanks.

Civic rotten

A must for any Civic, but especially necessary on a Coupe like ours, a rear spoiler makes a very clear statement to the car you just passed - do not mess. Our very fine Wings West Sky-Liner should **01** do the trick. The first thing we noticed were the T-strips under each leg - must be there for a reason, don't think we'll remove those just yet.

First (and this is good advice for fitting any spoiler), apply a few strips of masking tape where it's going to sit. This lets you mark the spoiler leg **02** profiles if necessary, and makes drilling any holes a lot easier.

Offer up the new bodywork, and get it straight. A mate can help here - at least you can share the blame if it goes on crooked. Check inside the panel you're mounting onto for any interesting features. On our Civic boot lid, the metal's only single-skinned towards the back, so our spoiler went all the way back **03** it could. Measure both sides so it's straight.

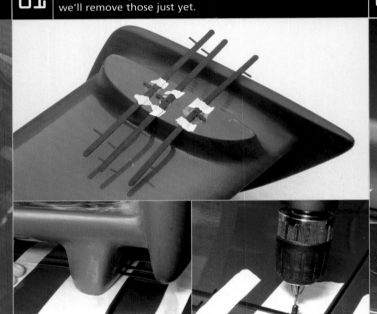

04 With this spoiler, the T-strips are a very neat way of getting the mounting holes in the right spot. When the spoiler's lined up, you tape down the ends of the strips, then unstick them from the spoiler, and lift it carefully away.

05 What you're left with are little tubes sticking up from the surface, marking the positions of your mounting holes. All you do is run a pilot drill down first, then remove the strips and enlarge the holes to the size given in the instructions. What a brill idea - but then, with all their experience, you'd expect something clever from this kit's manufacturers.

06 Most spoilers also come with a foam or rubber strip which fits between the spoiler and the body. This doesn't just prevent possible paintwork damage - it also seals out the elements (remember, you've just made some holes) If your spoiler seems a bit inadequate in this area, some silicone sealant or mastic will have to be used to keep your boot install dry.

07 All our spoiler needs now is a coat of paint. This is one item you probably could DIY paint yourself with cans, but when there's a pro like Kevin from Avon Customs on hand to do a proper job...

Wheelarch mods

The law states that your wide rubber shouldn't be so wide that it sticks out from your arches, and the MOT crew will not be impressed if your new rubber's rubbing, either. This presents something of a problem, if you're determined to get 18s on, especially if the car's also having a radical drop job (like our Civic, on coilovers). If you've got rubbing problems on 17s, check that your wheels are the right offset (see *'Wheels 'n' tyres'*), or chat to your wheel supplier about spacers. Civic arches are quite roomy, so you should only hit major problems above 17-inch rims.

Sometimes, all you need to stop those nasty grinding noises is a small amount of violence. Any non-vital protrusions into the under-arch area can be trimmed off or flattened with a hammer. Also, try removing those (oh-so-practical) wheelarch liners.

Serious wheelarch mods are best done at a bodyshop. Having the arches professionally rolled, using the proper tool, should only cost about £50 per arch (assuming they haven't also got rust or filler to deal with as well). Less satisfactory would be having the arch edges cut or ground off - this leaves a bare-metal edge, and encourages rust (as well as weakening the wings).

The best answer to arches which just aren't roomy enough is, of course, a wide-arch bodykit. And bank loans are so cheap these days.

Bonnet vents

Once you've got your bodykit on, it's only natural you'll want a bonnet vent, isn't it? Respect. But this is one scary job to tackle yourself, unless you're really that good, or that brave. Plenty of options - you can get little louvres stamped in as well, to complement your Evo, Impreza, Integrale or F50 main vent. A more recent trend is the Focus WRC vent, and there's even been a feature car with a bonnet scoop from a (sensible) Kia Sedona people carrier! Truly, anything goes.

For maximum respect in the bonnet department, you can't beat carbon fibre - on a street-racing Civic, it's pretty much expected these days. Kit yourself out with a ready-vented carbon bonnet, and it's not even hard to fit (just hard to pay for??). Unless you're us, and have nice friends like ABC Design who donate these things free.

Carbon fibre bonnet

01 You'll probably want to refit your original bonnet one day, so take a bit of care removing it - get a mate to help, or you could damage more than one body panel. The first bit's pretty easy - pull off the washer jet pipes inside the bonnet.

02 Making sure your chosen assistant is well-briefed on what will happen to them if they drop the bonnet, have them stand one side, with you on the other. There's two bonnet hinge bolts to undo each side, after which the whole thing's free to move. Or fall on your foot. And yes, it is heavy.

03 Assuming everything's still under control, you can now lift off the bonnet, and put it somewhere safe. Put some rags under the bonnet corners, to stop the paint getting damaged.

04 The worst time with any new panel is when you still don't know how good a fit it'll be. Nervous? Offer the new bonnet into place (again with the help of your trusty assistant), and check the fit. This is another quality item from ABC Design, so we're laughing. Line it all up, and tighten the hinge bolts.

 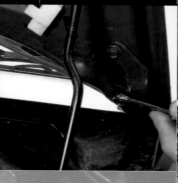  

05 Carefully lower the bonnet, and see whether the catch goes in centrally. If not, you can either give the bonnet a tweak by re-aligning it on the hinges, or by moving the striker.

06 With the bonnet shut, does it line up nicely with the front wings? Side-to-side alignment is again corrected using the hinges, but if the bonnet height is a problem, use the bump stops to cure it - these screw up or down as needed.

07 And that's it. Have to say this is one of the finest bonnets we've ever seen, especially with the bonnet vent that comes perfectly built in and meshed – superb!

Respraying

Not happy with your Civic's 'pensioner blue' paint? Time to call in the pros. There's no such thing as a simple DIY respray (not one that'll look good afterwards, at any rate). We just thought you'd like to see some of the stages involved.

01 Doing a full respray means getting all those door shuts and other areas of painted metal inside, but not the dash, seats, and carpets (unless you're going to completely gut the entire dash and interior afterwards). You can never do too much masking, and the lads at Avon Customs know this better than anyone.

02 Hang on, are you sure that's still our Civic under there? For a full respray, it's often better to remove fixed glass completely, rather than spend time masking it all up. That means windscreen, tailgate, and all the side glass. Still fancy having a go yourself?

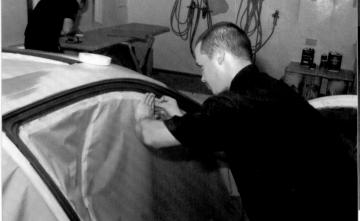

03 Mixing the paint is an important, but often overlooked, stage in any spraying process - even ambient temperatures have a bearing on the final paint mix. Topcoats and lacquer especially have complex mixing ratios for the thinners, hardener, activator, and any 'flex' additives for bumpers and such - get it wrong, and even top-notch paint like this won't work.

If you haven't got some kind of stand to support them, you'll struggle to get things like bumpers sprayed properly. Hanging items like this up for spraying may not be an option, either. Notice that the bumper mesh has been removed rather than masked-up.

06

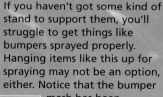

04 The smaller bits like mirrors and lights are obviously better removed for spraying. The plastic mirrors receive a special primer of their own - any suspect items may also require the use of an adhesion promoter (makes sure the later coats actually stick).

Making sure the paint surface is clean between steps is another often-overlooked essential item. Our chaps use a water-based wash, as solvent-based products can lift the paint (or react with the next coat). The final stage is cleaning using tack-rags (net-like material, impregnated with resin - very sticky, picks up any bits).

07

05 Here's our very illegal rear lights, which you may remember seeing elsewhere. Not the easiest things to get body-colour, as those lenses can't be separated from the surrounds. But if you're a dab hand with the masking tape, this is no challenge.

Now we're ready for some real paint. We're keeping the same colour base coat as standard, but adding a House of Kolor pearl over the top for a more-special look. The choice in pearls is bewildering - ask your bodyshop for some test cards before you decide! After the pearl will be several 'flow-coats' of lacquer to give it the deep shine. Can't wait to see the finished car now…

08

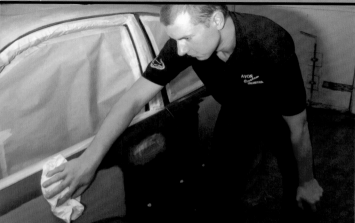

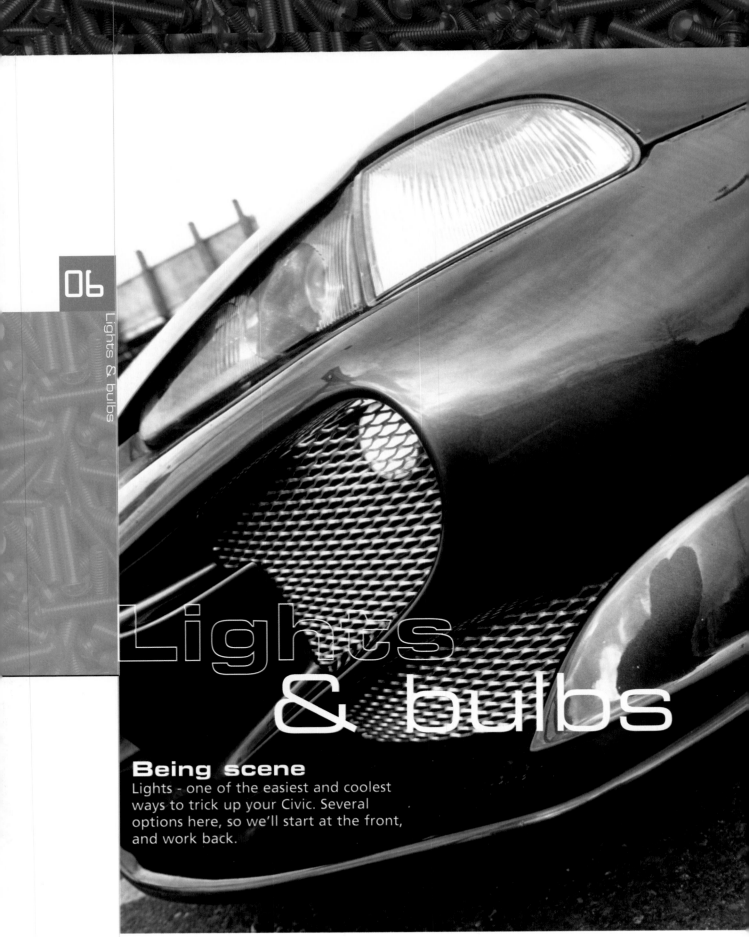

Lights
& bulbs

Being scene

Lights - one of the easiest and coolest
ways to trick up your Civic. Several
options here, so we'll start at the front,
and work back.

Headlights

Almost nothing influences the look of your Civic more than the front end, so the headlights play a crucial role.

What's available?

The popular cheap option is stick-on headlight 'brows', which do admittedly give the rather bland Civic front end a tougher look. The brows are best sprayed to match the car, before fitting - most are fitted using stick-on Velcro pads. Street-cred on the cheap, and (if you choose the Fox-style brows) a cheap alternative to a proper 'badboy' bonnet.

Another cheap option is again stick-on - this time, it's stick-on covers which give the twin-headlight look. This is basically a sheet of vinyl/plastic (shaped to the headlights, and colour-matched to your car) with two holes cut in it. Dead easy to fit, but dare we say, a bit tacky? Just our opinion. A cheap and simple way to get close to the twin-light look.

If you want tinted headlights, you could try spray-tinting them, but go easy on the spray. Turning your headlights from clear glass to non-see-through is plain daft, even if it's done in the name of style. A light tint is quite effective, and gives you the chance to colour-match to your Civic. With tinted headlights, you'd be wise to tint those clear front indicators too, of course.

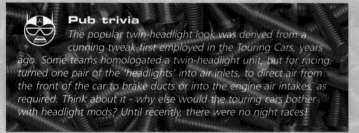

Pub trivia

The popular twin-headlight look was derived from a cunning tweak first employed in the Touring Cars, years ago. Some teams homologated a twin-headlight unit, but for racing, turned one pair of the 'headlights' into air inlets, to direct air from the front of the car to brake ducts or into the engine air intakes, as required. Think about it - why else would the touring cars bother with headlight mods? Until recently, there were no night races!

Another 'headlight' option sometimes featured on Civics actually belongs in the bodywork section - it's the 'badboy' bonnet. By cunningly welding-in a couple of triangular plates to your standard Civic bonnet, a bodyshop (or handy DIY-er) can create a really mean look, using just the standard lights. Excellent.

About this point, we'd normally start telling you about Morette twin headlights - but unfortunately, Morette don't cover the EG Civic, so we have to look elsewhere for twin-light action. Luckily, we don't have to look far, and there's loads of different options in twin lights, including crystals and halo-effect items - ours were sourced from Invo Auto. Pricey, but so worth it - you don't even start a Civic project unless you've got cash to splash. Maximum cred, and no-one's gonna accuse you of owning a 'boring' Civic ever again!

Headlight brows

This is the cheap 'n' cheerful approach, and it really doesn't get much simpler than this. This is even a mod you can 'undo' easily, if your MOT geezer objects. So what do you get? Two bits of triangular plastic, and two strips of Velcro. It's worth doing a quick trial fitting first, to make sure you've been sent the right ones.

Unless you like black brows, the first job's painting. Which means preparation - don't assume those fresh-from-the-packet bits of plastic will take paint straight away. A little roughing-up with fine emery paper or Scotchbrite, then a wipe with meths or thinners, and we're off. If you want the best finish on your brows, and like the idea of not having the paint flaking off, you must give them a coat of plastic primer. Any lumps in the primer, and you'll need to do a quick rubdown with fine paper. If all's well, now's the time for the top coats. Build the finish up in thin layers, to avoid runs.

Give the paint a good few hours to dry, or you'll end up wrecking the finish. Now the strips of Velcro go on the back of the brows. Don't rip the Velcro apart - stick both bits on the brows, and peel off the self-adhesive backing, ready to stick to the light. Give the headlight glass a good clean, if you want the sticky to stick. Slide the brow into place, and press firmly - job done. Now the brows can be removed easily by separating the Velcro, leaving one strip still on the light for refitting.

Twin
headlights

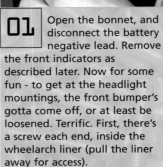

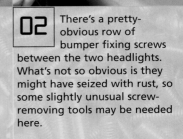

01 Open the bonnet, and disconnect the battery negative lead. Remove the front indicators as described later. Now for some fun - to get at the headlight mountings, the front bumper's gotta come off, or at least be loosened. Terrific. First, there's a screw each end, inside the wheelarch liner (pull the liner away for access).

02 There's a pretty-obvious row of bumper fixing screws between the two headlights. What's not so obvious is they might have seized with rust, so some slightly unusual screw-removing tools may be needed here.

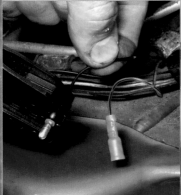

07 Now crimp on some bullet connectors (female on the red live lead, please), and the old wires are ready to be joined to the red and white wires from the new lights (red-to-red, black-to-white in our case).

08 Next, we've got two hefty red leads which connect to a permanent live supply. The obvious spot for this in the engine bay is the battery - but wait. Take off the fusebox lid next to the battery . . .

09 . . . and we find a ready-made tap-in point where the engine bay wiring harness starts. Remove the bolt, and add your new wires to the terminal that those cunning Japanese blokes at Honda provided for you.

10 These new wires contain fuses, so route the wires neatly round, and don't bury the fuses where you'll never find them again.

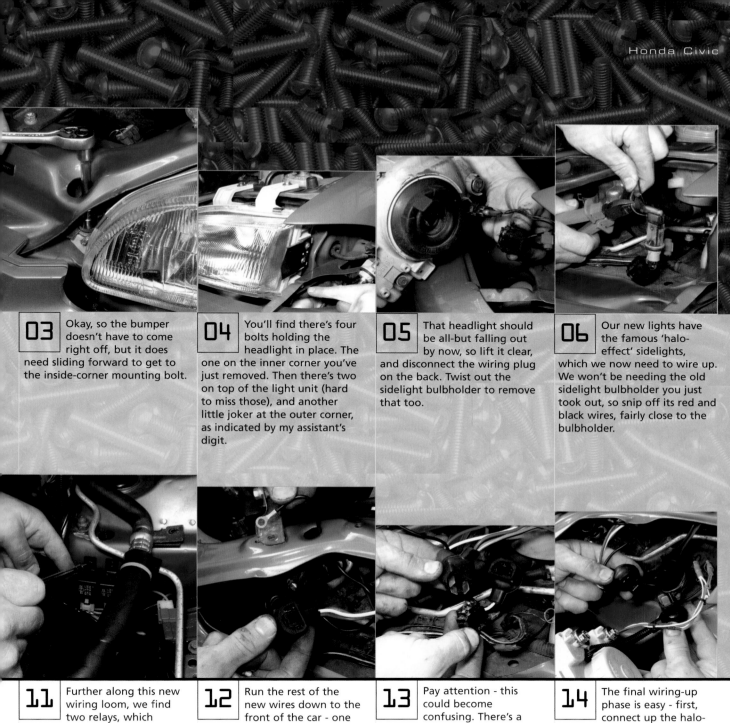

03 Okay, so the bumper doesn't have to come right off, but it does need sliding forward to get to the inside-corner mounting bolt.

04 You'll find there's four bolts holding the headlight in place. The one on the inner corner you've just removed. Then there's two on top of the light unit (hard to miss those), and another little joker at the outer corner, as indicated by my assistant's digit.

05 That headlight should be all-but falling out by now, so lift it clear, and disconnect the wiring plug on the back. Twist out the sidelight bulbholder to remove that too.

06 Our new lights have the famous 'halo-effect' sidelights, which we now need to wire up. We won't be needing the old sidelight bulbholder you just took out, so snip off its red and black wires, fairly close to the bulbholder.

11 Further along this new wiring loom, we find two relays, which we've chosen to mount on our suspension turret after drilling through a couple of holes. Just make sure there's nothing vital in the way before you start drilling.

12 Run the rest of the new wires down to the front of the car - one of the big plugs should be fed across to the driver's-side headlight area. On each of the new headlight plugs, there's a short black wire, which is the earth connection. Trap its ring connector under a screw going into the car's bodywork, and you're sorted. We used the bolt from this funny little bracket on the front slam panel to pin ours - make your own hole if you have to.

13 Pay attention - this could become confusing. There's a big plug for each new headlight, with blue, white and black wires - these we'll plug in shortly. For now, there's another large plug (brown, grey and green wires) to deal with - this connects to the old headlight's big wiring plug. We learned this from reading the kit's instructions - always a good idea - and yours might be different to ours, so check.

14 The final wiring-up phase is easy - first, connect up the halo-sidelight bullet connectors we did earlier. Then all you do is plug in the large wiring plug to the back of the new light, and refit it using the old headlight mountings. Repeat this challenging (not) process for the other light, and your headlight makeover is complete.

Headlight
bulbs

Make your Civic look like an Audi or a Beemer, the easy way. Bad-weather and 'blue' headlight bulbs are an excellent way to boost headlight performance, and are perfect with other blue LED accessories like washer jets and number plate screws. The blue bulbs you buy in most accessory shops will be legal, 60W/55 bulbs, and are no problem. Don't be tempted to buy the mega-powerful bulbs you can get from rallying suppliers (any over 60W/55 are in fact illegal for use in this country) - as with all other non-standard lights, the boys in blue will love pulling you over for a word about this, so ask before you buy.

Even if you're not bothered about the legality of over-powerful bulbs (and you might well argue that being more powerful is the whole point of fitting), there's other problems with monster bulbs.

First, they give off masses of heat, and loads of people have melted their headlights before they found this out. Don't believe us? Try fitting some 100W/90s and put your hand in front of the light, close to the glass. Hot, isn't it? The excess heat these bulbs generate will damage the headlights eventually, either by warping the lens, burning off the reflective coating, or melting the bulbholders. Maybe all three.

The increased current required to work big bulbs has also been known to melt wiring (this could lead to a fire) and will almost certainly burn out your light switch. There's no headlight relay fitted as standard, so the wiring and switch were designed to cope only with the current drawn by standard-wattage bulbs; if you're going for high power, a relay must be fitted (much as you'd have to, to fit foglights or spots).

Tricks 'n' tips
Put the old bulbs in the glovebox - carrying spare bulbs is a good way to get a let-off from Plod, if they stop you for having a bulb gone. Be smart. Carry spares.

Front fog/spotlights

Extra lights are useful for adding features to the Civic's rather bland front end, even if they are a bit harder to fit than mesh. Most front bumpers have the facility for one or more pairs of lights, so it's gotta be done, really.

If you're fitting fogs, they must be wired in to work on dipped-beam only, so they must go off on main beam. The opposite is true for spotlights. Pop out the main light switch (or pull down the fusebox) and check for a wire which is live ONLY when the dipped beams are on. The Haynes wiring diagrams will help here - on our Civic, it was a red/white wire we needed, fed by fuse number 21 (pull the fuse to check you've got the right wire).

Once you've traced your wire, this is used as the live (+ve) feed for your foglight relay. Did we mention you'll need a relay? You'll need a relay. A four-pin one will do nicely. Splice a new wire onto the feed you've found, and feed it through to the engine (use one of the bulkhead grommets). Decide where you'll mount the relay (next to the battery seems obvious) and connect the new wire onto terminal 86.

For your other relay connections, you'll need an earth to terminal 85 (plenty of good earth spots around the battery). You also need a fused live supply (buy a single fuseholder, and a 15 or

20-amp fuse should be enough) and take a new feed straight off the battery positive connection - this goes to terminal 30 on your relay.

Terminal 87 on your relay is the live output to the fogs - split this into two wires, and feed it out to where the lights will go. Each foglight will also need an earth - either pick a point on the body next to each light, or run a pair of wires back to the earth point you used earlier for your relay. Simple, innit?

With the wiring sorted, now you'd best fit the lights. Over to you. Most decent foglights come with some form of mounting brackets - you must be able to adjust the aim, even if only slightly. To look their best, hopefully your new lights can slot into pre-cut holes in your new front bumper/bodykit.

To connect the wiring to the lights, you'll probably need to splice on your wires from terminal 87 to the new wiring plugs which came with the lights - not too difficult. Plug it all together, and test - you should now have some rather funky fogs!

Front
indicators

Like most small hatches, the Civic's front indicators blend into the headlights, to give a wrap-round effect. Can't fit trick headlights and not do the indicators, then, can we? Plenty of styles here too - just match up the look, and you're there. For us, choosing a Coupe wasn't such a neat idea when it came to these lights - Civic Hatch indicators (of which there are dozens to choose from) don't seem to fit the Coupe, leaving us with a tadge of a problem. But, knowing that our moody black twin lights would soon be joined by a carbon-fibre bonnet, we chose light-tinting as our best alternative. Smokin'!

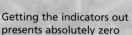

01 Getting the indicators out presents absolutely zero challenge to anyone. Remove one screw next to the headlight . . .

02 . . . then pull it out (there's a couple of moulded clips which slot into lugs on the side of the headlight) . . .

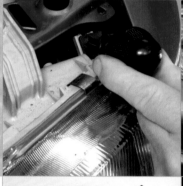

03 . . . and twist out the bulbholder. Now it's off, do we mod it or scrap it?

04 Spraying your lights is a top idea if funds are too tight for replacements, or if you simply don't fancy paying loadsamoney for illegal lights which also don't fit very well. The first job before spraying is to get the old lights clean - we used meths, which works well enough to get off all the old silicone products and polish residue.

05 As with most spray-painting, the trick is to get the stuff on evenly, which means applying light coats. Blasting it on too thick will give you the runs, which is never pleasant.

06 How thick is too thick? Well, this is what one of our standard Civic lights looked like, after a couple of light coats. This might be too subtle a look for you, but don't go too mad if you want to avoid attention from the Law.

There's a range of 'standard' colours that side reps come in, but most people go for clear or smoked, to colour-code with their rear clusters. Clear lenses can be coloured using special paint, but the paint must be applied lightly and evenly to the lens, or this will invite an easily-avoided MOT failure. Bodyshops can colour clear lenses to the exact shade of your car, by mixing a little paint with loads of lacquer - very trick.

Side repeaters must still show an orange light, and must be sufficiently bright (not easy to judge, and no two coppers have the same eyesight!). The stock bulbs are clear, so make sure you get orange bulbs too. You can actually get orange bulbs that look clear, to avoid the 'fried egg' effect. Alternatively, get LED side repeaters, like we did on our Fiesta project car.

Besides the various colour effects, side repeaters are available in many different shapes. Any shape other than standard goes, really - one popular choice for now are the Focus-style triangular lights, but the standard Civic items are so dull, even clear/crystal repeaters would be an improvement.

Or how about ditching the repeaters altogether, and get some tasty Merc-style mirrors, with side reps built-in? You could smooth your front wings, then…

Fitting new side repeaters wasn't actually that easy on our Civic, so pay attention. This shows the kind of problems you could have, if your new reps don't exactly fit (and also shows how you could fit totally-non-Honda items - like M3 repeaters, available cheap from your local Beemer dealer).

Side
repeaters

Don't just prise the old repeater light out with your biggest screwdriver. It's effective at light removal, but also a good way to wreck your wing. Using a small screwdriver, press the tang at the back of the repeater forwards, then carefully prise the light out at the back edge.

01

The old orange lens just twists off the bulbholder. Incidentally, while you're swapping these lights over, don't let the bulbholder fall back inside the wing panel, or you'll swear. A lot. If it's not just a simple swap over, tape the bulbholder to the wing.

02

With virtually any replacement side reps, you'll need a new bulb (check whether your chosen items come with new bulbs - not all do). Side reps still have to show an amber light, so if you've chosen clear lenses, you need an amber bulb. Pull the old one straight out, push in the new one.

03

Houston, we have a problem. Maybe we ordered the wrong lights here. Anyway, the new lights are too big. Do we get the right ones, or carry on regardless?

04

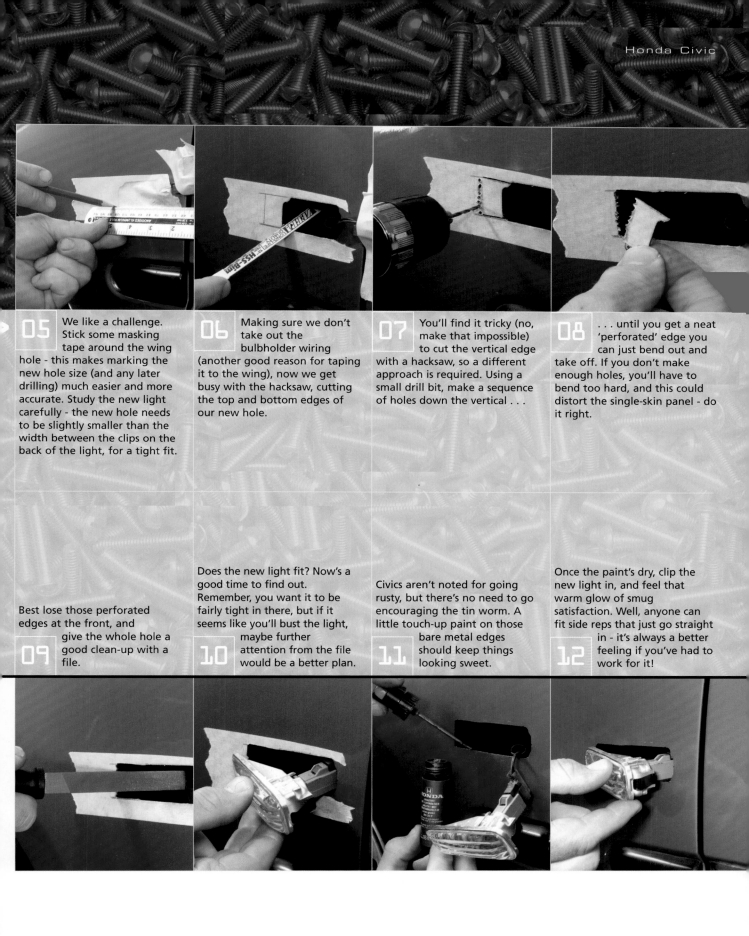

05 We like a challenge. Stick some masking tape around the wing hole - this makes marking the new hole size (and any later drilling) much easier and more accurate. Study the new light carefully - the new hole needs to be slightly smaller than the width between the clips on the back of the light, for a tight fit.

06 Making sure we don't take out the bulbholder wiring (another good reason for taping it to the wing), now we get busy with the hacksaw, cutting the top and bottom edges of our new hole.

07 You'll find it tricky (no, make that impossible) to cut the vertical edge with a hacksaw, so a different approach is required. Using a small drill bit, make a sequence of holes down the vertical . . .

08 . . . until you get a neat 'perforated' edge you can just bend out and take off. If you don't make enough holes, you'll have to bend too hard, and this could distort the single-skin panel - do it right.

09 Best lose those perforated edges at the front, and give the whole hole a good clean-up with a file.

10 Does the new light fit? Now's a good time to find out. Remember, you want it to be fairly tight in there, but if it seems like you'll bust the light, maybe further attention from the file would be a better plan.

11 Civics aren't noted for going rusty, but there's no need to go encouraging the tin worm. A little touch-up paint on those bare metal edges should keep things looking sweet.

12 Once the paint's dry, clip the new light in, and feel that warm glow of smug satisfaction. Well, anyone can fit side reps that just go straight in - it's always a better feeling if you've had to work for it!

Rear lights

Oh boy - we're spoilt for choice again (as long as you like the Lexus-look, that is). No surprise that the main choice in rear lights for a Jap car just happens to be those that look like another Jap car. It's just that it's getting a bit boring on Civics now. Do you want to go with the flow, or strike out on your own? Some people are now coming back to clear rears as an option, or even M3-style (half-clear, half-red). Your car, your look, of course. When Wings West came to us and said "we've got something new, d'you fancy it?" we couldn't say no - this is what we got...

Light legality

Lots of Civic rear clusters there may be, but - often, they're not UK-legal (even lights which are E-marked sometimes have no rear fogs or reflectors). Our lights are a bit more extreme, and don't even have UK amber indicators - beware of this if you're sourcing clusters from the US, as they can't be adapted to UK spec (we're keeping ours, but our finished Civic will only see shows, not the road). Mr. Plod is well-informed on this point, and those sexy rear lights are way too big a come-on for him to ignore.

Bought E-marked, but need a way round reflectors and a rear fog? You can buy stick-on reflectors, but these are about as sexy as NHS specs, so there's no easy answer on this. You'd have to be pretty unlucky to get pulled just for having no rear reflectors, but don't say we didn't warn you. And what happens if your car gets crunched, parked at night with no reflectors fitted? Will your insurance try and refuse to pay out? You betcha.

The rear foglight problem could perhaps be solved by spraying the clear bulb itself red (you can also buy ready-made red bulbs), but it won't fool every MOT man. Other ideas? Cut a hole in your new rear bumper/mesh, and find a cool-looking rear fog to mount inside (the Peugeot 206 unit's pretty sweet). If you don't mind a bit extra work, source an exhaust tailpipe trim roughly the same size as your existing single pipe, mount it on the opposite side of the car, and fit a round foglight inside the end.

The best solution? Only buy UK-legal lights (if you can find some) or lightly spray-tint your standard units. Any questions on light legality? Why not check out the ABC Design website tech tips page - if you've any questions after that, you can E-mail them. We're so good to you.

Rear lights

01 First, those gakky old rear lights have to go. Open the boot, and unclip this cover . . .

02 . . . then disconnect the main wiring plug (grey) and undo the four mounting nuts. One of the nuts secures the (green) earth wire - pull the wire off before you try yanking out the light cluster. You may need this wire for your new lights to work.

03 If the light unit won't part company from the car, it's probably just been on there a while, and it's got stuck on. Persuade it. We know this is a Coupe, but the same basic procedure applies to you Hatch owners, so don't panic.

04 The inner set of lights obviously has to go too, and this is remarkably the same as before. This time, you have to disconnect the wiring plug to get at the mounting nuts . . .

05 . . . and off she comes (persuasion optional).

06 If you've chosen quality lights, fitting the new items shouldn't tax your brain. If the mountings don't line up, you complain (or file out the holes a bit). If the fit seems poor, you could end up with leaks into the boot where the light meets the bodywork, so apply a little clear silicone to keep the weather out. Connect up, and check it all works before venturing out into Plod-land.

Rear foglight

Our very sexy rear light clusters from MSI Online are one of the latest products to take the market by storm. However, it's worth remembering that they were designed for the American market and exported to the UK, so they don't have a built-in fog light. Due to the nature of the MOT beast we gotta have one...so here goes. We're using the Peugeot 206 standard foglight as it's small, saucy and easy to fit!

01 First, swallow your pride and ring the good guys at your local Peugeot garage to order one – nicking one from a 206 sat in a car park is neither big nor clever. Offer it to the bumper and find the best position for it. We chose the centre of the mesh in the rear bumper – but it's up to you.

02 Second, make a template of the foglight by drawing around the shape on a piece of card, then cutting the shape out.

07 Drill a hole in each end of the light's metal lugs . . .

08 . . . then attach a spring (back to the DIY shop again) to each of the metal lugs.

09 There wasn't a bulb supplied with our foglight (French cheapskates), so we used the bulb from our old rear foglight and slotted it into the holder. You'll also need two a length of twin-core wire at this point – black for earth, red for live. Attach a female spade terminal to each wire and cover in heat-shrink to protect them from contacting on each other. Then slot them onto the contacts built into bulbholder.

03 Using the template, mark on the bumper exactly where the light will be positioned. If you're putting it in the centre of the bumper, make sure you've measured correctly - don't want that light off to one side. Keep the template in place by sticking it down with masking tape.

04 Next job is to chop off the plastic retaining lugs on the side of the 206 unit. You can snap them off if you're feeling strong, but we don't recommend it.

05 Back to the bumper to snip out the required hole, and check to see that the light fits the hole – if not, do some fettling.

06 Next, we need a bracket to hold our light in place. An L-bracket (from any DIY/hardware shop) is great for this job. When your bracket is ready, drill a hole and mount the bracket to the back panel of the car using a self-tapping screw.

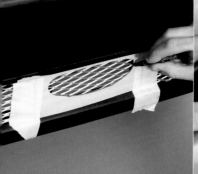

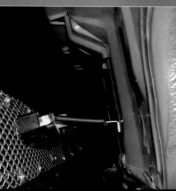

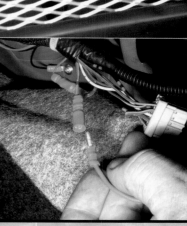

10 From underneath the car, hook the end of each spring into the hole on the L-bracket. These springs will hold the unit firmly in place.

11 Feed the wire up into the car by drilling a hole and adding a grommet. In the words of Blue Peter, this is one we made earlier, for our under-car neon set.

12 The black wire goes to a suitable earth point - in our case we used a ring terminal and fastened it with a nut to the body of the car. Now, we need to find a live feed for the red wire.

13 After rooting around in the boot area, we discovered what can only be described as a wiring plug for a tow bar (how cool is this Civic?). Careful probing with a test light found us the wire from our old foglight. Crimp a female spade to the existing wire, a male to the red wire from the fog and connect them. Legality never felt this good.

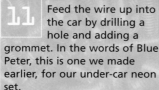

Wheels & tyres

Your most important decision ever?

This is where it's at - alloy wheels are the most important styling decision you'll ever make. No matter how good the rest of your car is, choose the wrong rims and your car will never look right. Choose a good set and you're already well on the way to creating a sorted motor. Take your time and pick wisely - wheel fashions change like the weather, and you don't want to spend shedloads on a set of uncool alloys.

1

None of the standard alloys cut it, and should very quickly be dumped. Advice on which particular wheels to buy would be a waste of space, since the choice is so huge, and everyone will have their own favourites. For what it's worth, though, something in a multi-spoker usually looks sweet on a Civic, so maybe some OZ's? For something more Jap-style, have a look at wheels from SSR, Volk Racing, Mugen or Enkei. If your Civic's going all-American, this year's look is chrome, and the US-based sites have plenty to see (check MSI Online, for starters, and DM Tech America). Even Wolfrace have recently jumped on the chrome bandwagon - our Cam chromes were supplied through Wolfrace.

One point not to overlook when choosing wheels is the wheel offset. Most normal cars fall somewhere in the mid-30s to early 40s, but the Civic is right at the top of this range, at 45. Make sure you mention they're for a Civic at an early stage in negotiations. Going lower than a 45 offset makes the wheel 'stick out' more - for really big rims, your arches won't just have to be 'trimmed' - they'll be butchered! Fitting wheels with the wrong offset may also do unpleasant things to the handling.

Lead us not into temptation

Before we go any further into which wheels are right for you, a word about insurance and security. Fitting tasty alloys to your Civic is one of the first and best ways to make it look cool. It follows, therefore, that someone with dubious morals might very well want to unbolt them from your car while you're not around, and make their own car look cool instead (or simply sell them, to buy spot cream and drugs).

Since fitting a set of top alloys is one of the easiest bolt-on ways to trick up any car, it's no surprise that the market in stolen alloys is as alive and kicking as it currently is - your wheels will also look very nice on any number of other cars, and the owners of those cars would love to own them at a fraction of the price you paid... It's not unknown for a set of wheels to go missing just for the tyres - if you've just splashed out on a set of fat Yokohamas, your wheels look even more tempting, especially if you've got a common-size tyre.

Tell your insurance company what you're fitting. What will probably happen is that they'll ask for the exact details, and possibly a photo of the car with the wheels on. Provided you're happy to then accept that they won't cover the extra cost of the wheels if they get nicked (or if the whole car goes), you may find you're not charged a penny more, especially if you've responsibly fitted some locking wheel nuts. Not all companies are the same, though - some charge an admin fee, and yes, some will start loading your premium. If you want the rims covered, it's best to talk to a company specialising in modified cars, or you could be asked to pay out the wheel cost again in premiums. The dumbest thing you can do is say nothing, and hope they don't find out - we don't want to go on about this, but there are plenty of documented cases where insurance companies have refused to pay out altogether, purely on the basis of undeclared alloy wheels.

How **cheap** are you?

Hopefully, you'll be deciding which wheels to go for based on how they look, not how much they cost, but inevitably (for most ordinary people at least), price does become a factor. Surely buying a cheaper wheel must have its pitfalls? Well, yes - and some of them may not be so obvious.

Inevitably, cheaper wheels = lower quality, but how does this manifest itself? Cheap wheels are often made from alloys which are more 'porous' (a bit like a sponge, they contain microscopic holes and pockets of air). Being porous has two main disadvantages for a wheel, the main one being that it won't be able to retain air in the tyres. The days of tyres with inner tubes are long gone (and it's illegal to fit tubes to low-profile tyres), so the only thing keeping the air in are the three 'walls' of the tyre, with the fourth 'wall' being the inside of the wheel itself. If you like keeping fit by pumping up your tyres every morning, go ahead - the rest of us will rightly regard this as a pain, and potentially dangerous (running tyres at low pressure will also scrub them out very effectively - what was that about saving money?).

Porous wheels also have difficulty in retaining their paint, lacquer, or chrome finish, with flaking a known problem, sometimes after only a few months. This problem is made worse by the fact that porous wheels are much harder to clean (brake dust seems to get ingrained into the wheels more easily) - and the more you scrub, the more the lacquer comes off.

The final nail in the coffin for cheap wheels is that they tend to corrode (or 'fizz') more. This not only looks terrible if visible from outside, but if you get corrosion between the wheel and the hub, you won't even be able to take the damn things off! Yes seriously, grown men with all the specialist tools in the world at their disposal will be scratching their heads when faced with wheels which simply **will not** come off.

Buying an established, popular make of wheel has another hidden benefit, too. Choosing a popular wheel will mean more suppliers will stock it, and the manufacturers themselves will make plenty of them. And if you're unlucky enough to have an accident (maybe a slide on a frosty road) which results in non-repairable damage to one wheel, you're going to need a replacement. If you've chosen the rarest wheels on the planet, you could be faced with having to replace a complete set of four, to get them all matching... A popular wheel, even if it's a few years old, might be easier to source, even second-hand.

The Sunday morning ritual

It's a small point maybe, but you'll obviously want your wheels to look as smart as possible, as often as possible - so how easy are they going to be to clean?

The real multi-spokers and BBS-style 'wires' are hell to clean - a fiddly toothbrush job - do you really want that much aggro every week? The simpler the design, the easier time you'll have. For those who like nothing better than counting their spokes, though, there are several really good products out there to make your life less of a cleaning nightmare.

Other options

If you're on a really tight budget, and perhaps own a real 'basic' model Civic, don't overlook the possibility of fitting a discarded set of standard alloys, possibly from another Honda entirely (Prelude wheels are a good bet) - check that the stud pattern's the same, obviously.

If the Honda range of wheels is too limiting, don't be too quick buying (for instance) alloys from other car makes altogether. For instance, some Renault, Rover, BMW, Vauxhall, Toyota and VW alloys have the same stud pattern (4 x 100), so they'll go on alright, but the offset may be different. In the case of some alloys (Ford, for example), the stud pattern may be only fractionally different (4 x 108), but if you put these on, the strain on the wheel studs is too great, and they can fracture...

Bound to drive you nuts

Don't forget about locking wheel nuts (see *'Hold on to your wheels'* further on) - bargain these into a wheel/tyre package if you're buying new.

A word of warning about re-using your existing wheel nuts, should you be upgrading from steel wheels. Steel-wheel nuts may not be suitable for use with alloy wheels (and vice-versa, incidentally). Make sure you ask about this when buying new wheels, and if necessary, bargain a set of nuts into the price. Most nuts for use with alloys will have a washer fitted, for two very good reasons - 1) the nut will pull through the wheel hole without it, and 2) to protect the wheel finish.

Size **matters**

For us Brits, biggest is best - there are Civics out there with 18s and up. And yes, the mags all say you can't be seen with anything less than 17-inchers. In Europe, meanwhile, they're mad for the small-wheel look, still with seriously dropped suspension of course.

While the Civic will take 17-inch rims without sorting the arches, remember that 17s often don't do wonders for the ride or handling. If you're bothered about how your Civic takes the bends, consider getting some tidy 15s or 16s instead. Providing the rest of the car's up together, get the car low and you'll still get respect. A comment we saw on one chat room was "get 18s for the look, 16s if you wanna drive it" - or 17s if you wanna compromise? Seems Civic Coupes are easier to get 18s on than Hatches - certainly looks like we could've put our coilover-kitted Coupe on 18s if we'd wanted to.

Tricks 'n' tips
When you have your new wheels balanced, make sure the fast-fit centre knows to use stick-on weights, inside the wheel (not on the rim edge) - old-type knock on lead weights look lame on the outer wheel edges, and on the inner edges may foul the suspension. Stick-on weights are, however, notorious for falling off easily, even when applied to pristine new alloys.

We like a challenge

To be honest, successfully fitting big wheels in combination with lowered suspension is one of life's major challenges. As much as anything, tyre width is what ultimately leads to problems, not so much the increased wheel diameter.

If the tyres are simply too wide (or with wheels the wrong offset), they will first of all rub on the suspension strut (ie on the inside edge of the tyre). Also, the inside edges may rub on the arches on full steering lock - check left and right. Rubbing on the inside edges can be cured by fitting offsets or spacers between the wheel and hub, which effectively pull the wheel outwards, 'spacing' it away from its normal position (this also has the effect of widening the car's track, which may improve the on-limit handling - or not). Fitting large offsets must be done using special longer wheel studs, as the standard ones may only engage the nuts by a few threads, which is highly dangerous.

Rubbing on the outside edges is a simple case of wheelarch lip fouling, which must be cured by rolling up (or trimming off) the wheelarch return edge, and other mods. If you've gone for REALLY wide tyres, or have already had to fit offsets, the outer edge of the tyre will probably be visible outside the wheelarch, and this is a no-no (it's illegal, and you must cover it up!).

The other trick with fitting big alloys is of course to avoid the 'Civic 4x4 off-road' look, which you will achieve remarkably easily just by popping on a set of 17s with standard suspension. The massive increase in ground clearance is fine for Farmer Palmer, but your 'fistable' arches won't win much admiration at cruises. Overcoming this problem by lowering can be a matter almost of inspired guesswork, as much as anything (see 'Suspension').

Speedo error? Or not?

One side-effect of fitting large wheels is that your car will go slower. Yes, really - or at least - it will appear to go slower, due to the effects of the mechanically-driven speedometer.

As the wheel diameter increases, so does its circumference (distance around the outside) - this means that, to travel say one mile, a large wheel will turn less than a smaller wheel. Because the speedometer is driven from the gearbox final drive, the apparent vehicle speed is actually based on the number of complete revolutions of the wheel. Therefore, for a given *actual* speed, since a larger-diameter wheel will be turning at a slower rate than a smaller wheel, and the method for measuring speed is the rate of wheel rotation, a car with larger wheels will produce a lower *speedo reading* than one with smaller wheels - but it's NOT actually going any slower in reality. So don't worry if you think you've reduced your Civic's performance somehow with the monster rims, 'cos you 'aven't.

With the ever-increasing number of those lovely grey/yellow roadside boxes with a nasty surprise inside, spare a thought to what this speedo error could mean in the real world. If (like most people) you tend to drive a wee bit over the posted 30s and 40s, your real speed on 17s could be a bit more than the bit more you thought you were doing already, and you could get an unexpected flash to ruin your day. What we're saying is, don't drive any faster, to compensate for the lower speedo reading. Actually, the speedo error effect on 17s really is tiny at around-town speeds, and only becomes a factor over 70. But then, Officer, you couldn't possibly have been going over 70, could you? Officer?

Jargon explained

Rolling Radius - You may have come across the term 'rolling radius', which is the distance from the wheel centre to the outer edge of the tyre, or effectively, half the overall diameter. The rolling radius obviously increases with wheel size, but up to a point, the effects are masked by fitting low-profile tyres, with 'shorter' sidewalls. Above 16-inch rims, however, even low-profiles can't compensate, and the rolling radius keeps going up.

PCD - this isn't a banned substance, it's your Pitch Circle Diameter, which relates to the spacing of your wheel holes, or 'stud pattern'. It is expressed by the diameter of a notional circle which passes through the centre of your wheel studs, and the number of studs/nuts. Unlike the offset, the PCD often isn't stamped onto the wheels, so assessing it is really a matter of eyeing-up and trying them on the studs - the wheel should go on easily, without binding, if the stud pattern is correct. On a Civic, the PCD is 100 mm with four studs, which is given as 100/4, or 4 x 100.

Offset - this is determined by the distance from the wheel mounting face in relation to its centre-line. The offset figure is denoted by ET (no, I mustn't), which stands for einpress tiefe in German, or pressed-in depth (now I KNOW you're asleep). The lower the offset, the more the wheels will stick out. Fitting wheels with the wrong offset might bring the wheel into too-close contact with the brake and suspension bits, or with the arches. Very specialised area - seek advice from the wheel manufacturers if you're going for a very radical size (or even if you're not). The correct offset for Civics of all sizes is ET 45.

Hold on to your wheels

The minute you bang on your wicked alloys, your car becomes a target. People see the big wheels, and automatically assume you've also got a major stereo, seats and other goodies - all very tempting, but that involves breaking in, and you could have an alarm. Pinching the wheels themselves, now that's a doddle - a few tools, some bricks or a couple of well-built mates to lift the car, and it's easy money

The trouble with fitting big wheels is that they're only screwed on, and are just as easily screwed off, if you don't make life difficult for 'em. If you're unlucky enough to have to park outside at night (ie no garage), you could wake up one morning to a car that's *literally* been slammed on the deck! Add to this the fact that your car isn't going anywhere without wheels, plus the damage which will be done to exhaust, fuel and brake pipes from dropping on its belly, and it's suddenly a lot worse than losing a grand's worth of wheels and tyres…

The market and demand for stolen alloys is huge, but since most people don't bother having them security-marked in any way, once a set of wheels disappears, they're almost impossible to trace. Thieves avoid security-marked (or 'tattooed') wheels (or at least it's a pretty good

deterrent) - and it needn't look hideous!

When choosing that car alarm, try and get one with an 'anti-jacking' feature, because thieves hate it. This is sometimes now called 'anti-tilt', to avoid confusion with anti-hijacking. Imagine a metal saucer, with a metal ball sitting on a small magnet in the centre. If the saucer tilts in any direction, the ball rolls off the magnet, and sets off the alarm. Highly sensitive, and death to anyone trying to lift your car up for the purpose of removing the wheels - as we said, the crims are not fond of this feature at all. Simply having an alarm with anti-shock is probably not good enough, because a careful villain will probably be able to work so as not to create a strong enough vibration to trigger it - mind you, it's a whole lot better than nothing, especially if set to maximum sensitivity.

Locking nuts/bolts

Locking wheel nuts will be effective as a deterrent to the inexpert thief (kids, in other words), but will probably only slow down the pro.

Thieves want to work quickly, and will use large amounts of cunning and violence to deprive you of your stuff. If you fit a cheap set of locking nuts, they'll use a hammer and thin chisel to crack off the locking heads. Some nuts can easily be defeated by hammering a socket onto them, and undoing the locking nut as normal, while some of the key-operated nuts are so pathetic they can be beaten using a small screwdriver. So - choose the best nuts you can, but don't assume they'll prevent your wheels from disappearing. Insurance companies seem to like 'em - perhaps it shows a responsible attitude, or something...

There seems to be some debate as to whether it's okay to fit more than one set of locking nuts to a car - some people we know value their wheels so highly that they've fitted four sets of nuts - in other words, they've completely replaced all the standard nuts! The feeling against doing this is that the replacement locking nuts may not be made to the same standard as factory originals, and while it's okay to fit one set on security grounds, fitting more than that is dangerous on safety grounds (nut could fail, wheel falls off, car in ditch, owner in hospital...).

Obviously, you must carry the special key or tool which came with your nuts with you at all times, in case of a puncture, or if you're having any other work done, such as new brakes or tyres. The best thing to do is rig this onto your keyring, so that it's with you, but not left in the car. The number of people who fit locking nuts and then leave the key to them cunningly 'hidden' in the glovebox or the boot... You don't leave a spare set of car keys in your glovebox as well, do you?

How to change a set of wheels

You might think you know all about this, but do you really?

Okay, so you know you need a jack and wheelbrace (or socket and ratchet), but where are the jacking points? If you want to take more than one wheel off at a time, have you got any axle stands, and where do they go? If you've only ever had wheels and tyres fitted by a garage, chances are you're actually a beginner at this. It's surprising just how much damage you can do to your car, and to yourself, if you don't know what you're doing - and the worst thing here is to think you know, when you don't...

What to use

If you don't already have one, invest in a decent hydraulic (trolley) jack. This is way more use than the standard car jack, which is really only for emergencies, and which isn't really stable enough to rely on. Lifting and lowering the car is so much easier with a trolley jack, and you'll even look professional. Trolley jacks have a valve, usually at the rear, which must be fully tightened (using the end of the jack handle) before raising the jack, and which is carefully loosened to lower the car down - if it's opened fully, the car will not so much sink as plummet!

Axle stands are placed under the car, once it's been lifted using the jack. Stands are an important accessory to a trolley jack, because once they're in place, there's no way the car can come down on you - remember that even a brand new trolley jack could creep down (if you haven't tightened the valve), or could even fail completely under load (if it's a cheap one, or knackered, or both).

Under NO circumstances use bricks, wooden blocks or anything else which you have to pile up, to support the car - this is just plain stupid. Civics are small cars, sure, but they still weigh quite enough to damage you convincingly if they land on top of you - if you don't believe us, try crawling under it when it's resting on a few poxy bricks.

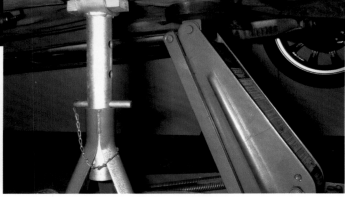

Where to do it

Only ever jack the car up on a solid, level surface (ideally, a concrete or tarmac driveway, or quiet car park). If there's even a slight slope, the car's likely to move (maybe even roll away) as the wheels are lifted off the ground. Jacking up on a rough or gravelled surface is not recommended, as the jack could slip at an awkward moment - such as when you've just got underneath...

How to do it - jacking up the front

Before jacking up the front of the car, pull the handbrake on firmly (you can also chock the rear wheels, if you don't trust your handbrake).

If you're taking the wheels off, loosen the wheel nuts BEFORE you start jacking up the car. It's easily forgotten, but you'll look pretty silly trying to undo the wheel nuts with the front wheels spinning in mid-air.

We'll assume you've got a trolley jack. The next question is - where to stick it? Up front, there's a chunky-looking section just inside the sill (remember, this is a Coupe - Hatches should be the same, but check first). If you use this for jacking, put a flat offcut of wood on your jack head first, to spread the load. You can jack on the sill jacking points, which are marked by large arrows under the sill edges, but it's better to leave those for your axle stands.

Once you've got the car up, pop an axle stand or two under the front sill jacking points - this is the only part of the sill it's safe to jack under or rest the car on. With the stands in place, you can lower the jack so the car's weight rests on the stands. For maximum safety, spread the car's weight between the stands and the jack - don't lower the jack completely unless it's needed elsewhere.

I'm sure we don't need to tell you this, but don't jack up the car, or stick stands under the car, anywhere other than kosher jacking and support points. This means - not the floorpan or the sump (you'll cave it in), not the suspension bits (not stable), and not under the brake/fuel pipes (ohmigawd).

How to do it - jacking up the rear

When jacking up the rear of the car, place wooden chocks in front of the front wheels to stop it rolling forwards, and engage first gear.

If you're taking the wheels off, you don't have to loosen the wheel nuts before lifting the car, but you'll be relying on your handbrake to hold the wheels while you wrestle with the nuts. Much cooler (and safer) to loosen the rear wheel nuts on the ground too.

Jacking and supporting the Civic back-end is a little trickier. Have a good look under there before making your choice. On our Coupe, there's a central jacking point right at the back of the car - we've made life a bit trickier for ourselves by mounting our under-car neon tube near it. Certainly not one to use without any axle stands as well - being in the centre, it makes the car rock from side to side - only with a stand under the rear sill point would it really be safe.

Although Honda certainly wouldn't recommend it, you can jack under the rear shock absorber mounting, on the suspension arm - just go slowly, as the arm will move and compress the suspension as the jack rises. Jacking under the suspension arm is obviously no use if you're working on the rear suspension itself.

For axle stands, it's the rear sill jacking point, again marked with a large arrow underneath. Not so much need for a block of wood here, but still not a bad idea to use one if you can - saves your paint, spreads the load into the car.

Remember not to put your axle stands under any pipes, the spare wheel well, or the fuel tank, and you should live to see another Christmas.

Finally...

As far as possible, don't leave the car unattended once it has been lifted, particularly if kids are playing nearby - football goes under your car, they go under to get it, knock the jack, car falls... it would almost certainly be your fault.

Changing wheels

01 Have you got a nice ally/plastic ring inside the wheel hub? Make sure it's there, as it acts to centre the wheel properly, and may help to stop the wheel rusting on. Ever had a rusted-on wheel? Your local fast-fit centre will have, and they'll tell you it ain't funny.

02 Even with the plastic ring of confidence, the metal bits can still corrode on. Equip yourself with some copper brake grease, and smear some on the hub. The pros 'paint' it on with a brush - the rest of us get messy. It's not a bad idea if some of that grease finds its way onto the wheel studs/nuts, too.

03 Pop the wheel onto the hub, then on with the nicely-greased nuts, and tighten up as far as possible by hand. Don't you just love the bling-bling of chrome?

04 You have got some locking nuts, haven't you? Keep your locking tool somewhere safe, but not obvious. The glovebox is convenient, but way too obvious!

05 With the wheel on the ground, tighten the wheel nuts securely (ideally, to the correct torque - 109 Nm). Don't over-tighten, or you'll never get them if you have a flat! If you've really blown some serious cash on your new rims, why not treat them to a special protected socket for tightening the nuts? Companies like Draper do a set of special sockets with plastic protector sleeves fitted, to stop the metal scratching your fine alloys. Makes sense to us.

06 Some wheels look better without their centre cap (not all wheels have one to start with), but even this might slow down a particularly stupid wheel-thief, as it covers up the nuts. Remember to also carry the tool used to secure it (in this case, a humble screwdriver), or a puncture would leave you stranded. And embarrassed.

Always nice to see a good brand of tyre on a decent alloy. How cool do cheap tyres look?

Tyres

To some people, tyres are just round and black - oh, and they're nearly all expensive, and don't last long enough. When you're buying a new set of wheels, most centres will quote prices with different tyres - buying a tyred-up set of rims is convenient, and usually quite good value, too.

Some people try and save money by fitting 'remould' or 're-manufactured' tyres. These aren't always the bargain they appear to be - experience says there's no such thing as a good cheap tyre, with wheel balancing problems a well-known downside, for starters.

Choosing a known brand of tyre will prove to be one of your better decisions. Tyres are the only thing keeping you on the road, as in steering, braking and helping you round corners - what's the point of trying to improve the handling by sorting the suspension if you're going to throw the gains away by fitting naff tyres? Why beef up the brakes if the tyres won't bite? The combination of stiff suspension and cheap tyres is inherently dangerous - because the front end dives less with reduced suspension travel, the front tyres are far more likely to lock and skid under heavy braking.

Cheap tyres also equals more wheelspin - might be fun to disappear in a cloud of tyre smoke, but wouldn't you rather be disappearing up the road? Another problem with really wide tyres is aquaplaning - hit a big puddle at speed, and the tyre skates over the water without gripping - it's seriously scary when your car starts

Tricks 'n' tips
When buying tyres, look out for ones which feature a rubbing strip on the sidewall - these extend over the edge of the wheel rims, and the idea is that they protect the rim edges from damage by 'kerbing'. Any decent tyre has them - discreet and very practical, and much better than a chewed-up rim.

steering for you. Fitting good tyres won't prevent it, but it might increase your chances of staying in control. The sexiest modern low-profile tyres have a V-tread pattern, designed specifically to aid water dispersal, which is exactly what you need to prevent aquaplaning - try some, and feel the difference!

Finally, cheap tyres ruin your Civic's appearance - a no-name brand emblazoned in big letters on your tyre sidewalls - how's that going to look? If you're spending big dosh on wheels, you've gotta kit 'em out with some tasty V-tread tyres, or lose major points for style. Listen to friends and fellow modifiers - real-world opinions count for a lot when choosing tyres (how well do they grip, wet or dry? How many miles can you get out of them?) Just make sure, before you splash your cash on decent tyres, that you've cured any rubbing and scrubbing issues, as nothing will rip your new tyres out faster.

Marks on your sidewalls

Tyre sizes are expressed in a strange mixture of metric and imperial specs - we'll take a typical tyre size as an example:

205/40 R 17 V
for a 7-inch wide 17-inch rim
205 width of tyre in millimetres
40 this is the "aspect ratio" (or "profile") of the tyre, or the sidewall height in relation to tyre width, expressed as a percentage, in this case 40%. So - 40% of 205 mm = 82 mm, or the height of the tyre sidewall from the edge of the locating bead to the top of the tread.
R Radial.
17 Wheel diameter in inches.
V Speed rating (in this case, suitable for use up to 150 mph).

Pressure situation

Don't forget, when you're having your new tyres fitted, to ask what the recommended pressures should be, front and rear - it's unlikely that the Honda specs for this will be relevant to your new low-low profiles, but it's somewhere to start from. If the grease-monkey fitting your tyres is no help on this point, contact the tyre manufacturer - the big ones might even have a half-useful website! Running the tyres at the wrong pressures is particularly stupid (you'll wear them out much faster) and can be very dangerous (too soft - tyre rolls off the rim, too hard - tyre slides, no grip).

Speed ratings

Besides the tyre size, tyres are marked with a maximum speed rating, expressed as a letter code:

T up to 190 km/h (118 mph)

U up to 200 km/h (124 mph)

H up to 210 km/h (130 mph)

V inside tyre size markings (225/50 VR 16) over 210 km/h (130 mph)

V outside tyre size markings (185/55 R 15 V) up to 240 km/h (150 mph)

Z inside tyre size markings (255/40 ZR 17) over 240 km/h (150 mph)

Suspension

If your Civic's still sitting on standard suspension, it's safe to say it doesn't cut it - yet. If you've decided you couldn't wait to fit your big rims, the chances are your Civic is now doing a passable impression of a tractor. An essential fitment, then - so how low do you go, and what nasty side-effects will a lowering kit have?

The main reason for lowering is of course, to make your car look cool. Standard suspension nearly always seems to be set too soft and too high - a nicely lowered motor really stands out instantly. Lowering your car should also improve the handling. Dropping the car on its suspension brings the car's centre of gravity closer to its roll and pitch centres, which helps to pin it to the road in corners and under braking - combined with stiffer springs and shocks, this reduces body roll and increases the tyre contact patch on the road. BUT - if improving the handling is really important to you, choose your new suspension carefully. If you go the cheap route, or want extreme lowering, then you could end up with a car that don't handle at all…

As for what to buy, there are basically three main options when it comes to lowering, arranged in order of ascending cost below:

1 *Set of lowering springs.*

2 *Matched set of lowering springs and shock absorbers (suspension kit).*

3 *Set of 'coilovers'.*

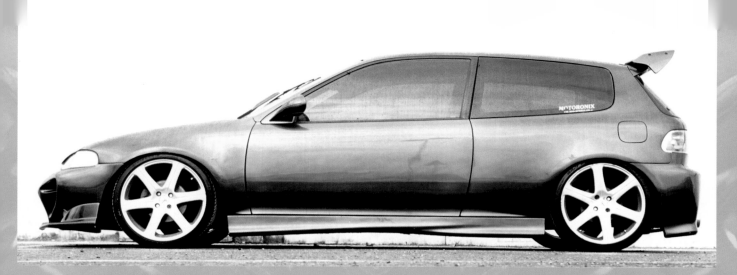

Lowering springs

The cheapest option by far, but with the most pitfalls and some unpleasant side-effects. Lowering springs are, effectively, shorter versions of the standard items fitted to your Civic at the factory. However, not only are they shorter (lower), they are also uprated (stiffer) - if lowering springs were simply shorter than standard and the same stiffness (the same 'rate'), you'd be hitting the bump-stops over every set of catseyes. With lowering springs, you just fit the new springs and keep the original shock absorbers ('dampers'), so even if the originals aren't completely knackered, you're creating a problem caused by mis-matched components. The original dampers were carefully chosen to work with the original-rate springs - by increasing the spring rate without changing the dampers, you end up with dampers that can't control the springs properly. What this usually does before long is wreck the dampers, so you don't even save money in the end.

The mis-matched springs and dampers will have other entertaining side-effects, too. How would you like a Civic which rides like a brick, and which falls over itself at the first sign of a corner taken above walking pace? A very choppy ride and strange-feeling steering (much lighter, or much heavier, depending on your luck) are well-documented problems associated with taking the cheap option, and it doesn't even take much less time to fit, compared to a proper solution. Even if you're a hard man, who

doesn't object to a hard ride if his car looks cool, think on this - how many corners do you know that are completely flat (ie without any bumps)? On dodgy lowering springs, you hit a mid-corner bump at speed, and it's anyone's guess where you'll end up.

If cost is a major consideration, and lowering springs the only option for now, at least try to buy branded items of decent quality - some cheap sets of springs will eat their way through several sets of dampers before you realise the springs themselves have lost the plot. Needless to say, if riding around on mis-matched springs and shocks is a bit iffy anyway, it's downright dangerous when they've worn out (some inside 18 months!).

Assuming you want to slam your suspension so your arches just clear the tops of your wicked new rims, there's another small problem with lowered springs - it takes some inspired guesswork (or hours of careful measuring and head-scratching) to assess the required drop accurately, and avoid that nasty rubbing sound and the smell of burning rubber. Springs are generally only available in a very few sizes, expressed by the amount of drop they'll produce. On many Civics, even 40 mm is quite a major drop on 17s. If scraping the deck's your thing, you can usually get 60 mm springs - there's 30 or 35 mm springs too if you're less brave (or if you've simply got massive rims). Take as many measurements as possible, and ask around your mates/'net forums - suppliers and manufacturers may be your best source of help in special cases.

Suspension **kit**

A far better choice, Sir - a matched set of springs and dampers is a genuine 'upgrade', and respect is due. There are several branded kits available, and some Honda specialists do their own. With a properly-sorted conversion, your Civic will handle even better, and you'll still be able to negotiate a set of roadworks without needing dental work afterwards. Actually, you may well be amazed how well the Civic will still ride, even though the springs are clearly lower and stiffer - the secret is in the damping.

Some of the kits are billed as 'adjustable', but this only applies to the damper rates (don't mistake them as being cheap coilovers), which can often be set to your own taste by a few minutes' work. This Playstation feature can be a good fun thing to play around with, even if it is slightly less relevant to road use than for hillclimbs and sprints - but don't get carried away and set it too stiff, or you'll end up with an evil-handling car and a CD player that skips over every white line on the road!

Unfortunately, although you should end up with a fine-handling car, there are problems with suspension kits, too. If you don't have your steering geometry (camber and tracking) reset, you'll eat tyres, and once again, you're into guesswork territory when it comes to assessing your required drop for big wheels. Generally, most suspension kits are only available with a fairly modest drop (typically, 35 to 40 mm).

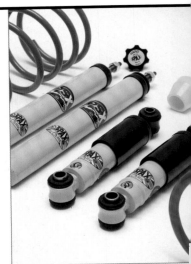

Coilovers

If you've chosen coilovers, well done again. This is the most expensive option, and it offers one vital feature that the other two can't - true adjustability of ride height, meaning that you can make the finest of tweaks to hunker down on your new rims (coilovers are an almost-essential choice if you're trying for 18s). Coilovers give you more scope to fit those big rims now, lower it down as far as poss, then wait 'til next month before you have the arches rolled, and drop it down to the deck. Coilovers are a variation on the suspension kit theme - a set of matched variable-rate springs (some have separate 'helper' springs too) and shocks, but their adjustability might not guarantee as good a ride/handling mix as a normal kit.

A coilover set replaces each spring and shock with a combined unit where the coil spring fits over the shocker (hence 'coil' 'over') - nothing too unusual in this, because so far, it's similar to a normal front strut. The difference lies in the adjustable spring lower seat, which can lower the spring (and car) to any desired height, within limits.

Unfortunately, making a car go super-low is not good for the ride or the handling. Coilover systems have very short, stiff springs, and this can lead to similar problems to those found with cheap lowering springs alone. If you go too far with coilovers, you can end up with a choppy ride, heavy steering and generally unpleasant handling. Combine a coilover-slammed car with big alloys, and while the visual effect may be stunning, the driving experience might well be very disappointing. At least a proper coilover kit will come with shock absorbers (dampers) which are matched to the springs, unlike a 'conversion' kit.

Coilover conversion

A better-value option is the 'coilover conversion'. If you really must have the lowest, baddest machine out there, and don't care what the ride will be like, these could be the answer. Offering as much potential for lowering as genuine coilovers (and at far less cost),

these items could be described as a cross between coilovers and lowering springs, because the standard dampers are retained (this is one reason why the ride suffers). What you get is a new spring assembly, with adjustable top and bottom mounts - the whole thing slips over your standard damper. Two problems with this solution (how important these are is up to you):

1 Your standard dampers will not be able to cope with the uprated springs, so the car will almost certainly ride (and possibly handle) like a pig if you go for a really serious drop - and okay, why else would you be doing it?

2 The standard dampers are effectively being compressed, the lower you go. There is a limit to how far they will compress before being completely solid (and this could be the limit for your lowering activities). Needless to say, even a partly-compressed damper won't be able to do much actual damping - the results of this could be… interesting…

Front Suspension

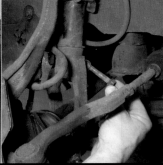

Tricks 'n' tips

A few days before attacking your suspension, spray some WD-40 on the various mounting nuts and bolts. Shearing off one of the suspension mountings is a great way to ruin your weekend. If any of the nuts/bolts proves really tough to loosen (or goes a little way, then sticks), try tightening it a small amount before getting out the cracker bars - a little movement, even if it's the wrong way, might prevent a fastener from shearing.

Tricks 'n' tips

Don't start this job without coil spring compressors, or you'll be sorry! A torque wrench is also pretty important.

01 Loosen the wheel nuts, jack up the corner of the car you're working on (see 'Wheels 'n' tyres' for more info on jacking up) and take off the wheel. The first bits we need to unbolt are the two mounting brackets for the front brake hoses. Move the hoses to one side, and make sure they don't get hooked up or crushed while you're working - tie them back if poss.

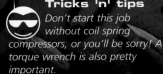

02 Now the anti-roll bar must be disconnected from the suspension lower arm - two spanners will be needed for this, and you might need a bit of leverage to separate the roll bar from its mounting.

03 This Civic suspension's a bit weird if you're used to Fords. At the base of the front strut, there's a horseshoe-shaped section called the strut fork which joins to the lower control arm. To remove the strut (the bit we're interested in), the fork's got to go, and this means taking out two big (rusty?) bolts. First, put a jack under the lower control arm . . .

04 . . . then remove the pinch-bolt at the top . . .

05 . . . and another at the bottom. If the nut/bolt looks well-rusty, first give it some tlc with a wire brush and some WD-40.

06 The final stage in removing the fork is separating it from the base of the strut, which could be harder than it sounds if rust has had its way. Try twisting it sideways, as well as giving it the treatment with a large hammer.

07 Just the two top mounting nuts in the engine bay to undo now. These nuts have a 'self-locking' plastic thread insert to stop them coming loose - this feature might not work if you re-use the old nuts, so it's best to get new ones, or use thread-locking fluid when you put the old ones back later.

08 If the strut doesn't fall out on your foot you can work it down through, and out.

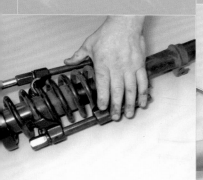

09 There are two clamps, each with two hooks, which sit over one of the spring coils. You may not get the hooks over the top and bottom coils, but try the next nearest. Fit the two clamps opposite each other, then tighten the big bolt up the middle of each to compress one side of the spring - this must be done evenly, one side after the other, or the un-clamped side might fly off. Compress the spring until the tension is off the strut top mounting plate.

10 Undo the strut inner nut, using an Allen key to hold the strut piston from turning.

11 Take care when pulling the old strut apart - that spring's still under major tension. Most of the old bits won't be needed again, but one that will is the strut top mounting plate. Loosen off the spring clamps slowly and evenly, or you'll end up having a really bad day.

Respect

For this next bit, you MUST use coil spring compressors ('spring clamps'). Medical attention will be required if you don't. Do we have to draw you a diagram? The spring's under tension on the strut, even off the car - what do you think's gonna happen if you just undo it? The spring-embedded-in-the-forehead look is really OVER, too.

>>

12 Ah, that's more like it. Start assembling your new strut by slipping on the shiny spring (if it's not obvious which way up it goes, be guided by the writing on it). Which springs are the fronts? You could be on the phone to the makers, if it's not clear. Even if your springs all look the same, they could be different rates (stiffness). Pays to check these things...

13 When you're happy with your spring, slip on the spring seat . . .

14 . . . followed by the bearing washer and the old strut top mounting plate (looking suspiciously like someone's cleaned it) . . .

15 . . . then, on our Spax kit at least, there's another bearing washer on top, and a dished washer (your kit may be slightly different to ours - always check your instructions). All of this gets secured with a new nut supplied - this nut has to be tightened while the strut piston is held using a spanner on the flats provided.

16 With coilovers, you'll be doing yourself a favour if you set the adjustable lower spring seat now, using the C-spanner provided. When it's set, lock the spring seat in place with the second locking ring. Might be an idea to give those coilover threads a shot of lube (or even Waxoyl) once they're on the car - stops 'em seizing up.

17 If you set both sides to exactly the same height (measure with a ruler), at least the car will start off level. When you set the ride height finally with the wheels on the ground, you can keep it level by turning each side the same amount. Simple, innit?

Suspension

18 The freshly-assembled coilover unit can now be fed into position under the arch. Hold it in position for now by loosely fitting the two top nuts.

19 Everything works better with a little lube, and this is very true when you're trying to poke the strut base into the strut fork we took off earlier.

20 Slip on the strut fork, and tighten the pinch-bolt just by hand for now. At least clean and re-lubricate the old bolt, if you don't buy a new one, like us (remember how rusty this was, coming off?). This bolt must be fully tightened when the weight of the car's back on its wheels - don't worry, we'll remind you later on.

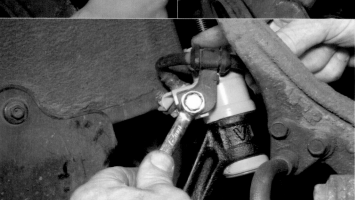
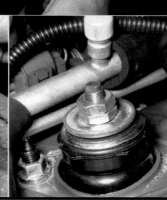

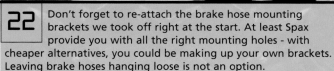

21 Another rather vital bolt is the one fitted at the base of the strut fork - if the old one's really bad, rust-wise, getting a new one should be a no-brainer. Torque this one up to 64 Nm (you'll need to jack under the control arm again, to get the bolt in). Another bolt not to leave out is one for the anti-roll bar (tighten its nut to 22 Nm).

22 Don't forget to re-attach the brake hose mounting brackets we took off right at the start. At least Spax provide you with all the right mounting holes - with cheaper alternatives, you could be making up your own brackets. Leaving brake hoses hanging loose is not an option.

23 The wheel's back on, car's on the ground. It's time to check everything's tight - like the two top mounting nuts (64 Nm, using new nuts or thread-lock fluid). The piston rod nut in the centre should be tight already, but on this kit, there's a second locknut to tighten onto that (use thread-lock on this, too). Underneath, tighten the strut fork pinch-bolt to 43 Nm (and you thought we'd forgotten).

Rear Suspension

Working in the boot, remove all the fasteners securing the boot carpet, and peel it back for access to the rear strut top mountings. Loosen off just the outer two nuts - don't touch the one in the centre, or things will go off with a bang.

01

Loosen the rear wheel nuts, then jack the whole back end of the car, and support with axle stands under the sill rear jacking points. Have a look in *'Wheels 'n' tyres'* for more info on jacking up. Remove the rear wheels. In theory, all you have to do is loosen the shock lower mounting bolt, take out the bolt, and drop the whole strut out. Just like that.

02

07 Dismantling the rear strut is exactly the same deal as it was up front. Use spring clamps, undo the piston rod nut while holding the rod still with an Allen key, take apart carefully, loosen the spring clamps evenly.

Respect

For this next bit, you MUST use coil spring compressors ('spring clamps'). Medical attention will be required if you don't. Do we have to draw you a diagram? The spring's under tension on the strut, even off the car - what do you think's gonna happen if you just undo it? The spring-embedded-in-the-forehead look is really OVER, too.

08 Assembling the new rear strut is also a carbon-copy of the front procedure (but again, check your kit's instructions to be sure). If you've already done the fronts, at least there should be no confusion on which springs to use. As with the front strut, about the only bit that gets recycled is the top mounting plate.

09 Now we get to see how easy this job's supposed to be. Just slip the new strut into place, securing it loosely with the two nuts at the top . . .

Life isn't always that easy, though - as we found out. Our lower mounting bolt was totally seized, so instead we removed the inner and outer bolts from the suspension lower arm . . .

03

. . . and took off the strut with the lower arm attached. There's none of this "here's one we did earlier" stuff with us (well, hardly ever).

04

Getting that bolt out was - a challenge. First, we decided to hacksaw off the nut, which might let us drive out the bolt. See, not only was the nut rusted-on, the bolt was also rusted inside the shock lower bush. Who bought this ******* car?

05

In the end, it took some pretty unusual methods to get the bolt out - here's one example. Mount the shock in a vice, and use another bolt and socket either side to press the bolt out. If it's really bad, you'll probably need professional help. Or a complete new lower arm.

06

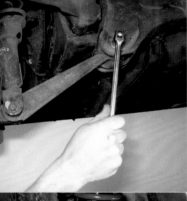   

10 . . . while the bottom end hooks over the lower arm, and the lower mounting bolt just slips into place. Sigh. Tighten the strut lower bolt (obviously a new one, in our case) to 54 Nm. It's the same torque for the bolt at either end of the lower arm if you had the same trouble as us.

11 Inside the boot, make sure the piston rod nut's fully tight, and lock it using the second nut provided (some kits give you just one nut, with a self-locking plastic thread insert).

12 Finally, tighten the two top mounting nuts to 49 Nm. Or just as tight as you sensibly can, so it won't fall off. Set your adjustable dampers/ride heights to your liking, and enjoy.

Nasty side-effects

Camber angle and tracking

With any lowering 'solution', it's likely that your suspension and steering geometry will be severely affected - this will be more of a problem the lower you go. This will manifest itself in steering which either becomes lighter or (more usually) heavier, and in tyres which scrub out their inner or outer edges in very short order - not funny, if you're running expensive low-profiles! Sometimes, even the rear tyres can be affected in this way, but that's usually only after some serious slammage. Whenever you've fitted a set of springs (and this applies to ALL types), have the geometry checked ASAP afterwards.

If you've dropped the car by 60 mm or more, chances are your camber angle will need adjusting. This is one reason why you might find the edges of your fat low-profiles wearing faster than you'd like (the other is your tracking being out). The camber angle is the angle the tyre makes with the road, seen from directly in front. You'll no doubt have seen race cars with the front wheels tilted in at the top, out at the bottom - this is extreme negative camber, and it helps to give more grip and stability in extreme cornering (but if your car was set this extreme, you'd kill the front tyres VERY quickly!). Virtually all road cars have a touch of negative camber on the front, and it's important when lowering to keep as near to the factory setting as possible, to preserve the proper tyre contact patch on the road. Trouble is, there's not usually much scope for camber adjustment on standard suspension, which is why (for some cars) you can buy camber-adjustable top plates which fit to the strut tops. Setting the camber accurately is a job for a garage with experience of modified cars - so probably not your local fast-fit centre, then.

FUJI RDPII 1 2

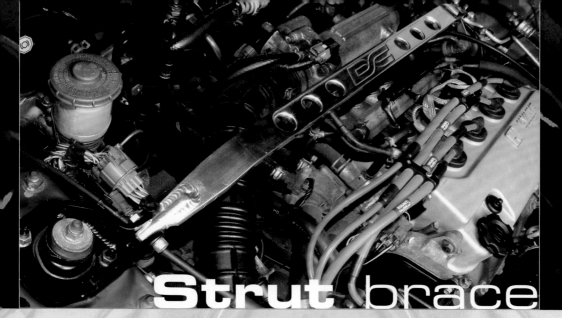

Strut brace

Another item which is inspired by saloon racing, the strut brace is another underbonnet accessory which you shouldn't be without. Some of them might even work...

The idea of the strut brace is that, once you've stiffened up your front suspension to the max, the car's 'flimsy' body shell (to which the front suspension struts are bolted) may not be able to cope with the 'immense' cornering forces being put through it, and will flex, messing up the handling. The strut brace (in theory) does exactly what it says on the tin, by providing support between the strut tops, taking the load off the bodyshell.

Where this falls down slightly (for road use) is that 1) no-one's going to have the car set that stiff, 2) no-one's going to drive that hard, and 3) the Civic shell isn't exactly made out of tin foil (allegedly). The strut brace might have a slight effect, but the real reason to fit one is for SHOW - and why not? They look great in a detailed engine bay, and are available in lots of designs and finishes. You're looking at parting with up to a hundred of your finest English pounds, but your mates will be impressed and the girls will love it - and you can't put a price on that!

The first step with any brace is to put it in its place - by doing this, you can see how much stuff it interferes with, and whether they've sent you the right one! Surprisingly, there's quite a lot in the way on our Civic, so we'll deal with one side at a time. On the driver's side, unclip the throttle cable . . .

01

. . . then unbolt this wiring plug bracket, and move it out of the way (don't disconnect any plugs or stretch any of the wires).

02

The car must be sitting on its wheels for this bit, or your front suspension will fall out. Undo the two strut top mounting nuts (don't touch the middle one) . . .

03

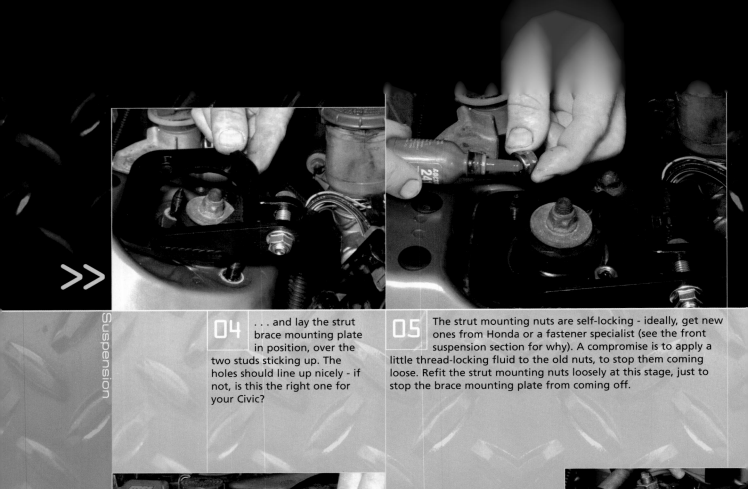

04 . . . and lay the strut brace mounting plate in position, over the two studs sticking up. The holes should line up nicely - if not, is this the right one for your Civic?

05 The strut mounting nuts are self-locking - ideally, get new ones from Honda or a fastener specialist (see the front suspension section for why). A compromise is to apply a little thread-locking fluid to the old nuts, to stop them coming loose. Refit the strut mounting nuts loosely at this stage, just to stop the brace mounting plate from coming off.

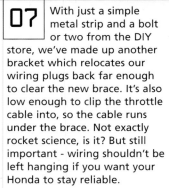

06 Not all strut braces are the same - on this one, the brace itself is separate from the two plates. Fit it to the plate using the through-bolt, and tighten it by hand for the moment. Remember that wiring plug bracket we took off earlier? With the brace temporarily in position, we can see where the bracket will sensibly fit.

07 With just a simple metal strip and a bolt or two from the DIY store, we've made up another bracket which relocates our wiring plugs back far enough to clear the new brace. It's also low enough to clip the throttle cable into, so the cable runs under the brace. Not exactly rocket science, is it? But still important - wiring shouldn't be left hanging if you want your Honda to stay reliable.

08 With one end of the brace sorted, it's time to see what's happening at the other end. If you're lucky enough to have a Civic with air-con, you could be feeling unlucky right now - the air-con pipes are in the way. Care is needed with these pipes - if they get damaged the refrigerant could leak out, and it's highly dangerous. We're going to raise ours up slightly. Release the large pipe from its holding clips, then unbolt the pipe mounting bracket.

09 Having taken off the strut top mounting nuts on this side, the other brace mounting plate can be slipped under the now-loose air-con pipe, onto its studs . . .

10 . . . and the air-con pipe bracket refitted. But hang on - look closely, and you'll see the bracket's had the Haynes workshop treatment too. Using a longer bolt, with two large nuts underneath as spacers, we've raised the pipe up so it sits better over the new brace plate. Make sure your pipes and wiring can't rub through on metal edges, or you'll be sorry.

11 If you're lucky, the brace will now drop straight into the right place - if not, some fine-tuning may be needed, using a spanner on the adjuster nut provided. On some braces the length is adjusted by turning the brace end fitting.

12 Now tighten the brace-to-plate through-bolts . . .

13 . . . and take up any slack in the brace using the adjuster nut again.

14 Lastly, tighten those two strut mounting nuts either side (use new nuts or thread-lock). Remember - they also hold the front struts to the car, so It would be nice if they didn't come loose unexpectedly. Ideally, do them to the correct torque (64 Nm). Time to stand back and admire your handiwork - give the brace a quick polish, so people notice it as soon as you lift the bonnet.

Brakes

Remember the middle pedal?

It's the one next to the throttle - some people don't use it much. Uprating the brakes is actually a very easy bolt-on upgrade, but there are some points to consider.

One of the strangest, given that improving the brakes should in theory also improve your chances of avoiding an accident, is that insurance companies do not like performance brakes. You should still tell them, but be prepared for bad news. To them, it seems that fitting sporty brakes must automatically make you drive like Colin McRae - the clear implication is that if you need better brakes, you've either also uprated the engine (and not told them?), or you simply drive on the limit everywhere. Shame. We just like to know our cars will stop quickly. That, actually, might be another reason why they don't like better brakes - you stop better, but does the old dodderer behind you? Crunch.

Uprating the brakes will be a complete waste of time if you're a cheapskate on tyres. Cheap, no-name tyres (or ones with no tread left) won't always be able to translate extra braking power into actual vehicle-stopping power - they'll give up their grip on the tarmac and skid everywhere. Something like 90% of braking is done by the front wheels - ie the ones you steer with. If you consider that locked-up wheels also don't tend to steer very well, you'll begin to see why top brakes and lame tyres are a well-dodgy mixture.

Groovy discs

Besides the various brands of performance brake pads that go with them, the main brake upgrade is to fit performance front brake discs and pads. Discs are available in two main types - grooved and cross-drilled (and combinations of both).

Grooved discs (which can be had with varying numbers of grooves) serve a dual purpose - the grooves provide a 'channel' to help the heat escape, and they also help to de-glaze the pad surface, cleaning up the pads every time they're used. Some of the discs are made from higher-friction metal than normal discs, too, and the fact that they seriously improve braking performance is well-documented.

Cross-drilled discs offer another route to heat dissipation, but one which can present some problems. Owners report that cross-drilled discs really eat brake pads, more so than the grooved types, but more serious is the fact that some of these discs can crack around the drilled holes, after serious use. The trouble is that the heat 'migrates' to the drilled holes (as was intended), but the heat build-up can be extreme, and the constant heating/cooling cycle can stress the metal to the point where it will crack. Discs which have been damaged in this way are extremely dangerous to drive on, as they could break up completely at any time. Only fit discs of this type from established manufacturers offering a useful guarantee of quality, and check the discs regularly.

Performance discs also have a reputation for warping (nasty vibrations felt through the pedal). Justified, or not? Well, the harder you use your brakes (and we could be talking serious abuse), the greater the heat you'll generate. Okay, so these wicked discs are meant to be able to cope with this heat, but you can't expect miracles. Cheap discs, or ones which have had a hard time over mega-thousands of miles, will warp. So buy quality, and don't get over-heroic on the brakes.

Performance pads can be fitted to any brake discs, including the standard ones, but are of course designed to work best with heat-dissipating discs. Unless your Civic's got an over-boosted Spoon engine under the bonnet, don't be tempted to go much further than 'fast road' pads - anything more competition-orientated may take too long to come up to temperature on the road. Remember what pushbike brakes were like in the wet? Cold competition pads feel the same, and old dears always step off the pavement when your brakes are cold!

Lastly, fitting all the performance brake bits in the world is no use if your calipers have seized up. If, when you strip out your old pads, you find that one pad's worn more than the other, or that both pads have worn more on the left wheel than the right, your caliper pistons are sticking. Sometimes you can free them off by pushing them back into the caliper, but this could be a garage job to fix. If you drive around with sticking calipers, you'll eat pads and discs. You choose.

Brake discs and pads

Have a look in *'Wheels 'n' tyres'* for more info on jacking up.

Loosen the wheel bolts, jack up the corner of the car you're working on, and take off the wheel. Make sure you've got an axle stand under a solid part of the car in case the jack gives out. Have a look in *'Wheels 'n' tyres'* for more info on jacking up. First job is to undo the caliper bolt top and bottom . . .

01

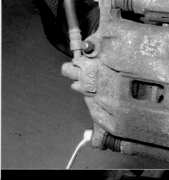

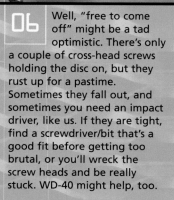

05 With the caliper carrier out of the picture, the disc is free to come off.

06 Well, "free to come off" might be a tad optimistic. There's only a couple of cross-head screws holding the disc on, but they rust up for a pastime. Sometimes they fall out, and sometimes you need an impact driver, like us. If they are tight, find a screwdriver/bit that's a good fit before getting too brutal, or you'll wreck the screw heads and be really stuck. WD-40 might help, too.

07 Sorry, more bad news (possibly). Even if the screws come out, the disc might not just fall off for you. If it's rusted on, first try a few well-aimed blows with a blunt instrument. If that doesn't work, find two bolts which screw into the larger pair of holes in the disc. Tighten them equally and hard, and additional persuasion with that hammer should see the disc come off.

02 . . . then lift off the caliper. You won't be able to remove it completely, as it's still attached by the fluid hose - tie the caliper up with string or wire so the hose isn't stretched (don't let it hang on the hose).

03 If all you're doing's changing the pads, this is the end of the road. Take 'em out, slap in the new ones, put it back together. But we know you're more dedicated than that.

04 To get the disc off, the caliper carrier bracket comes off next. There's two bolts to remove, and they will be tight (they'd better be tight, anyway). Seen from inside, it's pretty obvious which two big bolts we're on about.

08 Alright, so your disc just fell off. What do you want? A medal? If your discs had to be beaten off, they're only fit for scrap (no point in keeping them to re-convert the car later).

09 Any rust on the hub now has to go, along with any other crud. If the wheel hub isn't totally pristine, the new disc won't sit on quite straight, and will eat its way through the new pads in no time. All for the sake of a few minutes with a wire brush.

10 If you want to spare yourself the misery of stuck-on discs in future, a little copper grease on the wheel hub will be a big help.

>>

>>

11 Like the hubs, the new discs must be clean before fitting - give 'em a wipe over with meths, or a squirt of brake cleaner. Your new discs probably are not identical, and should only be fitted with the grooves facing a certain way (this is the left front). Check your paperwork - our new multi-grooved discs were supplied by Red Dot Racing Ltd, with matching pads. Cheers, chaps!

12 Tighten the disc screws securely (use new screws if the old ones were caned during removal). Painting your calipers? Now would be an excellent time. Well, that's what we thought - so don't adjust your set, those brake bits really have gone luminous green. Refit the caliper carrier bracket, and tighten the bolts to 109 Nm - that's very, very tight if you don't have a torque wrench.

13 To make room for your new pads, the caliper piston must be pushed back into the caliper. If the piston's partly seized, effort will be needed. You can lever it back in with a screwdriver and block of wood, or squeeze it back using water pump pliers (or even this, a cheap ratchet clamping tool from a local DIY store). Watch the brake fluid level in the underbonnet reservoir - it mustn't overflow.

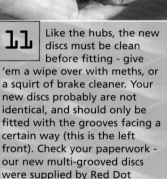

14 Smearing a bit of copper grease on the pad backplates shows you're serious about not having annoying squealing brakes (but don't overdo it). Carefully apply a bit more grease to the edges of the pad backplates. If any grease gets on the disc, get it all off with meths and a rag.

15 Slip the new pads into position on the caliper carrier (greased backplates facing away from the disc, obviously), then hook over the caliper. If it won't go on, you haven't pushed the piston back in enough (Step 13).

16 Fit the caliper upper and lower mounting bolts (wiggle the caliper to get them in) and tighten them to 33 Nm. Give the brake pedal several good shoves to bring the new pads up to the new disc, and you're ready for a road test. When you've done both sides, that is. Your calipers may be slightly different to this - if so, refer to the Haynes manual for details.

 Remember!
New pads of any sort need careful bedding-in (over 100 miles of normal use) before they'll work properly - when first fitted, the pad surface won't have worn exactly to the contours of the disc, so it won't actually be touching it, over its full area. This will possibly result in very under-whelming brakes for the first few trips, so watch it - misplaced over-confidence in new brakes is a fast track to hospital…

Cool
coloured
stoppers

One 'downside' to fitted massive multi-spoked alloys is that - gasp - people can see your brakes! So don't be shy about it - paint some of the brake bits so they look the biz, to match (or clash completely) with your chosen colour scheme. Red is the colour inspired by the racing/touring-car boys, but isn't the only choice.

Many Civics don't have rear discs, but painting the brake drums is acceptable under the circumstances - but then, do you paint 'em black, to de-emphasise them, or in your chosen colour for the fronts? It's all tough decisions, in modifying. If you're really sad, you can always buy fake rear discs... For the less-sad among you, Honda performance specialists may be able to sell you a rear disc brake conversion kit - pricey, but maybe necessary if there's a B16A engine going in soon. A rear disc conversion's going a bit far, just to have red calipers front and rear - and remember, the rear brakes don't do much actual stopping...

Painting the calipers requires that they're clean - really clean. Accessory stores sell aerosol brake cleaner, which (apart from having a distinctive high-octane perfume) is just great for removing brake dust, and lots more besides! Some kits come complete with cleaner spray. Many of the kits advertise themselves on the strength of no dismantling being required, but we don't agree. Also, having always successfully brush-painted our calipers, we wouldn't advise using any kind of spray paint.

We know you won't want to hear this, but the best way to paint the calipers is to do some dismantling first. The kits say you don't have to, but trust me - you'll get a much better result from a few minutes' extra work. The best time to paint would be while you're fitting new discs, but nobody thinks that far ahead.

Painting calipers

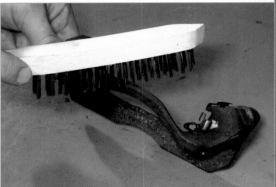

01 Strip the front brakes down as for fitting new discs, but leave the disc in place. Getting stuff clean is the name of the game, and you'll do a way better job with it all apart. This is the caliper carrier bracket getting the wire-brush treatment . . .

02 . . . and by the time we're done, it's so shiny, it's almost a shame to paint it. This is one bit you can bolt back on. Very tight (109 Nm).

03 The caliper itself also needs a thorough scrub with the wire brush (breathing-in the black dust not advisable) . . .

Achtung!
Brake dust from old pads or shoes may contain asbestos. Wear a mask to avoid inhaling it.

04 . . . followed by a good squirt of the brake cleaner supplied in most kits. Don't just spray it and leave it - get wiping as soon as possible. Spraying alone will only loosen the muck. If you don't get it spotless, you'll get black streaks in the paint later, which looks really cack.

05 We found the best way to paint was to refit the caliper by its top bolt, and swing it up, supporting it with a piece of wire. So as not to get our new disc covered in green paint, some masking tape was applied.

06 Most caliper paint comes in two tins, which you mix together - if yours is like this, remember it goes off fast. You really should have all four brakes scrubbed and ready to paint before mixing (do all four brakes in the same morning/afternoon).

07 Stick some card or paper under the brake, 'cos this paint's a bugger to get off your driveway. Remember that you only have to paint the bits you'll see when the wheels are on. It's best to do more than one coat, and don't bother with the brushes they give you - a good brush gives a better result. Wait 'til the paint's totally dry (like overnight, or longer) before reassembling.

Tricks 'n' tips
If you have trouble reassembling your brakes after painting, you probably got carried away and put on too much paint. We found that, once it was fully dry, the excess paint could be trimmed off with a knife.

Painting drums

At least there's no dismantling with drums - get the rear end jacked up, wheels off (see *'Wheels 'n' tyres'* if you need jacking info) and just get stuck in with the wire brush, sandpaper (to smooth the surface), then it's spray on the brake cleaner and wipe thoroughly. Wiping is important - don't rely on the spray alone, as you won't get the surfaces clean. **01**

You definitely don't want any paint on the wheel studs, nor where the wheels will touch the drum. Masking-up shouldn't be necessary if your hand is steady. Painting the drums is much easier than the fiddly calipers, but use a better-quality brush than the one they give you, for a smooth paint finish. Let off the handbrake and turn the drum half a turn every so often until the paint's dry. Nobody likes the runs, after all. **02**

Interiors

The Civic dash is best described as functional. It does the job, and that's about it. It might have no style whatsoever, but at least it doesn't feel like it's about to fall apart, or come off in your hands, unlike certain popular French superminis we could mention. Yes, the Civic interior (with the exception of some really awfully-nice seat fabrics - not) is pretty damn dull. But you need suffer no longer, because the interior really is one area where most of the goodies are pretty easy to fit, and provided you go for one particular 'theme' (rather than a mixture), the end result can certainly help you forget you're in a poverty model, if indeed you are…

when you compare them with the sort of look that can easily be achieved with the huge range of product that's out there. As with the exterior styling, though, remember that fashions can change very quickly - so don't be afraid to experiment with a look you really like, because chances are, it'll be the next big thing anyway. Just don't do wood, ok? We've a feeling it's never coming in, never mind coming back…

Removing stuff

Take it easy and break less

Many of the procedures we're going to show involve removing interior trim panels (either for colouring or to fit other stuff), and this can be tricky. It's far too easy to break plastic trim, especially once it's had a chance to go a bit brittle with age. Another 'problem' with the Civic is that the interior trim is pretty well-attached (and the designers have been very clever at hiding several vital screws), meaning that it can be a pig to get off. We'll try and avoid the immortal words 'simply unclip the panel', and instead show you how

properly, but inevitably at some stage, a piece of trim won't 'simply' anything.

The important lesson here is not to lose your temper, as this has a highly-destructive effect on plastic components, and may result in a panel which no amount of carbon film or colour spray can put right, or make fit again. Superglue may help, but not every time. So - take it steady, prise carefully, and think logically about how and where a plastic panel would have to be attached, to stay on. You'll encounter all sorts of trim clips (some more fragile than others) in your travels - when these break, as they usually do, many of them can be bought in packs from accessory shops, and rarer ones will be available from a Honda dealer, probably off the shelf. Even fully-trained Honda mechanics aren't immune to breaking a few trim clips!

Door trim panel

You'll find plenty of excuses for removing your door trim panels - fitting speakers, re-trimming the panel, de-locking, even window tinting, so we'd better tell you how ...

01 Removing the door card is really easy, and takes just a few minutes. Begin by lowering the door window, then remove the door trim panel screw as shown . . .

02 . . . then remove the hidden screw inside the door pull.

03 Gently prise the door pull out of its recess and disconnect the wiring plug. If you have one, this will be for the electric windows. If you don't, do not despair - we'll help you off with those window winders shortly.

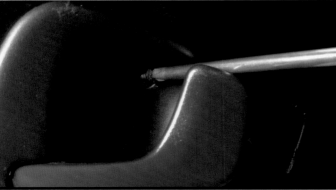

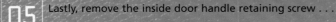

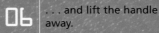

05 Lastly, remove the inside door handle retaining screw . . .

06 . . . and lift the handle away.

07 Push the door card up to disengage the retaining clips, and lift it away.

Wind-up windows? No worries

For those of you without the benefit of electric motors for your window winding operations, here's how to take off those luvverly plastic handles. The little beggars are held on by a spring clip, which has two small 'legs' sticking out at the bottom. Work the edge of a piece of (clean) cloth/rag into the gap between the handle and the plastic disc, from underneath. Using a 'sawing' action, work the cloth side to side - this catches on the legs, and releases the clip. Takes a while, but it does work - just watch where the spring clip goes!

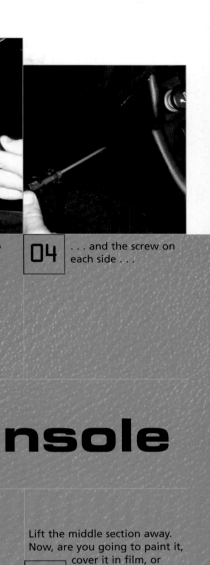

01 Remove the ashtray by lifting it from its housing. The rear of the handbrake console is held in place by two plastic retaining lugs. Prise away the trim panel directly below the handbrake handle to gain access to the two hidden retaining screws.

02 With the screws removed, gently lift and pull the console back towards the rear of the car, then lift it over the handbrake lever. If your console has any switches in, reach under the console and pull off the wiring plugs.

03 Next, remove the two front console upper retaining screws . . .

04 . . . and the screw on each side . . .

Centre **console**

05 . . . before lifting the front part out.

06 Finally remove the remaining two retaining screws (one either side) on the middle section of the console.

07 Unscrew the shift knob and remove it.

08 Lift the middle section away. Now, are you going to paint it, cover it in film, or what? Don't put it back standard, please.

Anything but black?

The interior trim on the Civic at least hides its age well, and doesn't rattle much. And that's about it - for a lover of elephant-hide grey, it's heaven. For normal people, it's something else. Fortunately, there's plenty you can do to personalise it, and there are three main routes to take:

1) Spray paint - available in any colour you like, as long as it's… not black. This Folia Tec stuff actually dyes softer plastics and leather, and comes in a multi-stage treatment, to suit all plastic types. Don't try to save money just buying the top coat, because it won't work! Special harder-wearing spray is required for use on steering wheels. Ordinary spray paint for bodywork might damage some plastics, and won't be elastic - good primer is essential. Make sure you also buy lots of masking tape.

2) Adhesive or shrink-fit film - available in various wild colours, carbon, ally, and, er… walnut (would YOU?). Probably best used on flatter surfaces, or at least those without complex curves, or you'll have to cut and join - spray is arguably better here. Some companies will sell you sheets of genuine carbon-fibre, with peel-off backing - looks and feels the part (nice if you have touchy-feely passengers).

3) Replacement panels - the easiest option, as the panels are supplied pre-cut, ready to fit. Of course, you're limited then to styling just the panels supplied.

If you fancy something more posh, how about trimming your interior bits in leather? Very saucy. Available in various colours, and hardly any dearer than film, you also get that slight 'ruffled' effect on tighter curves.

Get the cans out

Any painting process is a *multi-stage* application. With the Folia Tec system (thanks to Eurostyling for supplying ours), many of you apparently think you can get away just buying the top coat, which then looks like a cheap option compared to film - WRONG! Even the proper interior spray top coat won't stay on for long without the matching primer, and the finish won't be wear-resistant without the finishing sealer spray. You don't need the special foaming cleaner - you could get by with a general-purpose degreaser, such as meths. Just watch the grey/black plastic doesn't suddenly turn white - if it does, you're damaging the finish! This might not be too important to you, as it's being sprayed over anyway, but if you take out the grey too far on a part that's not being sprayed all over, you'll have to live with a cacky-looking white-grey finish to any non-painted surface...

Providing you're a dab hand with the masking tape, paint gives you the flexibility to be more creative. For instance, you could try colour-matching the exterior of the car - but will ordinary car body paint work on interior plastics? Course it will, as long as you prep the panels properly.

Choice of paint's one thing, but what to paint? Well, not everything - for instance, you might want to avoid high-wear areas like door handles. Just makes for an easier life. The glovebox lid and instrument panel surround are obvious first choices, as are the ashtray and fusebox lid. The centre console's not lighting anyone's fire in standard Honda grey, so hit it with some spray too. Any panels which just pop out are targets, in fact (lots less masking needed) - just make sure whatever you're dismantling was meant to come apart, or it'll be out with the superglue instead of the cans.

Don't be afraid to experiment with a combination of styles - as long as you're confident you can blend it all together, anything goes! Mix the painted bits with some tasteful carbon-fibre sheet or brushed-aluminium film, if you like - neutral colours like this, or chrome, can be used to give a lift to dash bits which are too tricky to spray.

Painting **trim**

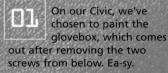

01 On our Civic, we've chosen to paint the glovebox, which comes out after removing the two screws from below. Ea-sy.

02 Place the glovebox on clean, flat surface, and attack with sandpaper. Our aim is to remove the nasty injection-moulded design that looks like elephant hide! In order to save total disintegration of your hands, wear gloves!

03 When you're satisfied that enough of the design has been removed by sandpaper (remember that you carry on the smoothing process by priming the area, rubbing the primer back and repeating the process), clean the area with a suitable degreaser. Try 'panel-wipe' from a bodyshop.

04 Plaster the surrounding area with newspaper (to avoid parental unrest), then add your first layer of plastic primer and leave to dry as per instructions on the can.

05 Rub the primer back with fine grain sandpaper. Do not rub the primer off; we're aiming partly to fill any gaps left from the elephant hide by building up layers of primer.

06 Repeat this process of building up the primer until the glovebox is totally smooth. Ours took three layers until we were happy that all elephant hide had been eliminated. It's time to paint. We've chosen to paint our box that same colour as the car, but the possibilities are endless. One coat of paint should be enough – but use two coats if you feel it needs it. End by adding a nice layer of lacquer to make it really shiny!

Dynamic dashes

A far easier route to the brushed-ally or carbon look, pre-finished ('here's some we did earlier') panels are available from suppliers. Dash kits are available for the Mk 1 Civic from companies like Dash Dynamics, and offer a simpler way of livening-up the dull Civic dash. Did we say simple? It's sometimes not too obvious where the various kit bits are supposed to go! A trial fitting isn't a bad idea, before peeling off the backing. Make sure your chosen trim piece is lined up nice and square, and keep it square as you press it on - the adhesive's usefully-sticky, meaning it will stay stuck whether you get it right or wrong. Still, it's easier by far than trying to mask up and spray the edges of the vents, which is what you'd have to do otherwise.

Filming your Civic

If you fancy creating a look that's a bit more special than plain paint colours, film is the answer - but be warned - it's not the easiest stuff in the world to use, and so isn't everyone's favourite. If you must have the brushed-aluminium look, or fancy giving your Civic the carbon-fibre treatment, there really is no alternative (apart from the lazy-man option of new panels, of course).

01 Cut the film roughly to size, remembering to leave plenty of excess for trimming - it's also a good idea to have plenty to fold around the edges, because thin film has a nasty habit of peeling off, otherwise.

02 Next, we gently warmed up both the panel, and the film itself. Just following the instructions provided, and who are we to argue?

03 Peel off the backing, being careful that the film stays as flat as possible. Also take care, when you pick the film up, that it doesn't stick to itself (our stuff seemed very keen to do this!).

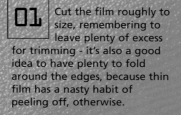

Stick the film on straight - very important with any patterned finish. Start at one edge or corner, and work across, to keep the air bubbles and creases to a minimum. If you get a really bad crease, it's best to unpeel a bit and try again - **04** the adhesive's very tacky, and there's no slide-age available.

Work out the worst of the air bubbles with a soft cloth - get the stuff to stick as best you can before trimming, or it'll all go horribly wrong. To be sure it's stuck (especially important on a grained surface), go over it firmly with the edge of your **05** least-important piece of 'plastic' - ie not a credit card.

Once the film's laid on, it's time for trimming - which (you guessed it) is the tricky bit. We found it's much easier to trim the tricky bits once the film's been warmed up using a hairdryer or heat gun, but don't overdo it! Make sure you've also got a VERY sharp knife - a blunt one will ripple the film, and may tear it (one **06** good thing about film is that blood wipes off it easily!).

To get the film to wrap neatly round a curved edge, make several slits almost up to the edge, then wrap each sliver of film around, and stick on firmly. If the film's heated as you do this, it wraps round and keeps its shape - meaning it **07** shouldn't try and spring back, ruining all your hard work.

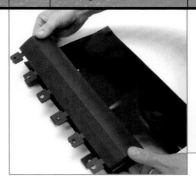

Bum notes

There are limitations to using film, and the quality of the film itself has a lot to do with that. We had major problems doing any kind of job with one particular make of brushed-aluminium-look film - it was a nightmare to work with, and the edges had peeled the next day. Buying quality film will give you a long-lasting result to be proud of, with much less skill requirement and LOTS less swearing. But it still pays not to be too ambitious with it.

Gear knob jobs

Gear knobs and gaiters are a fairly inexpensive way of modifying the interior look of your car. You spend a lot of time in contact with that knob, so why not treat it to a new look?

01 Firstly remove the centre console (refer to section on removing stuff). When you have the console apart, select the middle section (part that holds the gear gaiter), flip it over and remove the four screws that hold the gaiter in place . . .

02 . . . then unclip the gaiter from the surround.

03 To fit our very saucy Richbrook gear gaiter, we drilled a number of holes into the surround . . .

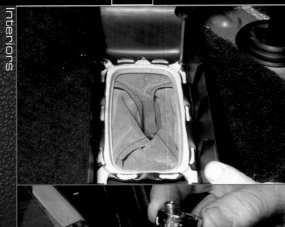

07 Begin by adding the threaded ring to the gear lever . . .

08 . . . then add the correct size rubber cap, for a firm fit over the gear lever.

09 Insert the grub screws into the threaded holes in the neck of the knob.

04 . . . and used the trusty self-tapping screws to fasten the gaiter in place.

05 Pop the gaiter back into in the console . . .

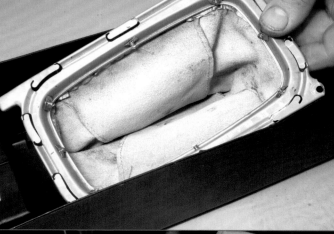

. . . and refit the console. At this point, we're fitting a new gear knob - kinda seems wrong not to fit a spankingly gorgeous new knob to match the gaiter. If you're new-knob-less, go ahead and screw the old one in place.

06 . . . and refit the console. At this point, we're fitting a new gear knob - kinda seems wrong not to fit a spankingly gorgeous new knob to match the gaiter. If you're new-knob-less, go ahead and screw the old one in place.

10 Pop the knob back onto the lever, push down firmly and tighten the three screws uniformly to ensure the knob sits centrally on the lever. They'd better be tight, the amount of stick the new knob will get.

11 Screw the threaded ring up underneath the knob . . .

12 . . . and the job's a good 'un. Isn't she a beauty? Slide your gaiter fully up under the knob, and either secure it with its Velcro collar, or tie its laces for it (best to have any join at the front of the gaiter, where you won't see it).

A Civic that really shifts

Fractions of a second count on the strip, and off the lights. Even if you're not a racer (we don't believe you), you might just like the feel of a quick-shifting Civic with a short-throw change. Not saying there's anything wrong about the standard gear linkage, but it's just, you know, standard.

This short shift kit by B&M is easy to fit and gives fantastic results. It's advisable to let the car cool for at least 1 to 2 hours before you begin fitting the kit, since a lot of the time will be spent under the car near the exhaust system. Remove the centre console (as described in 'removing stuff'). Then get the car (safely) about two feet in the air - see 'wheels 'n' tyres' for jacking information.

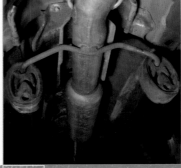

01 Unhook the rubber exhaust mountings and carefully lower the exhaust pipe - check first that it really has cooled down.

02 It's helpful to wedge a piece of wood between the exhaust pipe and floorpan to increase access to the two bolts we'll be removing next.

03 The pivot bolt that holds the gear lever to linkage rod is the first to be removed . . .

04 . . . lower the linkage rod and allow to it to hang out of the way.

05 Now remove the two gear linkage mounting bolts right at the back. The fixed/stabiliser rod will then drop down slightly.

06 To the bottom of the gearbox now, to remove the bolt holding the fixed/stabiliser rod in place. The linkage rod remains in place, hanging to one side.

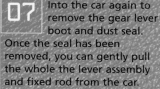

07 Into the car again to remove the gear lever boot and dust seal. Once the seal has been removed, you can gently pull the whole the lever assembly and fixed rod from the car.

08 Place the assembly on a clean flat surface, and begin by removing the two gear lever mounting plate bolts.

09 Next, slide the mounting plate away, and remove the lever by sliding out of the end of the assembly. At the bottom of the lever, slide out the bush and remove the four rubber O-rings fitted to it - we'll be fitting some new O-rings later on.

10 Remove the rubber gaiter by sliding it off the lever. Take out the plastic bush from inside the gaiter, and give it a good clean. You can now fit the plastic bush to the new lever.

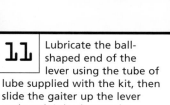

11 Lubricate the ball-shaped end of the lever using the tube of lube supplied with the kit, then slide the gaiter up the lever and work it back over the plastic bush.

12 Refit the original mounting plate up under the gaiter/bush, then slide the lever back through the assembly and into place. Someone's been cleaning this lot, haven't they?

13 Select the correct-size new O-rings from those supplied with the kit, and fit a set to the bush. Apply a little more lube to the newly-ringed-up bush, and slide it back into place on the new lever.

14 Return the assembly to the car, and refit it, the exact same way it all came out (shouldn't be a challenge). Inside, you end up with something like this. Well, it'll look a lot better with a centre console, gear gaiter and gear knob, obviousl

Handbrake
knobs & gaiters

01 Now you've done it - fitting a sexy new gear knob and gaiter's only made the sad black handbrake stick look even worse. Get it sorted. If you haven't already, remove the rear section of the centre console (see 'removing stuff'). First, some violence - chop the old knob off with a hacksaw.

02 With the knob chopped, now you can also slide off the nasty plastic 'gaiter' below the knob.

03 Richbrook again for the handbrake gaiter - and why not? Slip it on . . .

04 . . . and secure it round the base with a few self-tappers, keeping it away from the handbrake cables.

Last job is the knob itself, and it's the easiest part. Slip it over the handle, and tighten the grub screws round the base. Make sure it's capable of releasing the handbrake knob before going any further - not all manufacturers seem to have considered whether these things are meant to just look cool, or work as well.

Now the console rear section can be slipped back over, which unfortunately hides most of your hard work. Never mind - and you can always paint that console.

05

06

07 Fold the gaiter round the base of the knob to hide those screws, and we're there. Now imagine the look with something other than a grey plastic console...

The personal touch – re-trimming

Okay, so you're definitely not happy with how the inside of your Civic looks, but you're not sold on any of the off-the-shelf options for tricking it up, either. You know how you want it to look, though, so get creative!

There are any number of upholstery companies in Yellow Pages, who will be able to create ANY look you want (we got one in our own back yard, almost - Pipers of Sparkford, Somerset, and very helpful lads they are, too). If your idea of Civic heaven is an interior swathed in black and purple leather, these guys can help. Don't assume that you'll have to go to Carisma, to get a car interior re-trimmed - they might well be the daddies at this, but any upholsterer worth the name should be able to help, even if they normally only do sofas!

Of course, if you're even slightly handy with things like glue and scissors, you might be inspired to get brave and DIY. An upholsterers will still be a useful source for materials (and maybe advice too?).

Seats

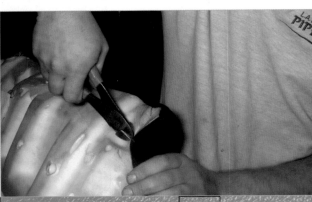

This is really one for a pro upholstery outfit - it involves pulling your seats to bits.

For what it's worth, if you're determined to try trimming your seats on your own, our advice is to practice on a seat from the scrapyard first, 'til you've got the hang of it! Good luck, and we salute you! Let's see how the professionals do it.

01 If you can't stand seeing a lovely Granny-grey Honda seat ripped apart, look away now. This, by the way, is the rear seat cushion, but it'll tell you most of what you need to know for any seat. First, the cover's clipped to the foam base around the edges, using a number of 'hog-rings' (a bit like large circular staples), which the pros release using special pliers.

02 So does the old cover get binned, once it's removed? Not a bit. We know it fits perfectly, so it gets 'dismantled' and used as a template for the new material. If anyone else were doing this, it would probably be vandalism - but not if it's the skilled hands of the professionals. Any seat cover worth having is made up of sections, stitched together. Each section now has to be carefully unpicked . . .

03 . . . and laid out for marking-up. Notice how adjoining sections have been marked across each other, in case our man should forget how it's supposed to fit together (no chance).

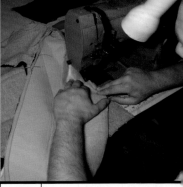

04 At last we get a glimpse of some new tweed. Tweed? Yes, really - several different shades of. It's an American thing. Here, our man's marking out the piece for one of the rear seat side panels.

05 Once the section's been marked up, it's out with the scissors. And here's another little trick to spot - he's not cutting these pieces right to the lines he's marked. Is he cutting it out roughly, to trim to the lines later? No. Leaving half-an-inch or so outside the required size gives you enough material to stitch to - of course.

06 Here's some we cut out earlier - but what's that stuff they've been laid on top of? Is it - foam? Virtually every section of this seat cover's going to end up being foam-backed. Why? To make the seat more comfy? Well, it does do that, but the real reason is to improve the visual effect. Any material looks too flat and lifeless without the foam backing, and it 'puffs up' the stitched sections.

07 So now it's over to the sewing machine (well, you didn't think all that stitching was fake, did you?) to join the trimmed panels to a matching piece of foam. When each section's complete, they each get stitched together to form a complete seat cover, which then gets clipped back over the original seat foam. As easy as that (well, not really, but it is to a pro).

Door card
trimming

We decided we'd like the removable centre section of our door cards re-trimmed to match our interior theme, so we gave the job to our local upholstery experts. It's always easiest to choose a section which can be removed - in this **01** case, the first stage is trimming off the blobs of glue . . .

02 . . . then remove a few screws, and out comes the piece we want.

03 The most satisfying bit of all? Ripping off the old grey stuff. Won't be wanting that again.

04 Lay the now-naked section of door card onto your new fabric, and trim it up, leaving plenty for folding over.

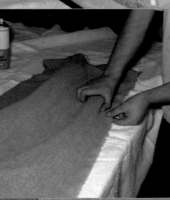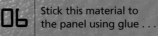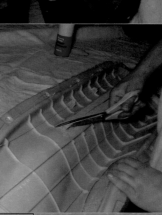

05 Things are about to get slightly sticky at this point. A decent layer of spray glue is all we need to secure the fabric. By the way, just in case you thought we're re-trimming in grey, we're not - it's actually oatmeal-coloured tweed. Which might not be your thing, but it's very US of A custom-car-type stuff, so no laughing.

06 Stick this material to the panel using glue . . .

07 . . . then trim up the tricky bits - notice how our man Royston is trimming across the corner, to make a neat fold later.

08 Screw-and-glue the freshly-trimmed section back in place, and admire the results. Colour choice is of course up to you - how cool would it've looked if we'd gone for red alcantara, for instance? Then you could always paint or re-trim the still-black part of the door card. Have we given you something to think about?

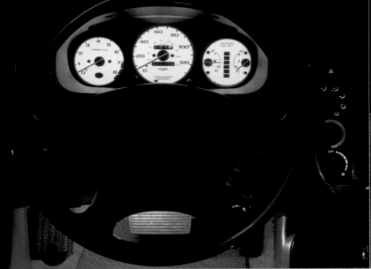

Under neon **light**

So how much of a poser are you? How'd you like to show off all this shiny chequer floor and sexy pedals to full effect, in the midnight hour? You need some neons, baby! Yeah!

01 There's not a great deal to this, really - decide where you want 'em, where you're going to get a live and an earth (and a switch, if necessary), then fit 'em. We wanted our neons up under the dash, to light up the footwells. The first thing to do is offer one in place - remember, it would be sort-of useful if your feet don't hit them as you work the pedals...

02 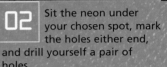 Sit the neon under your chosen spot, mark the holes either end, and drill yourself a pair of holes.

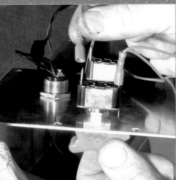

03 To make extra-sure your neons don't fall off, try sticking them in place with double-sided tape. But use some self-tappers as well, or small nuts and bolts, like us. Okay, so neons don't exactly weigh lots, but take some pride in the job - how careful are your front-seat passengers?.

04 That's the 'mechanical' side of fitting dealt with - how about the electrical stuff? Join the two black wires together, using a ring terminal, and fit the ring terminal to a good earth point. This can be one you make by drilling a hole in the car's metal body, and fitting a self-tapping screw, or look in the section on fitting the starter button for another earth-point solution.

05 Join the neon red wires together into a spade terminal, and run it to one side of your new switch. Mount the switch somewhere you can get at it quickly (remember what we say about the legal issues here).

06 Now we need a live feed, to the other side of the switch. This means poking about with a test light and your Haynes wiring diagrams for an existing wire to splice into, running one into the car from the battery, or making an auxiliary fusebox of your own (refer to the security section).

Bum notes

It appears that interior neons have recently been declared ILLEGAL, and this means, in the first place, you're unlikely to find anywhere that even sells them any more. Exterior neons have been illegal from day one. If you fit interior neons, make sure they're at least easily switched off, should you get pulled. Remember that driving at night with a brightly-lit interior makes it even harder to see out. Neons are best used for show purposes.

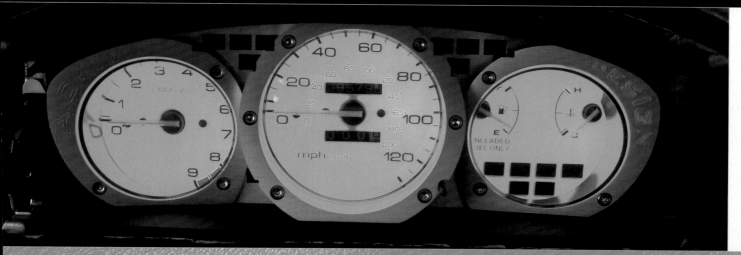

Are your dials all white?

White dial kits aren't that difficult to fit, but you will need some skill and patience not to damage the delicate bits inside your instrument panel - the risk is definitely worth it, to liven up that dreary grey Civic dash, anyway.

Just make sure you get the right kit for your car, and don't start stripping anything until you're SURE it's the right one - look carefully. Most dial kit makers, for instance, want to know exactly what markings you have on your speedo and rev counter. If they don't ask, be worried - the kit they send could well be wrong for your car, and might not even fit. If you're ordering a kit from the US, remember they get slightly different-spec Civics to us - don't order without checking your clock layout with their website pics.

We're going one better than just white dials - we've chosen some electro-luminescent jobs from the US. Here you get the best of both worlds - white dials by day, glowing blue dials by night. Will the trick finished effect mean more work? Let's see.

01 Unpack the illuminated gauges and read the instructions - it's always a good idea to familiarise yourself with a product before you fit it. If you're a little nervous about any part of this procedure, make sure you have someone nearby that knows a bit about wiring, dash removal and fitting illuminated gauges!

02 First job is to remove the large trim panel that the clocks sit behind. Start by prising out the hazard lights switch – be careful not to pull the switch out too far, as there's a wiring plug that needs to be unplugged. But you knew that already.

03 When the switch has been removed, you'll see a cross-head screw to the right of the recess - remove it.

04 Remove the two upper retaining screws . . .

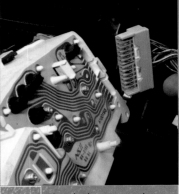

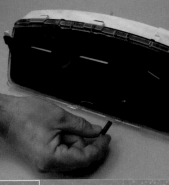

05 . . . and ease the panel out slightly. This will give you access to remove the wiring plug to the clock on the dash. After this has been unplugged, lift the panel away and store in a safe place. Like - not on the floor.

06 Remove the two retaining screws at either end of the instrument podule. Sorry, bit of a technical term there.

07 The clocks are nearly free to come out. Ease the unit out, and turn over to reveal two large wiring plugs that need to be disconnected before lifting the unit away.

08 Move the unit to a clean area, and start by removing the trip meter reset pin.

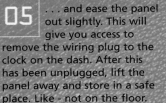

Next job is to route the wires. Turn the clocks over, and you'll see a piece of tape - remove it to reveal a perfect-sized hole for our requirements. Route the wires along the edge of the dials and down through this hole. Ensure that the path the wires follow means they won't be crushed once the lens cover has been replaced. Use your trusty small screwdriver to route the wires **13** between the new dial faces and the edge of the unit.

Replace the original lens cover. Or better still, look at our new very sexy lens covers from ADI **14** (see the lens cover section for more on those).

As our new dials are of the illuminated variety, we can lose the existing illuminating bulbs. Turn the clocks over and **15** remove the five brown bulbholders - they just twist 'n'go.

The little black box supplied with the kit has two wires (red and white), and a separate brightness switch. The red wire we splice into a sidelight live feed. Under the dash in the main fuse box area, we found a whole unused multi-plug with wires that are live when the sidelights are on - bonus. You might not be this lucky, but a squint at a Haynes manual **16** wiring diagram should find you a suitable light feed.

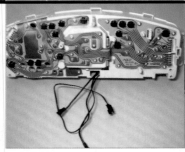

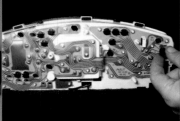

09 Using a screwdriver, prise the lens cover from the unit by unclipping the six retaining lugs.

10 Remove the two retaining screws on the tacho and speedometer dials (the fuel and temperature gauges don't have any). Don't lose the screws - a small bowl to keep them in's a good thing to have right now.

11 Carefully slide the new dial over the top of the existing dials (on some types of dial kit, the original dials need to be removed, if you're not sure, check your instructions). Hook the needle through the hole in the centre of the dial, and over the little plastic needle stop.

12 Refit the original dial retaining screws to hold the new dials. To get access to the screw by the needle stop, very gently wind the needle a little way round the dial using your finger.

17 Our white wire goes to a suitable earth. We extended this wire with a piece of our own brown wire and located an earth point in the main fusebox area. Any bolt attached to the car's metal body should do for an earth point.

18 Turn the black box over to see two strips of double-sided tape – remove the tape and stick the box in suitable place behind the instruments (choose a place that won't interfere with refitting the instruments, of course).

19 Locate a blank switch to stick the brightness button onto. Route the wire to the switch from behind so that the least possible wire is seen. Peel back the sticky tape on the button, and stick it on. This is one strange button, but it looks kinda slinky, and it works a treat.

20 Connect the wires from the new dials to the black box. You might find there's an extra black wire from the black box – you can probably ignore this (it's for cars with more than three dials). Refit the clocks and turn out the lights for a spot of glow-in-the-dark action.

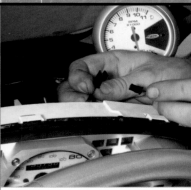

Designer frames

If you've got to wear specs, you wouldn't choose National Health frames - and your Civic feels the same way. Its instrument lens cover's just about the least exciting design you'll ever see, but thanks to the Civic's popularity in the land of Uncle Sam, we now have a choice in designer dash-ware. Bring on the new clock surrounds from ADI - some of the best we've ever seen. They're really easy to fit, easily obtainable, and look mighty fine - a must for your Civic.

01 Unpack the dials and read the back of the box. Although the instructions are a bit difficult to follow, keep the box handy as it contains very important information on the variety of lengths of Allen head screws supplied with the surrounds.

02 Rather than bore you again with the long-winded process of removing the clocks, turn to the white dials section and follow steps 2 to 9. Now we have our lens cover off, we're ready to roll. First job is to remove the clear plastic cover – prise off with trusty flat head screwdriver. Expect the plastic to crack – if it doesn't, lucky you.

03 Turn the cover over, and remove the three plastic rings in the same way.

04 Over it goes again, to put the new sexy brushed aluminium base into place.

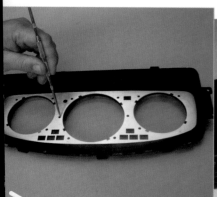

05 Using a pen/scribe, mark the twelve (count 'em) holes through the aluminium base, ready for drilling . . .

06 . . . then get brave, and drill some holes. Two possible options here - either remove the aluminium base before drilling, or leave the base in place. We chose to remove the base for fear of mincing the metal as we drilled, but it's your call. Don't forget the wood underneath.

07 Starting with the middle clock, lay the plastic lens cover in place.

08 Place the alloy surround over the lens cover, and after consulting the back of the box, select the correct-length Allen-head screw.

09 Turn unit over and add the nut. Tighten up using an Allen key and baby spanner.

10 Repeat processes for next two surrounds, then give the whole thing a good clean. Don't want grubby fingermarks ruining the effect, do we?

11 Re-attach the cover to the instrument pack, not forgetting to refit the trip-cancelling pin. Refit the clocks, and the job's a winner. Don't they look sweet? Dude?

Rev counter

Those of you who already have a rev counter (or tacho), ignore this bit. Or perhaps not - you might want a tidy little tacho mounted somewhere more helpful than in the instrument podule.

If so, we're here to help. Having one separate gauge mounted on the A-pillar, centre of the dash or centre console adds hugely to the racing look - so how smart would three look? If you don't want to give yourself a hard time, choose extra gauges which are easy to wire in - rev counter, voltmeter, water temperature, that kind of thing. Oil pressure and temperature gauges need dedicated sender units fitted, which makes things trickier (though not impossible). Then again, if you're just going for the look, who cares if they actually work or not?

Before fitting any new gauges, the engine should be cool and the ignition off (take out the key). Then disconnect the negative terminal at the battery. We're going to be installing this very trick rev counter available from MSI Online. The best thing about this particular tacho is that it lights up in six different colours – how cool is that?

01 The first job is to decide where you'd like it, and there's all sorts of positions for you to try (are we still talking about a tacho?). We've gone for the popular A-pillar choice for maximum race looks. Mark the pillar where you want to mount it.

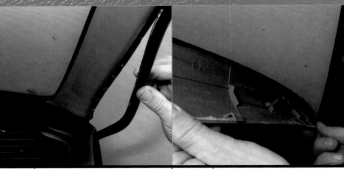

02 Remove the A-pillar trim panel by firstly pulling back the rubber door seal . . .

03 . . . then unclip it from the plastic lugs and lift away from the car.

04 Drill the bracket mounting hole . . .

05 . . . then position the bracket in place and mark a hole an inch behind the gauge, to feed the gauge wiring down the A-pillar. Pop a grommet in the hole earmarked for the wires – just to protect wires from any sharp edges.

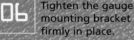

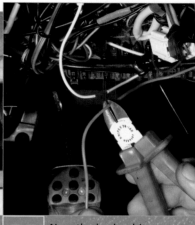

06 Tighten the gauge mounting bracket firmly in place.

07 On the rear of the actual tacho itself, you'll see a switch with 4, 6 and 8 on it. You're supposed to set this depending on whether you have a 4, 6 or 8 cylinder engine. Hmmm - bit of a no-brainer, but not everyone can live with a 1.5 litre, 4-cylinder engine forever, so there's some upgrade potential there.

08 Hold the gauge in position, then thread the tachometer nut up the wire and screw into place. Now feed the wire from the tacho through hole in the trim. Tape all the wires together, and feed them through the base of the A-pillar so that they eventually end up in the driver's footwell - this is a very fiddly job, but don't lose any wires on the way. When you're done, refit the A-pillar trim, without trapping any of the wires.

09 Now the boring bit – the wiring! After reading through the very detailed instructions supplied with the kit, we begin by finding a wire that's live when the ignition's on. We spliced the red tacho wire into the ignition live wire we found when wiring in our starter button. Temporarily reconnect the battery, turn the ignition on, and have a probe with a test light/meter to find a suitable feed.

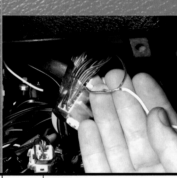

10 Next, the white tacho wire, which in our case is the illumination/ panel lights wire. Under the dash in the fusebox area we found an entire multi-plug that wasn't being used for anything. After checking with the test light, we found that the red and black wires in this multi-plug had a live feed when the panel lights were on, so we spliced our white into one.

11 The black (earth) wire is nice and easy. Use a ring terminal to connect the black wire to a suitable earth point in the fusebox area. Any bolt going to metalwork should do - if you can't find one, drill a hole into a suitable metal area, and fit your wire using a self-tapping screw.

12 The final green wire must be tapped into a suitable tachometer signal source. We decided to feed the wire through the bulkhead and go straight to the distributor. For a neat job, cable-tie the wire to the existing wiring loom.

13 When the wire arrives at the distributor, splice it into the blue wire. Check using a Haynes wiring diagram that your car's the same. Now the wiring-in's complete, turn the ignition on to check that the gauge illuminates and more importantly – works! Excellent.

Racing starts

Like to have a racing-style starter button on your Civic? Read on! A very cool piece of kit, and a great way to impress your passengers.

The idea of the racing starter button is the ignition key's made redundant, beyond switching on the ignition lights (it'd be a bit dumb, security-wise, if you could start the engine without the key at all).

The best (and easiest) part is deciding where the button's going to go. Somewhere highly-visible, obviously. Our Civic wasn't exactly bottom of the range, but still had a blank switch next to the one for the electric sunroof. Right next to the steering wheel, it was an obvious spot for the button. **01** Carefully prise out, then disconnect the wiring behind . . .

. . . mark the hole, and start drilling. You'll need a big drill bit, by the end. **02**

Fit the starter button into the hole, and tighten up the nut behind (you might need to trim some plastic behind to make room for the nut). **03** Feed the button wiring through . . .

. . . then reconnect the sunroof switch, and the switch panel's ready to fit back in the dash. **04** That's it then - time for a beer? Oh no - you've only just started.

The first wire we're going to play with is the earth. On our illuminated Pro-Start from Richbrook, the earth is a green wire (on the non-illuminated type, it's usually black). We already had an earth point sussed out - this nut's just above the fusebox. All we needed was a ring terminal on our green wire, **05** and we have an earth.

The main player in our starter button setup is the white relay provided in the kit, which has three wires coming off it (white, blue and black). Once we'd found a home for our relay (tucked inside the dash, above the fusebox), we tackled the black wire first. All we do here is join it to the black wire from our starter **06** button. Pretty easy, huh?

Before you go any further, now would be a great time to disconnect the battery. The ignition switch wiring is a prime source of volts, and we'll be chopping those wires about some. Better if they're **07** not carrying voltage at the time, really.

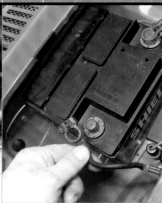

Now we need the ignition switch wire which feeds the starter motor (to reach the back of the ignition switch, take off the steering column lower shroud - just a few screws underneath). We know from our Haynes wiring diagram that we want a black/white wire, and here it is. Cutting it means the ignition key will no longer start the engine - the whole point of having a button. Tape up the end that goes back to the ignition switch.

08

Seems our black/white wire had been butchered previously, by whoever fitted our Civic's alarm - that's why we're now looking at a brown wire. Anyhow, the starter-motor end of the wire you just chopped now gets connected to the blue wire from the relay. We're using a soldered joint for this, which gives a more reliable connection than crimps. Tape up the soldered joint when you're done.

09

Achtung!
This is one job where you'll be messing with big wires, carrying serious current - more than any other electrical job, don't rush it, and don't skimp on the insulating tape. Do it properly, as we're about to show you, and there's no worries. Otherwise, at best, you'll be stranded - at worst, it could be a fire.

Only one more relay wire to go - the white wire, which is an ignition-live supply, protected by an in-line fuse. First job is to connect the white wire extension onto the fuseholder . . .

10

. . . and make a neat job of fixing the fuseholder to the relay. Our experience says that this fuse can sometimes blow, and you don't want it buried under the dash when it does.

11

We soon found the ignition-live we needed - a little probing with our test light found this heavy black/yellow wire under the fusebox. Rather than cut and join it (which might create problems with other circuits, if you don't do a very good job), we used the 'strip-and-solder' method. Use a knife to trim off a little insulation all round the wire . . .

12

. . . then bare the end of the white wire, twist it round the bared section you just made, and use solder to make the joint permanent.

13

Just one wire left (if you've got an illuminated button like ours) - it's the brown wire from the button itself. We need to find the wire which supplies the alternator warning light on the dash, and join the brown onto it. Our Haynes wiring diagram says it's blue/white, and it's not wrong. Hiding at the top of the fusebox, we soon had the brown soldered-on and taped up.

14

Fit the fuse into its holder, switch on the ignition, and give that button some action. You'll be so chuffed with yourself when your Civic bursts into life. You are a wiring God. When you're happy it all works, go back and make a neat job of all the wiring - loom it with tape, fix it in place with cable-ties, that sort of thing. Boring, but important.

15

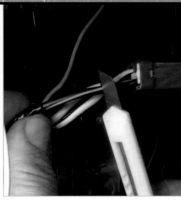

Boring flooring?

Alright, so carpets have always been a dull colour because they have to not show the dirt - when was the last time you heard of a car with white carpets? What goes on the floor needn't be entirely dull, though, and can still be easy to clean, if you're worried.

Ripping out the old carpets is actually quite a major undertaking - first, the seats have to come out (you might be fitting new ones anyway), but the carpets and underfelt fit right up under the dashboard, and under all the sill trims and centre console, etc. Carpet acts as sound-deadening, and is a useful thing to hide wiring under, too, so don't be in too great a hurry to ditch it completely. Unless, of course, your Civic is having a full-on race/rally style treatment, in which case - dump that rug!

Chequerplate is the current fashion in cool flooring, and it's easy to see why it'll probably have an enduring appeal - it's tough but flexible, fairly easy to cut and shape to fit, has a cool mirror finish, and it matches perfectly with the racing theme so often seen in the modified world, and with the ally trim that's widely used too.

Tips 'n' tricks

If you're completely replacing the carpet and felt with, say, chequerplate throughout, do this at a late stage, after the ICE install and any other electrical work's been done - that way, all the wiring can be neatly hidden underneath it.

Chequer mats

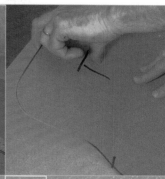

01 The halfway-house to a fully-plated interior is to make up your own tailored mats (hell, you can buy ready-mades if you're not allowed to play with sharp knives). Unless you buy real ally chequer, what you'll get is actually plastic, and must be supported by mounting it on hardboard. Take one of the lovely 'Granny' mats your car might have come with, and use it as a template to mark the shape onto the hardboard (you could always make a template from some thin card).

02 With the shape marked out, it's time for the jigsaw - next to a cordless drill, this has to be one of the most useful tools ever invented for the modder.

03 To make the hardboard fit better into the footwells, score it at the bend where it goes up under the pedals . . .

04 . . . then carefully 'fold' the hardboard back to the required shape - trust us, this will make your new chequer mats fit superbly.

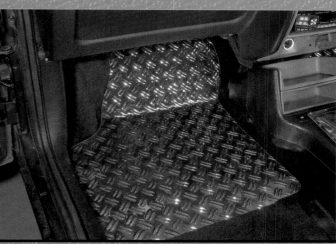

05 Not unlike this in fact. Try your hardboard mat in place, and trim the corners and edges as necessary to get it fitting as flat as poss.

06 Now you can use your hardboard as a template, for cutting out the chequer. Try to make the chequer fractionally bigger overall than the hardboard, so you don't see the wood edge (you shouldn't anyway, if your board is a tidy fit). Stick the chequer to the board, using some decent glue - spray glue's convenient, but usually not quite up to the job. You can't beat good old brush-on Evo-Stik (and no, we're not being paid to say that).

07 Do it right, and you too can have a floor like this - looks sweet, and the mats don't slip. Sorted.

Wheely cool

A new steering wheel is an essential purchase in personalising your Civic. It's one of the main points of contact between you and the car, it's sat right in front of you, and the standard ones are dull and massive!

Don't be tempted to fit too small a wheel - Civics never had power steering, and a tiny-rimmed steering wheel will make manoeuvring very difficult, especially with phat tyres.

One bit of good news is that, once you've shelled out for your wheel, it may be possible to fit it to your next car, too. When you buy a new wheel, you usually have to buy a boss (or mount) to go with it - the mounts are less pricey, so one wheel could be fitted to another completely different car, for minimum cost.

A trick feature worth investigating is the detachable wheel/boss. This feature comes in handy when you park up and would rather the car was still there when you come back (something most people find a bonus). It's all very well having a steering wheel immobiliser or steering lock, but I doubt many thieves will be driving off in your car if the steering wheel's completely missing! Also, removing the wheel may remove the temptation to break in and pinch… your wheel!

A word about **airbags**

Which Civics have airbags? Well, it all seems a bit of a random feature to us - from our information, if your Civic's older than 1994, and not an ESi, you don't have one - most Civics had an airbag by 1994, or got one just before the EG Civic died in 1995. So far, the market for replacement wheels with airbags hasn't materialised, so fitting your tasty new wheel means losing what some (old) people think is a valuable safety feature.

So just disconnect the damn thing, right? Wrong. Then your airbag warning light will be on permanently - not only is this irritating, your newly-modded motor will fail the MOT (having the airbag itself isn't compulsory, but if the warning light's on, it's a fail - at least at the time this was written). Two ways round this - either take out the clocks (see the section on fitting white dials) and remove the offending warning light bulb, OR bridge the airbag connector plug pins with two lengths of wire attached to either side of a 5A fuse. Bridging the pins this way 'fools' the test circuit (which fires up every time you switch on the ignition) into thinking the airbag's still there, and the warning light will go out as it should.

Disabling the airbag is yet another issue which will interest your insurance company, so don't do it without consulting them first. We're just telling you, that's all.

Warning: Airbags are expensive to replace (several £100s), and are classed as an explosive!!! Funny, that - for a safety item, there's any number of ways they can CAUSE injuries or damage if you're not careful - check this lot out:

a Before removing the airbag, the battery MUST be disconnected (don't whinge about it wiping out your stereo pre-sets). When the battery's off, don't start taking out the airbag for another 10 minutes or so. The airbag system stores an electrical charge - if you whip it out too quick, you might set it off, even with the battery disconnected. True.

b When the airbag's out, it must be stored the correct way up.

c The airbag is sensitive to impact - dropping it from sufficient height might set it off. Even if dropping it doesn't actually set it off, it probably won't work again, anyway. By the way, once an airbag's gone off, it's scrap. You can't stuff it back inside.

d If you intend to keep the airbag with a view to refitting it at some stage (like when you sell the car), store it in a cool place - but bear in mind that the storage area must be suitable, so that if the airbag went off by accident, it would not cause damage to anything or anyone. Sticking it under your bed might not be such a good idea.

e If you're not keeping the airbag, it must be disposed of correctly (don't just put it out for the bin men!). Contact your local authority for advice.

f Airbags must not be subjected to temperatures in excess of 90°C (194°F) - just remember that bit about airbags being an explosive - you don't store dynamite in a furnace, now do you? Realistically in this country, the only time you'll get THAT hot is in a paint-drying oven.

Removing a Civic airbag

Our Civic didn't have an airbag, but we're not leaving you poor guys with them out in the cold. First, in case you hadn't already got the message, disconnect that battery, then wait a while (like 10 minutes or so). From straight-ahead, spin the wheel round about 90°, and you should be able to feel one screw hole in the back of the steering wheel. The Torx screw is well-recessed inside this hole, and might well be tight. Undo the first screw, then spin the wheel through 180° and remove the other one.

All you have to do now is lift the airbag unit out of the wheel, and disconnect the yellow wiring plug behind.

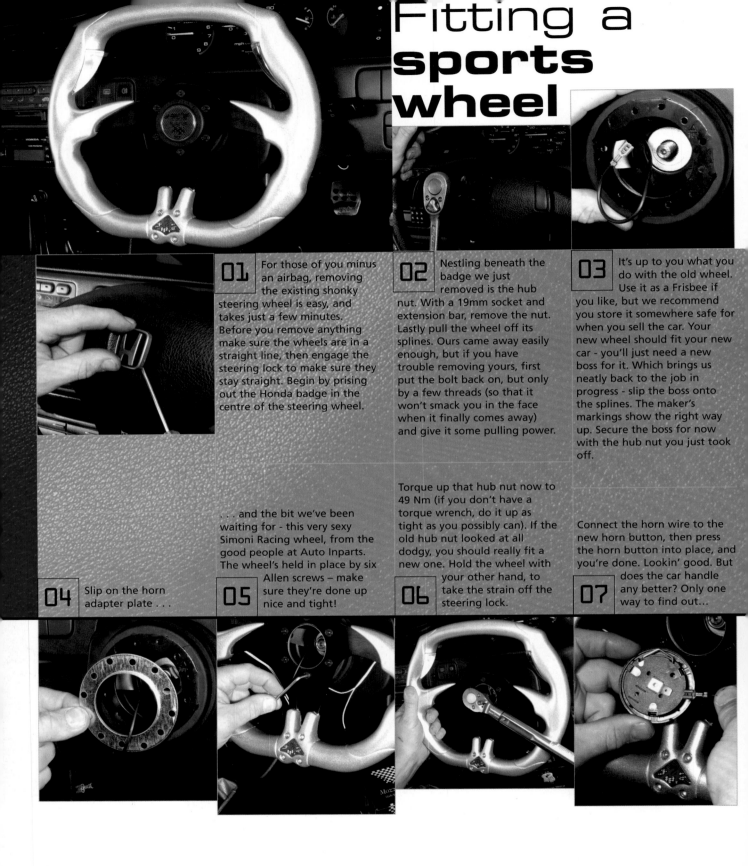

Fitting a sports wheel

01 For those of you minus an airbag, removing the existing shonky steering wheel is easy, and takes just a few minutes. Before you remove anything make sure the wheels are in a straight line, then engage the steering lock to make sure they stay straight. Begin by prising out the Honda badge in the centre of the steering wheel.

. . . and the bit we've been waiting for - this very sexy Simoni Racing wheel, from the good people at Auto Inparts. The wheel's held in place by six Allen screws – make sure they're done up nice and tight!

02 Nestling beneath the badge we just removed is the hub nut. With a 19mm socket and extension bar, remove the nut. Lastly pull the wheel off its splines. Ours came away easily enough, but if you have trouble removing yours, first put the bolt back on, but only by a few threads (so that it won't smack you in the face when it finally comes away) and give it some pulling power.

Torque up that hub nut now to 49 Nm (if you don't have a torque wrench, do it up as tight as you possibly can). If the old hub nut looked at all dodgy, you should really fit a new one. Hold the wheel with your other hand, to take the strain off the steering lock.

03 It's up to you what you do with the old wheel. Use it as a Frisbee if you like, but we recommend you store it somewhere safe for when you sell the car. Your new wheel should fit your new car - you'll just need a new boss for it. Which brings us neatly back to the job in progress - slip the boss onto the splines. The maker's markings show the right way up. Secure the boss for now with the hub nut you just took off.

Connect the horn wire to the new horn button, then press the horn button into place, and you're done. Lookin' good. But does the car handle any better? Only one way to find out...

04 Slip on the horn adapter plate . . .

05

06

07

Alternative thinking - steering wheel rim

The availability of aftermarket steering wheels complete with airbags has yet to develop fully in the modifying world.

Airbags are an important safety feature, and insurance companies may even charge you for the privilege of removing yours... So what do you do if you want to keep this valuable safety feature, whilst updating and creating a fresh interior look? The answer comes in the form of a Custom Styling Ring – a moulded cover that simply sits on top of your existing steering wheel. Custom rings are available in a variety of popular finishes including carbon fibre (or wood effect - lovely), and can instantly transform your boring, factory-fit wheel into a 'new' stylish fifth wheel.

01 Firstly unpack your custom ring, check that it is in perfect condition, with no rough edges.

02 Clean the steering wheel using a mild degreaser so that the adhesive from the ring will stick properly to the wheel. How grey is that standard wheel?

03 Clean any impurities from the inside of the wheel.

04 Then peel off the adhesive backing (that'll be the stylish red bit you can see here - and it's not staying!).

05 Position the custom ring over the steering wheel, making sure that the spokes on the ring are perfectly aligned with the steering wheel spokes. When you're satisfied it's positioned properly, press the ring onto the wheel. Work your way round the wheel pressing down firmly all the way, to ensure the adhesive sticks to the wheel. Well, it's better than it was...

And why not...

Although the 'new' steering wheel looks pretty sweet now, a big patch of nasty grey plastic still remains. Why not try painting the centre of your wheel using specialist paint - the elephant hide would be gone, and in return you've created a stylish and personalised interior.

Pedalling your Civic

A tasty race-equipment touch to your modded machine, pedal extensions really look the part when combined with full chequerplate mats, or alloy footwells - available in several styles and (anodised) colours. Not sure how well the anodising will wear, though...

The only other issue with pedals is the clutch and brake must have rubbers fitted - this is first of all sensible (so your feet don't slip off them at an awkward moment) and it's also a legal requirement. Don't buy extensions without.

01 Firstly peel off the old pedal rubbers. No worries so far.

> **Achtung!**
> *Check your insurance company's position regarding pedal extensions. A while ago there was a big fuss after a couple of cars fitted with pedal extensions crashed, which resulted in pedal extensions being withdrawn from sale at a lot of places.*

06 With the clutch and brake pedals done, it's the loud pedal's turn. Fitting the new throttle pedal extension proved to be just a little bit more difficult. Firstly the old rubber had to be cut off - it doesn't slide off as per the other two pedals.

07 After placing the new extension onto the throttle pedal, the two holes at the top of the extension were way out of line with the existing pedal. We can't have any extension held on by just one screw, so the pedal had to come off for modification. First job is to open the bonnet and locate where the throttle cable meets the quadrant, then disconnect the cable by unclipping the end fitting.

08 Back inside the car now to locate the split pin that retains the pedal arm in place, using a suitable tool push the pin up to remove.

09 Lastly, remove the pedal return spring by unclipping it at either end, and slide the pedal away.

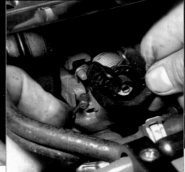

02 Hold the new pedal in place, and mark the holes ready for drilling using a pen or scriber. Ensure that these holes aren't too close to the pedal arm (behind the pedal footplate), as you won't be able to fit the nut to the mounting bolt if they are.

03 As you're going to be drilling into metal, use a centre-punch to mark the hole and help stop the drill skating all over the smooth, shiny surface. The block of wood behind the pedal is to stop it being pushed down while we drill our holes. It also eliminates the embarrassing possibility of drilling through the carpet.

04 The pedal extensions are held on by two Allen bolts. With the help of a spanner behind to hold the nut, make sure they're done up tight – loose pedals could mean problems. It's worth checking they're still tight after a few week's caning, too - especially the over-worked throttle pedal.

05 As is the case with most aftermarket pedal kits, the instructions with our superb 'Sport Action' pedals from Simoni Racing state that the pedals must be at least 50 mm apart. It really is important that the pedals are evenly spaced – we're sure everyone can appreciate the complications of having the brake pedal too near the throttle pedal.

These brackets (available from DIY/hardware shops) are perfect for this job. If you don't have a bracket, use a suitable strip of metal. Just by chance, the ready-drilled holes in the **10** bracket matched the holes on the extension perfectly.

The throttle pedal's still slightly too narrow for our new strip, so rather than try drilling two holes in the pedal, we used a round file to make two semi-circle cut-outs at the edges. Not as good as a proper hole, but the extension mounting nuts/bolts will still bite okay. We did drill a hole in the centre, for **11** the one hole in the extension that lines up with the pedal.

Another mod with the round file was to create a cut-out for the pedal arm, so our new **12** plate will fit flush to the back of the pedal.

Pop the new bracket into place behind the pedal, with the new extension on the front. Now tighten the nuts using the trusty Allen key and spanner routine. To tighten the centre mounting, you'll need long-nose pliers to get access to the **13** nut. When this has been done, refit the pedal to the car.

Are you **sitting stylishly?**

The perfect complement to your lovingly-sorted suspension, because you need something better than the standard seats to hold you in, now that you can corner so much faster... and they look brutal, by way of a bonus. Besides the seat itself, remember to price up the subframe to adapt it to the mounting points in your car. Most people also choose the three- or four-point harnesses to go with it (looks a bit daft to fit a racing seat without it), but make sure the harness you buy is EC-approved, or an eagle-eyed MOT tester might make you take 'em out.

Interiors

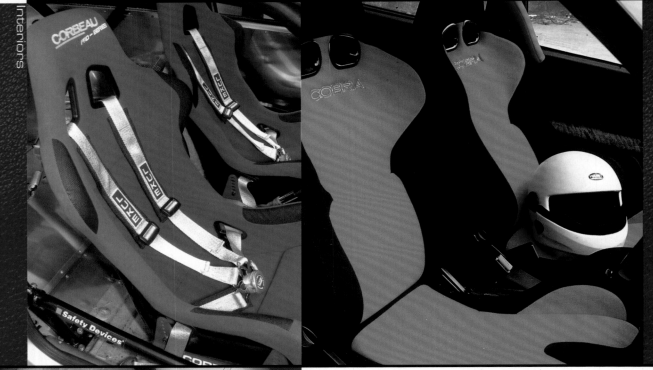

Reclining seats are pricier than non-recliners, but are worth the extra. With non-adjustable seats, how are your mates meant to get in the back? Through the tailgate? Or maybe there is no back seat... You can get subframes which tilt, so that non-reclining seats can move forward. Non-reclining racing seats should be tried for fit before you buy.

An alternative to expensive racing seats would be to have your existing seats re-upholstered in your chosen colours/fabrics, to match your interior theme. You might be surprised what's possible, and the result could be something truly unique. If you've got a basic model, try sourcing seats from a breakers (haggle if the side bolsters are worn away - a common fault). A secondhand interior bought here will be a lot cheaper than buying new goodies, and you know it'll fit easily (all Civics are the same underneath) - but - it won't have that unique style. Specialist breakers may be able to supply something more rad, such as a leather interior from a top-spec Accord/Prelude - might take some persuading to get it in, though!

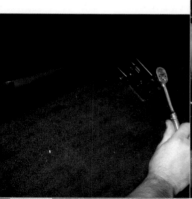

01 Removing the front seats is easy, and shouldn't take more than a few minutes. Begin by removing the two front track retaining bolts (slide the seat back for access). Then there's two more just the same behind, after you slide the seat forward . . .

02 . . . and out she comes. This Civic's looking less grey by the minute. Granny wouldn't like it.

03 We're fitting some front seats from a G-reg Prelude (found in our local scrappy), as they're much more sporty than the existing Civic ones. The front bolts on the Prelude subframes line up perfectly with the holes in the floorpan, but the back mountings will need some work. We had to start by removing the rear bracket, which was in the wrong place.

Removing
seats

Our new bracket needed to sit an inch from the tracks to give clearance to allow the seat to move. Measure and bend a strip of thick metal in a vice to create the bracket, then mark and drill a hole for mounting the seat to the floor.

04

Seat mountings have to be strong to be safe. Wimpy bits of metal and poor welding are not an option here. Don't forget to cover the seat, to prevent damage from welding or grinding sparks. When the welding expert's done his stuff, give the bracket a coat of paint for a factory look.

05

Our new seats are ready to be lifted back into the car. Refit the four track retaining bolts, and ensure that the seats move as they should. That's it – now we know it fits, the seat can come out again, to be sent off for a session with the trimmers (didn't think we'd leave it grey, did you?).

06

Fitting buckets and **harnesses**

Order your new buckets with proper Civic subframes to match, and you'll have wicked seats installed in minutes. The first job (apart from working out which base is for left and right) is to fit the subframes to the new seats. As we're talking about a fairly important safety item, do the frame-to-seat bolts up tight.

The new chairs are now ready to fit - hopefully, the bolt holes in the new bases will line up with the holes in the floor. The seat mounting bolts are, of course, the old ones you took out. Which are probably rusty as well, so treat them to some copper grease, instead of just bunging them straight back in. Another safety tip is to use some big washers under the bolt heads, to stop the bolts pulling through the subframes (which could happen if the accident's big enough).

Tips 'n' tricks
During fitting, the seats will have to slide forwards or back, to gain access to the mounting bolts. Make sure the subframes are bolted in firmly before you slide the seat, or there's a risk of twisting the seat relative to the base, and it will jam up solid. Trust us - we've been there.

It's true that not everyone likes racing harnesses, but anyone like that's just boring, or should probably eat less pies. Besides, you don't fit sexy race seats and then not fit race belts, do you?

The only problem with harnesses is caused by where you have to mount them. Even with a three-point harness, you end up using one of the rear seat belt mounts, and it seriously reduces your ability to carry bodies in the back seats (webbing everywhere). The MOT crew say that, if you've got rear seats, you must have rear seat belts fitted, so you either 'double-up' on your rear belt mounts (use the same mounting bolts for your harnesses and rear belts), or you take the back seats out altogether. Removing the rear seats leaves the rear deck free for chequerplate, speakers, roll cages - whatever you like. It's just important to understand how fundamental harnesses can end up being, to the whole look of your car - there's almost no half-measures with race belts, so you've got to really want 'em.

One thing you must **not** do is to try making up your own seat belt/harness mounting points. Honda structural engineers spent plenty of time selecting mounting points and testing them for strength. Drilling your own holes and sticking bolts through is fine for mounting speakers and stuff, but you're heading for an interview with the Grim Reaper if you try it with seat belts. The forces in a big shunt are immense. We're not convinced either that the practice of slinging harnesses round a rear strut brace is kosher, from the safety angle - the poxy strut braces available are so flimsy (they're usually ally) you can bend them in your hands. Nuts to trusting my life to one of those!

Your Haynes manual should help you to remove the old belts. After that, it's just a case of re-using the old belt mountings to fit the new harness 'eyes', which the harnesses clip onto. Tighten the eyes fully down to the floor, using an adjustable spanner. Check whether your new seat subframes have proper belt mountings on them - if so, you can use these for one of the front mounts (the other one comes from the old belt's sliding rail on the floor). Don't be shy about tightening things properly, and no bodges, please - these are safety harnesses, after all.

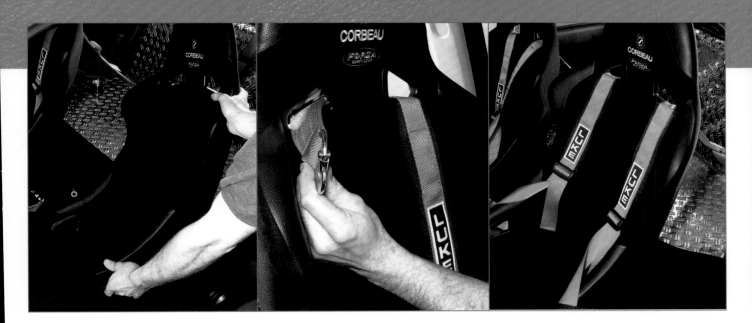

ICE

Headset

The cheaper your Civic, the nastier your standard head unit's going to be. Of course, by the time an Civic's passed through several owners, it's pretty unlikely to still have a standard Honda radio in anyway, but if all you've got is a hole, don't feel too bad. Standard sets are fine if all you want to do is aimlessly listen to the radio with your arm out the window, but not - definitely not - if you want to impress your mates with the depth and volume of your bass.

Or, of course, if you want to listen to CDs. It's got to go - and there's plenty of decent headsets out there which will give you a night-and-day difference in sound quality and features. The headset is the heart of your new install - always go for the best you can afford. Ask the experts which features matter most, if you're building a full system.

Our Alpine headset is pretty typical of the current single-CD state of the art - looks decent, good sound, plenty of features. The peak of in-car entertainment, so to speak.

01 First, the old set's got to be shifted. Resist the urge to just crowbar the thing out of the dash - you'll be needing two of the standard radio removal tools to do the job with less damage. And you could always sell it, or keep it, to stick back in when you sell the car.

02 Another reason not to get too excited when removing the old set is that most of the wiring behind is fully 'recyclable' - ie we'll be using it again. One bonus on our Civic - it's got ISO plugs for power and speakers, meaning our new set should plug straight in. Older Civics might require an adapter lead.

03 The old cage has to go too - you can't use this with your new set, or the locking pins won't engage. Most DIY-fitted cages have absolutely every last locking tab bent over, which makes it a long job with a small screwdriver to remove it.

ISO plug wiring **colours**

Black plug (power/earth)
Red - 12V permanent live
Yellow - radio memory live
Black - earth
Blue - Remote/P-cont
Orange - dimmer

Brown plug (speakers)
White pair - front left
Grey pair - front right
Green pair - rear left
Purple pair - rear right

With the old cage out of the picture, now's a good time to introduce the new set's cage into the equation. From behind the dash, feed in every wire that's going to be connected to the **04** headset (which includes any RCA leads, CD changer lead, P-cont/remote wire, and so on), and slip the cage loosely into place.

Having ISO plugs makes life much easier - one does power, the other speakers (the power one has red, yellow and black leads, among others). Plug in the power one, and all your lives and earths are taken care of. If you're in no-ISO-plug **05** hell, you only need to buy an adapter lead.

Look at that mass of wiring. But our man's doing the right thing, and consulting the Alpine manual. Well, it's a lot better than **06** blowing up your headset.

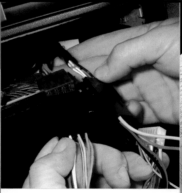

>>

07 If you're running amps in your system, you'll need a remote or P-cont lead, to switch them on (see the section on amps). The headset has a P-cont output wire, usually blue or blue/white. Any ordinary bit of wire will do for this - from the headset, feed it round the car to your amps. Our RCA lead had one built into it, which is a neat idea.

08 We're nearly ready for the new headset now, but the mass of wires inside the dash is giving us a headache. Rather than just cramming it all in, try making a neat job by looming some of it with tape.

09 Single-CD players are still prone to skipping - feed them a scratched disc, hard-riding slammed car, and a set of roadworks, and it's not surprising. But you can make things better by fitting the rear mounting peg (should be supplied), which then locates into the dash and stops the whole set wobbling about. It's there for a reason!

Those amps of yours also need a signal to work from, and that's what the RCA outputs on the headset provide. If your set's got more than one pair of connections (pre-outs), these may be marked 'front', 'rear' or 'sub'. Use whichever set makes sense for location and type of amped speakers you're running. **10** Connect red lead-to-red connection, white lead to...

And this is the headset main wiring plug going on. This is where all your power, earth and speaker wiring comes in, from the ISO plugs. It's a bit vital to the plot, this plug, so make sure it clips in tight. The same applies to the aerial lead, if you plan on listening to the radio. **11**

Test that everything's working at this point, before pushing the unit right into its cage. If all's well, push the headset home until it clicks. If it gets stuck, take the set out, and un-bunch all the wiring by hand. Do not force it in, or you could end up having a very bad day. If you have trouble, removing the front part of the centre console (see 'interiors') will give you more room to play. **12** Success? Now get out the instruction manual again, and set those levels properly. Enjoy.

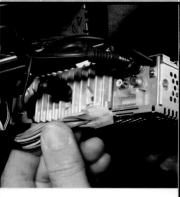

Front
speakers

The standard items in the Civic speak volumes (hur-hur) about any car manufacturer's desire to build things down to a price - ie spend as little as poss. What does it cost Honda for the speakers in a Civic? If it's more than a fiver a set, they're being robbed. Low on power, and with nasty paper cones which disintegrate after a few years, fitting ANY aftermarket speakers is going to be an upgrade.

So what are your options? Well, unless you've got plans for mahoosive door builds to take some 6x9s or the odd sub, you're limited to co-axial speakers (tweeter and woofer combined) or components (separate woofer and tweeter, with a crossover box). Components usually give the best sound, but you'll need space in your door for a tweeter, and the crossover also needs a home. Tricky. We're taking the easy option, with some quality Kenwood co-axials.

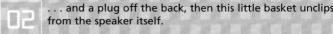

01 With the door trim panel off (see 'interiors'), removing the old speakers (for later burial) is easy-peasy. Four screws round the front . . .

02 . . . and a plug off the back, then this little basket unclips from the speaker itself.

>>

03 Before throwing both just-removed items out for the trash, we had a brainwave. Our new Kennies were chosen because they're similar size to the originals, to make life easier. So why not re-use the old mounting basket, if we can? Only trouble is, our new magnets are a bit too hefty. So we either give up and try mounting the speakers directly to the doors, or try Plan B. Which involves literally seconds of trimming with a hacksaw.

04 Now it fits like a glove . . .

. . . and even the speaker-to-basket holes line up. What a bonus. And of course, we know the basket fits the door just fine - so we're laughing. **05**

06 Looks like we're cheating, re-using the non-quality speaker wiring. Well, everyone else does it - we've even seen professional ICE installers avoid the trouble of routing oxygen-free into doors (which usually involves drilling holes, and a fair bit of grief which we don't want). The fronts are being amped, so fear not - quality wire will feature at some point.

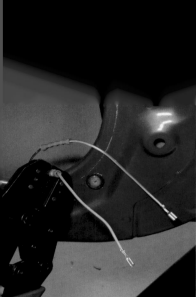

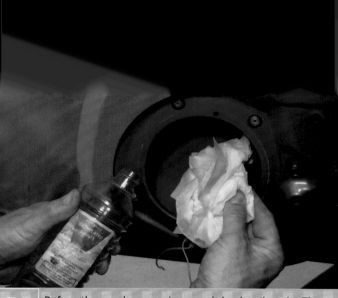

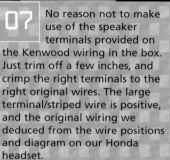

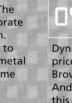

07 No reason not to make use of the speaker terminals provided on the Kenwood wiring in the box. Just trim off a few inches, and crimp the right terminals to the right original wires. The large terminal/striped wire is positive, and the original wiring we deduced from the wire positions and diagram on our Honda headset.

All you have to do is cut it, and get it onnn. Don't get too carried away in your quest for sonic perfection, but don't skimp on it, either. Treat the large 'floppy' areas of the door, and some round the speaker hole will help too. Two things - use it warm (warm it up with a heat gun, on a cold day), and watch your fingers on the

10 expensive stuff (the metal foil edges are sharp!).

08 Before the speaker goes in, sound-deaden that tin. The larger areas of the metal door panel will flex and vibrate with all the kicking power of your new sound system. Tizzing speakers we can live without. By sticking thick panels to the inside of your door inner and outer skins, you make the metal 'thicker', and vibration-free. Clean up the door panel with some decent solvent . . .

To get as much quality wire in as possible, splicing on our oxygen-free should be done right where the front speaker wire comes in from the front doors. But you try finding it on a Civic - it's buried. Instead, we traced it to the large wiring plug behind the old headset, where we snipped it off (taping the plug ends after) . . .

09 . . . then choose your material. The market leader in deadening is Dynamat - but - it comes at a price. What else is out there? Brown Bread. Sounds dead. And it's cheaper. Cheaper still is this stuff - flashing for roofing repairs, from a builder's merchants. Use the posh stuff if you prefer, but this works. Besides, who'll see it?

. . . and crimped on the far better-looking (and hopefully, - sounding) oxygen-free cable. As always, we're using the wire with the maker's writing on for speaker positive. This speaker wire now gets run to the boot,

12 where our four-channel amp's waiting to be powered up.

11

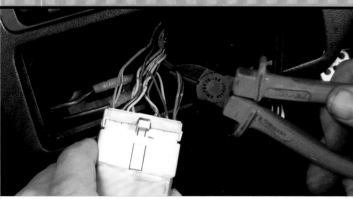

Rear speakers

Stealth
shelf 6x9s

First job with a new ready-made shelf is to mark the speaker positions. Not tricky.

01

If we're talking about a set of 6x9s, and a Civic Hatchback, rear shelf-mounting is the simplest option. If you don't want to butcher your standard shelf (always a flimsy item), either make a new one from MDF (using your stock shelf as a template), or buy a ready-made acoustic 'stealth' shelf. Either way, make hiding your new speakers a priority - tasty speakers on display in the back window could soon mean no rear window, and no speakers…

While shelf mounting has its advantages, Civics have another top spot for speakers - the rear side trim panels. Okay for speakers without huge, heavy magnets, you just cut a suitable-sized hole in the panel, and mount your speaker in from behind.

Our Civic Coupe's got a fixed shelf containing Honda speakers, packing a not-very-kicking 10 watts. An upgrade, therefore, is way overdue. We could butcher the shelf for some 6x9s, but a simpler option is replacing with some Pioneer co-axials. Run off the new headset, the speakers don't need to be mega-powerful, just quality.

Remember that the length of wire to each speaker should be the same (as near as poss), or you might find the speakers run slightly out of phase. Crimp on the right terminals, and connect up your speakers. For max neatness, use P-clips screwed along the edge of the shelf. To remove the shelf more easily, fit some bullet connectors in the speaker wiring, or ask your ICE dealer for a Neutrik connector plug.

With a speaker outline marked, remove the wood from the rest of the shelf, and drill a nice big hole somewhere inside the outline… then get busy with the jigsaw.

02

Use the speaker mounts (or even the speakers themselves) as a template to drill the mounting holes . . .

03

. . . then screw on the speakers themselves. Don't forget that 6x9s can be run off the headset, to provide a little 'rear fill' - if you have them amped-up, you might find that the sound's too biased to the back of the car.

04

05

 Achtung!
MDF dust is nasty stuff to breathe in. Wear a mask when you're cutting, drilling or sanding it.

Coupé rear speakers

01 Off with the wiring plug, out with the screws - not much grief to be found adios-ing the old shelf speakers.

02 Inside, we find a standard feature which we might actually refit - the Honda speaker grilles give a usefully discreet cover for our much-tastier new co-axials.

03 Nothing remotely tasty about these nasty items - we'd even be embarrassed about refitting these when the car gets sold.

04 Although the same diameter, our new speakers didn't go straight into the holes, so we had to do a little work. All we needed was one hole in a different spot, and a tiny bit of shelf-bending - not exactly a challenge, then.

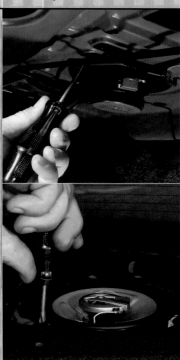

05 That looks so much better - let's hope they sound as good as they look. Might not be a bad idea to use a few strips of sound-deadening (like Dynamat or Brown Bread) on the metal rear shelf, to deaden any vibrations. More important if those rear speakers are getting seriously amped-up, especially.

06 The only bit left is the wiring-up. We're using the old speaker wire (no need to go for hefty stuff, if the speakers are being run off the headset), but the old wiring plug isn't much use to us - so off it comes.

07 To make our life even easier, we're going to use the connectors from the wiring supplied with our new speakers. Just trim off a few inches, and join to the existing wire with crimps.

08 On our car, the original grey wire was the speaker live (goes to the bigger terminal) - but we only worked this out from the wire positions at the headset. Guessing is not an option.

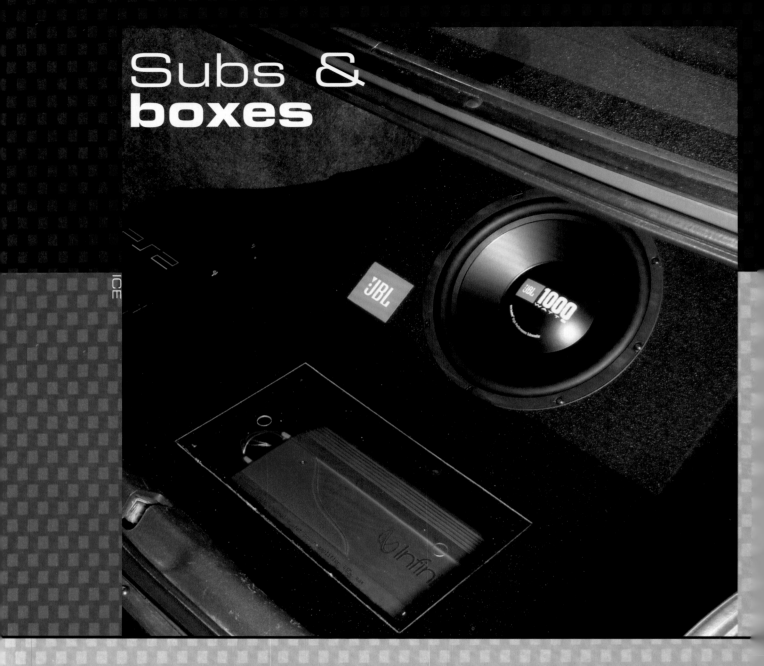

Subs &
boxes

No system's complete without that essential deep bass boom and rumble. Don't muck about with bass tubes - get the real thing to avoid disappointment. So you lose some of your boot space - so what? Is getting the shopping in an issue? We think not.

Most people opt for the easy life when it comes to boxes, at least until they're ready for a full-on mental install. The Civic at least has a roomy boot, so standard boxes will fit easily. Making up your own box isn't hard though, especially if you were any good at maths and geometry. Oh, and woodwork. Most subs come with instructions telling you what volume of box they work best in, but ask an expert (or a mate) what they think - the standard boxes are just fine, and none are pricey. The only real reason to build your own is if you've got an odd-shaped boot (or want something that looks trick).

Achtung!
MDF dust is nasty stuff to breathe in. Wear a mask when you're cutting, drilling or sanding it.

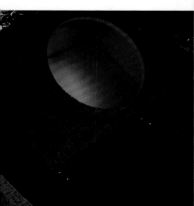

01 Take one standard sub box, and decide how you'd like it to fit your boot. Usually, you don't get too much choice, but our Civic Coupe's got masses of boot space. Thinking "outside the box", we decided to mount our box on its back, upside-down - it just looked better for our planned install's layout, and the sub won't mind.

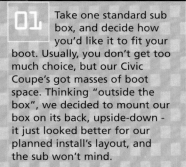

Make sure the sub's logo is lined up correctly (this won't affect the sound, just the pose-value), then drill through the mounting holes round the edge of the sub. Once the mounting holes are made, screw the sub down tight (unless you want bass all over the place).

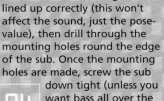

02 You don't want a heavy sub box sliding about in your boot, so nail it down. We're using our favourite DIY-store corner brackets again. Having lined our boot floor/spare wheel well with carpet, we're now using Tipp-Ex to mark the bracket holes for drilling.

The terminal plates on most ready-made boxes have either screw-type or spring-type terminals for connecting your speaker wire. You can just strip the end, twist it up and shove it in. Or you can do a more professional job, and 'tin' the end of your speaker wire, with solder . . .

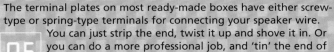

03 Once we're sure the box is a good fit, it can come out once more for the sub itself. Don't forget to wire up your sub before fitting it - a very common mistake, caused by being too keen. Most ready-made boxes come fitted with a terminal plate on the side of the box - with these, just run your speaker wire from the sub to the inside of the plate (keep the pos and neg wiring the right way round).

. . . this actually makes it easier to fit your speaker wire, and removes the chance of any stray strands (which could touch, and blow a channel on your amp or headset). Keeping to our wiring convention, we're joining the writing-on wire to the positive (red) terminal.

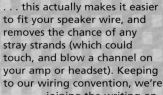
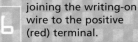

04

05

06

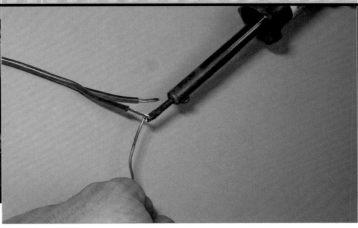
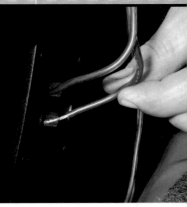

Wiring-up

For most people, this is the scariest part of an install - just the thought of masses of multi-coloured spaghetti sticking out of your dash might have you running to the experts (or a knowledgeable mate). But - if you do everything in a logical order, and observe a few simple rules, wiring-up isn't half as brain-numbing as it seems.

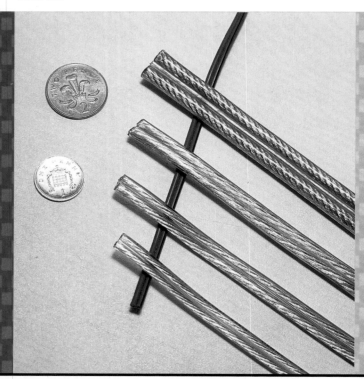

Live feeds

Although a typical head unit can be powered off the standard Honda wiring (the stock wire is good for about 15 amps, tops) running amplifiers means you'll be needing a new live feed, taken straight off the battery. Or in our case, straight off the junction box we fitted as part of our fusebox install (see 'security').

Get some decent 'eight-gauge' (quite heavy) or 'four-gauge' (getting on for battery cable thickness - serious stuff) wire, and a matching fuseholder. If you're running more than one item off this feed wire, get a distribution block too, which splits the feed up, with a separate fuse for each item - who'd have thought electrical safety can look trick too?

Pub trivia

Hands up, who knows what 'RCA' stands for? We use it every day in ICE-speak, but WHAT does it really mean? Really Clever Amplifier lead? Remote Control Acoustic lead? Well, the answer's a strange one. RCA leads and connectors are also known as 'phono' connectors in the world of TV and hi-fi, and they've been around a long, long time. How long, exactly? We're talking back in the days when you could only get radios - big suckers with valves in them, and long before anyone thought of putting one in a car. RCA actually stands for Radio Corporation of America, who hold the patent on this type of connector and lead. Not a lot of people know that.

Speaker and RCA wiring

As with all wiring, the lesson here is to be neat and orderly - or - you'll be sorry! RCA leads and speaker wires are prone to picking up interference (from just about anywhere), so the first trick to learn when running ICE wiring is to keep it away from live feeds, and also if possible, away from the car's ECUs. Another favourite way to interference-hell is to loop up your wiring, when you find you've got too much (we've all been there). Finding a way to lose any excess lengths of wire without bunching can be an art - laying it out in a zig-zag, taping it to the floor as you go, is just one solution.

Another lesson in neatness is finding out what kinds of cable clips are available, and where to use them. There's various stick-on clips which can be used as an alternative to gaffer tape on floors, and then 'P-clips', which look exactly as their name suggests, and can be screwed down (to speaker shelves, for instance). 'Looming'

your wiring is another lesson well-learned - this just means wrapping tape around, particularly on pairs of speaker wires or RCAs. As we've already said, don't loom speaker wire with power cables (or even with earths).

The last point is also about tidiness - mental tidiness. When you're dealing with speaker wiring, keep two ideas in mind - positive and negative. Each speaker has a pos (+) and neg (-) terminal. Mixing these up is not an option, so work out a system of your own, for keeping positive and negative in the right places on your headset and amp connections. Decent speaker cable is always two wires joined together - look closely, and you'll see that one wire has writing (or a stripe) on, and the other is plain. Use the wire with writing for pos connections throughout your system, and you'll never be confused again. While we're at it, RCA leads have red and white connector plugs - Red is for Right.

01 If you're running a live feed straight from the battery, you'll need to get it into the car at some point. Have a look at the fusebox fitting section in 'security' to see how we did ours. You'll also need an in-line fuseholder, containing a fuse that'll cover the total load for your system.

02 Our junction box gives us a real easy life for live feeds, and it's hard not to feel smug. Of course, wherever your live's come from, remember that it will be live even if the ignition's off - either remove the in-line fuse, or don't let it touch earth.

03 With the centre console removed (see 'interiors'), feeding essential ICE wiring down the centre of the car, under the carpet, is much easier. This is particularly good for the RCA leads, if you can.

04 The alternative to running your wires under the carpet is routing them down the sides of the car. You can achieve this by unclipping the sill trim/door seal - you'll be surprised how much wire can be hidden this way. Keep the power feeds and speaker wires separate by running them down the other side.

05 Looming the wires together keeps things neat, but don't pull those cable-ties too tight - it can be useful if the wires lie flat, and bunching them up might work against you. Also, if your sill trims are secured using screws, take great care when refitting them - a screw through your wiring is a good way to kill your system.

06 Here's where your live feed could end up - a distribution block. Split your power off to the amps as you need it - each amp gets its own fuse (downrated from the large one in the holder up front). Excellent electrical safety, trick looks. Pin the wire ends with the chunky Allen grub screws, then fit the plastic cover tight (or lives will touch earths, and sparks will fly).

Amplifiers

Achtung!
MDF dust is nasty stuff to breathe in. Wear a mask when you're cutting, drilling or sanding it.

We're doing the earth first - and why not?. Don't use skinny wires for earths - ideally, it should be the same-thickness wire as you've used for your live feed. Connecting it to the amp's the easy bit (make sure it's done up tight). **01**

Now we need a decent earth point somewhere in the boot, to join our wire to. The Coupe's got this handy bracket at the rear of the boot (it even has a pre-drilled hole). For a good earth connection, it's always best to clean off any paint. **02**

So, how many amps do we want in our car? One school of thought says each pair of speakers, and each sub, should have an individual amp - by setting the output from each amp separately, you can control each aspect of the sound, before you even need to think about adding a graphic equaliser. You can also better match your speakers to the level of power they need, to work best. Trouble is, running several amps means doubling-up on wiring, and you could end up drawing a monster amount of power from that battery.

Any starter system can be made to seriously kick, using just one 400W four-channel amp - choose the right one carefully (and the components to go with it), and just one will do. With a 'tri-mode' amp, you could run your front components off one pair of channels, bridge the other two for a sub, and run some 6x9s off the head unit. Don't forget that decent modern headsets chuck out fifty-per-channel now, so don't assume you'll need separate amps for everything.

Decide where you'll mount the amps carefully. Amps must be adequately cooled - don't cover it up so there's no airflow, and don't hang it upside-down from your shelf. With the back seat on our car chucked, we had ourselves a nice mounting platform, which we covered in carpet.

Our system set-up uses a large Infinity four-channel amp in tri-mode for our sub and the front speakers, with the rear speakers run off the headset. You may have your own ideas, but most ICE experts say you should have as much sound as poss coming from in front of you, with only a little from behind - that, apparently, is how our 'sound input' system was designed to work best (and who are we to argue?).

06 Read the amp's instruction book carefully when connecting any wires, or you might regret it, especially for bridged or tri-mode. Identify your speaker pos and neg/left and right wires, and get them screwed on. This is the bridged connection for our sub . . .

07 . . . while here, we're wiring up the front speakers. In all cases, you must check the manual for the right combination of speaker wires. As with the lives and earths, it's also vital there's no stray bits of wire left poking out.

By fitting a long-ish bolt, washer and nut, we've created an earth point. All we have to do is add our earth wire, and another nut, and we've got all the earth we can handle.

03

Next up, it's the humble P-cont (remote) lead going on. This performs the vital function of carrying the 'switch-on' signal from your headset - without this, you won't hear much. The good news is, this is one time when size doesn't matter - it doesn't carry much current, so the wire can be as skinny as you like.

04

The all-important live supply is one amp connection you should really use a ring terminal on, rather than just stuffing a bare wire into the hole. And insulate any bare metal on the terminal - that live touches anything else, and the results won't be good.

05

08 To get our large amp to work in tri-mode, we needed to split the RCA input across four channels, using an adaptor lead known as a splitter (cunning, eh?). These plug into each end of the RCA lead, and double the number of outputs.

09 Splitters aren't always clearly marked for left and right channels, so check what you're doing carefully. You can also use splitters to run more than one amp from one RCA lead (but the 'sound quality' experts say you shouldn't). Our headset actually had another set of RCA outputs, so we could've run another RCA lead down the car for this. But the system sounded great when we finished, so who cares?

10 A good tip is to leave the amps loose until after you've set them up - if you can, leave good access to the gain adjustment (volume) screws after final fitting, too. Starting at normal listening volume, with the amp gain turned down, put on a kicking track, then turn the gain up until the speakers just start to distort. Turn the gain down a tad from there, and you've a good basic setting. Amp gain and headset faders can now be tweaked to give a good balanced sound - or whatever tickles your lugholes.

Tricks 'n' tips

Very few systems work 100%, first time. If the amp LEDs don't light up, for instance, are they getting power? Are the p-cont/remote wires connected properly? If the sub doesn't kick, is the amp switch set to bridged or tri-mode, not stereo? Are the low-pass switches in the correct position? RTFM.

Playstation & screen

Bored of your CDs? Nothing on the radio? We have just the thing if you and a mate get bored, stuck in a 10-mile tailback on a bank holiday. Definitely a growing trend on the ICE scene, no top modded motor's complete these days without a games console, screen, DVD - where d'you stop? Just don't get caught playing it while you're moving, that's all.

01 Won't see much without a screen, so let's do that first. The trickiest bit of all is deciding where it'll go - obviously, both front seat people have to see it, so somewhere central, but how high up? Try the screen and its bracket in place, and check it adjusts how you want it. Is it accessible from below/behind, for feeding-in the wires? We chose this spot next to the centre vents.

02 With the pilot hole drilled, we found it would have to go quite a bit larger, to let the main video lead's plug through. We also modded the mounting bracket slightly, to route the lead more neatly. The less wires on show, the better it'll look. Talking of 'on show', it pays to plan ahead, and consider how the screen could come out easily, if you park in a dodgy area at night.

03 The Civic dash is quite strong, but we thought it a good plan to brace it from inside, using this large 'panel' washer - just spreads the load, stops the dash cracking.

04 Now the screen can be mounted on, and the video lead plugged together. This Centurion screen's a budget model, but still has built-in speakers and even a headphone socket. Looks good, but it's not working yet - let's finish the job.

05 Our screen came with an all-in-one lead containing the three-part video feed from the PS2 (or DVD), and also the power supply/earth. We'll connect up the PS2 later - for now, we want power to our screen. They give you a cigar lighter plug, but this looks a bit pants - let's do it properly. Prise apart the halves of your plug, and you get wires - chop the end off . . .

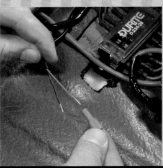

06 . . . strip the ends, and we have skinny red and black wires. The red's a live feed (you guessed it), which we're taking from our auxiliary fusebox (fitted in the 'security' section). Finding an earth point for the black wire's not difficult either. The little green lights now tell us the screen's ready for input - let's give it some.

01 inverter - ours was about £50 from Comet. What this does is take your car's 12-volt DC electrics, and turns it into 240-volt AC, giving you a domestic three-pin socket in your car - how cool is that? As with our screen, our inverter came with a fag lighter plug, which we dismantled. This time, we took the live feed and earth from the same places as our amplifier (heavier leads).

02 Our inverter had to be in the boot, to be near the PS2 itself - but we didn't want to make a feature of it. There was a handy gap between our sub box and amp (which would later be covered over by a false floor), so we mounted our inverter onto the box. We struggled a bit for some kind of mounting bracket, but we managed to make one from a huge Jubilee clip . . .

03 . . . and there he is, wired-up and looking sweet. The Playstation now has power - what else do we need?

04 There's a whole bunch of wires to run down the car, so this is a good excuse to remove a seat or two and lift the carpets (if you want to do a neat job, that is). Besides the two controllers, there's the video/audio outputs to our screen to connect. Luckily, they're so well colour-coded, there's no danger of messing this up.

05 Just to ensure nothing goes wrong when those carpets go back down, tape up each connection. This stops them coming apart, and also stops the connectors earthing-out on the car floor.

06 With power and video leads connected, and a screen that's ready to go, choose a suitable secure spot for the console, and it's plug . . .

07 . . . and play. Our first-ever Playstation install, and it goes like a dream. Total cost, including screen, inverter and PS2 (with free game) - about £400. Now that's what we call a bargain - true in-car entertainment, and maximum respect.

Engines

Faster, faster!

So - does your car talk the talk (sounds fast), or does it walk the walk (actually is fast)? There's no shame in just having a fast-sounding car - not everyone can afford mega-performance, which is why bolt-on goodies like induction kits and big-bore exhausts are such big business. Serious engine tuning costs, and not just in the engine parts - your insurance company will throw a wobbly at a gas-flowed head, and might refuse to cover you altogether if you go for that Type R engine conversion.

The induction kit and sports exhaust are an essential first choice, and usually it's as far as you can really go before your insurance company disowns you. Both mods help the engine to 'breathe' better, which helps when you go for the accelerator initially, improving the response you feel, while you also get a crowd-pleasing induction roar and rasp from the back box, so everyone's happy.

Now for the harsh and painful truth. On their own, an induction kit and back box may not gain you much extra 'real' power. Sorry, but it's a myth. Time and again, people fit induction kits and back boxes, expecting huge power gains, and those 'in the know' have a quiet chuckle. All these things really do is make the car sound sportier, and improve the response - accept this, and you won't be disappointed. Ask yourself why most insurance companies don't generally increase premiums for the likes of a performance rear box or induction kit. The answer is - because (on their own) they don't make enough difference!

The 'bolt-on' performance goodies have more effect as part of an engine 'makeover' package, and setting-up the engine properly after fitting these parts can make a huge difference. If you're halfway serious about increasing the go of your Civic, talk to someone with access to a rolling road, so you can prove what's been done HAS actually made a useful gain. If you've spent time and a ton of money on your car, of course you're going to think it feels faster, but is it actually making more power?

Fitting all the performance goodies in the world will be pretty pointless if the engine's already knackered, but it might not be as bad as you think. One of the best ways to start on the performance road is simply to ensure that the car's serviced properly - new spark plugs, HT leads (also dizzy cap/rotor arm), and an oil and filter change, are a good basis to begin from. Correct any obvious faults, such as hoses or wiring plugs hanging off, and look for any obviously-damaged or leaking components, too.

Breathe with me...

Replacement element

One of the simplest items to fit, the replacement air filter element has been around for years - of course, now the induction kit's the thing to have, but a replacement element is more discreet (if you're worried about such things).

While we're at it, don't listen to your mates who tell you to simply take out the air filter completely - this is a really lame idea. The fuel system's air intake acts like a mini vacuum cleaner, sucking in air from the front of the car, and it doesn't just suck in air, but also dust, dirt and leaves. Without a filter, all this muck would quickly end up in the sensitive parts of the fuel system, and will quickly make the car undriveable. Worse, if any of it makes it into the engine, this will lead to engine wear. Remember too, that cheaper performance filters can be of very suspect quality - if your new filter disintegrates completely inside six months, it'll do wonders for the airflow, but it'll also be letting in all sorts of rubbish!

Some performance filters have to be oiled before fitting - follow the instructions provided; don't ignore this part, or the filter won't be effective. If the filter won't fit, check whether you actually have the right one - don't force it in, and don't cut it to fit, as either of these will result in gaps, which would allow unfiltered air to get in.

Pancake filter

If your Civic's 'only' got a carb, you may find there's no induction kit you can get for it. So how do you boost its performance, and get that induction kit roar under the bonnet?

The old-school answer is a 'pancake' filter, which, like an induction kit, does away with the old air cleaner, in favour of a sweet-looking filter unit which bolts straight to the top of the carb. Try K&N - look under 'custom assemblies' on their website.

Bum notes

One potential problem of fitting a filter like this is carb 'icing' in cold weather. Your old air cleaner had an automatic warm-air supply system built in, to combat the problem - chuck the air cleaner, and you lose the benefit. Carb icing is caused by water vapour freezing inside the carb, which leads to the engine losing power and maybe stalling in cold weather. Curing the problem's not easy - refitting the warm-air pipe from the exhaust manifold will help, but if you leave it on in hot weather, you'll get fuel vapourisation and pinking. Certain fuel additives might help to reduce icing, and could be the simplest answer.

Induction kit

Kits can be had for most Civics, especially if you widen your search to the American suppliers, you'll be amazed at the choice out there (remember, the street racing scene is huge in the US).

With an induction kit, the standard air filter housing and ducting are junked, and the new filter bolts directly to the airflow meter or throttle body. Most kits also feature special air inlet ducting (hoses) to feed the new filter with the coldest possible air from the front of the car - cold air is denser, and improves engine power. Many Jap/US companies now supply 'cold air pipes', which are phat chromed tubes, shaped to direct the cool air where it's needed - again, massive power gains are claimed (and they look totally trick, which no-one's disputing). Feeding the filter with cold air is in theory good for maximum performance with a hot engine or in hot weather, but in colder conditions with a cold engine, driveability and fuel economy might suffer.

The fuelling arrangements for fuel injection are based largely on the volume of incoming air. If you start feeding the injection system an unusually large amount of air (by fitting an induction kit, for instance), the management system will compensate by throwing in more fuel. This could result in some more power - or the car will drink petrol and your exhaust emissions will be screwed up, inviting an MOT failure. We're not saying 'don't do it', just remember that power gains can be exaggerated, and that there can be pitfalls.

What no-one disputes is that an induction kit, which operates without all the standard ducting, gives the engine a real throaty roar when you go for the loud pedal. So at least it sounds fast. Pop the hood, and it looks wicked. Jubbly.

01 This Civic's certainly got plenty of 'induction kit' as standard - like this resonator box, fitted in front of the main air cleaner. This bit just unclips. If you're interested, there's an even bigger resonator box under the front wing - all designed to reduce induction noise, the exact opposite of what we're trying to do.

02 To remove the air cleaner itself, pull off the rubber inlet hose at the back (it'll probably put up a fight) . . .

06 The last part of fitting the cone is to mount it somewhere solid. We were supplied a clip which you slip round the cone, and a bracket/bolt which attaches this clip to one of the old air cleaner box mounting holes. Clever stuff.

07 An essential part of fitting any induction kit is the cool-air feed pipe, to direct cold air right at the cone. Our kit gave us a length of flexi-hose, and a very cool alloy trumpet. So where can we run that lot? First, attach one to the other with a Jubilee clip.

03 . . . then unscrew the three bolts and lift out the complete box.

04 Our 'Viper' induction kit was supplied by Pipercross, and it's possible we didn't get quite the right one for our Civic. But never ones to give up easily, we carried on fitting - simply because the thing looks totally awesome. First, there's an extension sleeve to fit to the main (carbon fibre) cone, secured with a Jubilee clip.

05 We offered the cone and its new pipe onto the end of the rubber air inlet hose, and found it wouldn't fit inside the engine bay, so the next job was trimming the extension sleeve to length. Notice we used masking tape to mark on, and to stop the saw slipping.

Getting in cold air means mounting the trumpet end at the front of the car, away from the radiator, preferably right in the airflow as the car moves forward. Our new Wings West front bumper has some rather huge meshed holes in, ideal for our air intake needs. With the old bumper off, we drilled the front panel and fitted a small mounting bracket . . .

08

09 . . . then fixed our alloy trumpet to it. It's not a good idea to set this too low, especially if your Civic's going to be hugging the deck anyway - too much risk of sucking in flood water and small mammals.

10 Feed the other end of the flexi-hose back up into the engine . . .

11 . . . and attach it to the cone with another Jubilee.

>>

12 What we have here isn't just a cold-air pipe, it's a ram-effect. Sports bikes have been known to make an extra ten brake at the top end, through their pukka ram-effect systems. We like.

13 Offer up our new bumper, and you see what we're getting at. Spotted the trumpet? The mesh will even help keep the bugs out.

14 Even if you're stuck with the standard bumper for a bit, there's no need to miss out on the ram-air action. Just make yourself some tidy holes in your old plastic - our Coupe bumper's even got some ready-made slats, just gagging to be trimmed out with a hacksaw.

Finally...

Once you've fitted your new filter or induction kit, even if you don't take the car to a rolling road for setting up, at least take it to a garage and have the emissions checked - any minor adjustments should ensure that the engine will, if nothing else, still tick over okay, and should ensure an MOT emissions pass.

Other air filter-type mods

One old favourite, if you've got an injection Civic with a square filter box and haven't gone for an induction kit, is drilling holes in the air filter box. Only drill the air filter box below the level where the filter element sits, or the air going into the engine won't be filtered. Making your airbox look like a Swiss cheese won't make the car faster, but it does give you the nice throaty induction roar at full throttle. So, incidentally, will removing all the resonator boxes from the system (Step 1 in induction kits, and also in the front bumper fitting section).

Adjustable fuel
pressure regulator
(power boost valve)

Only available for Civics with multi-point injection (1.6 litre models and the 1.5 Coupe), these valves allow the fuel system pressure to be increased over the standard regulator valve. Contrary to what you might think, they don't actually provide much more fuel (this is regulated separately by the injection ECU).

The effect of increasing the injection pressure is to improve the injector spray pattern, which helps the fuel to burn more efficiently, and has the effect of increasing engine power while actually reducing emission levels.

To see the true effect of these valves, they must be set up using emission test gear and ideally a rolling road - merely turning the pressure up to the maximum level might not produce the desired effect. Fitting one of these valves involves breaking into the high-pressure fuel line, which is potentially dangerous for the inexperienced - also, if the valve is poorly fitted (or the fuel lines are in poor condition), you could end up with fuel spraying out under pressure onto a hot engine. Make sure you know what you're doing - anything involving petrol requires talent - and watch carefully for any sign of fuel leakage after fitting, even if this is done by a professional.

No quicker but it looks nice

Looks are just as important as performance. No hot hatch is 'finished' without making it look sweet. Details to the engine bay as well as your interior and exterior mods are an important factor, especially if you were thinking about getting your motor featured in top magazines. Every one does it, and you're next.

First up - try cleaning the engine, for flip's sake! How do you expect to emulate the show-stopping cars if your gearbox is covered in grot? Get busy with the degreaser (Gunk's a good bet), then get the hosepipe out. You can take it down to the local jetwash if you like, but remember your mobile - if you get carried away with the high-power spray, you might find the car won't start afterwards!

When it's all dry (and running again), you can start in. Get the polish to all the painted surfaces you reasonably can, and don't be afraid to unbolt a few of the simpler items to gain better access.

We're assuming you've already fitted your induction kit, but if not, these nicely do away with a load of ugly plastic airbox/air cleaner and trunking, and that rusted-out exhaust manifold cover, in favour of decent-looking product. Take off the rocker cover, and paint it to match your chosen scheme (heat-resistant paint is a must, really, such as brake caliper paint), set off with a funky oil filler cap. A strut brace is a tasty underbonnet feature, especially chromed. Braided hose covers (or coloured hose sets), ally battery covers and bottles, mirror panels - all give the underbonnet a touch of glamour.

Braided hoses

01 Unroll your braiding, check the length against your freshly-removed hose, and trim it roughly to length - you might need something heftier than scissors for this.

02 Now expand the braiding to the right size using a suitable blunt object. Like a screwdriver handle, we mean - what were you thinking of? Once the braiding's roughly the right size, you can slip your pipe in (lovely). Smooth out the braiding round the bends, as it tends to gather up and look naff otherwise, then trim up the ends.

03 Slide a new Jubilee clip over the braiding at one end, then slip one of the coloured end fittings over the clip. Repeat this process at the other end of your chosen hose, and it'll be ready to fit back on. When you're sure the hose is fully onto its fitting, tighten the hose clip securely to avoid embarrassing leakage.

You's a hose

There are many ways to add detail and colour to otherwise boring components. Spraying your hoses is just one of those ways. Only apply paint that is suitable for engine bay use, as temperatures get very high under the hood. The good folk from ABC Design supplied our MHW Tube-It paint.

01

Choose the most visible hoses first, and be careful undoing the hose clips - there could be coolant or fuel in there. Don't even think about spraying the hoses in place - do you really want to colour-code the entire underbonnet area? Give the pipe a good clean to thoroughly degrease it - any oil or silicone-slippery stuff, and the paint won't stick.

02

Achtung!

The engine must be completely cold before you start. Even if you've only done a quick lap, it would be dangerous to attempt doing anything with a remotely warm engine, as the fluids inside the pipe are often a lot hotter than they appear. Be warned!

03 A preferred way of spraying, to ensure maximum coverage, is to hang the pipe from above. Use a stiff piece of wire inserted into the end of the hose (NOT poked through the hose) to hold onto.

04 Apply the paint in three or four light layers until pipe is evenly covered. You'll also have to wait a while (ideally, leave overnight) before that hose can go back on.

05 Given enough time to dry, this hose paint's really good stuff - doesn't crack or flake off. But we wouldn't advise going ballistic with the pressure washer, once the hose is back on - the paint might not be quite that good.

06 Tighten all hose clips securely - coolant leaks are not cool, and fuel leaks could be deadly. If you've lost any coolant, the system will need topping-up once you're done - you'll want a 50-50 mix of antifreeze and water, not just plain water.

Coloured HT leads

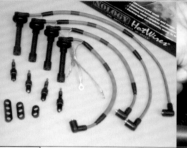

01 Brighten up the underbonnet, and maybe (if you believe what it says on the tin) make your car go better too? Gotta be worth a punt, to find out. First, make sure the ignition's off - take out the key, to be certain. Mark the old leads for position with tape, and work on one lead at a time here - pull one end off the spark plug . . .

02 . . . then trace it through and unclip from the distributor cap.

03 Lay the new leads out, and choose the lead closest in length to the one you've just pulled off. Always pays to check the leads look right, before you get too far in - and don't wreck the box they came in, when you open it up. Leads are often far too long, but this is easier than if they're too short. And there's only four leads on a Civic (no coil lead).

04 When you're happy with your choice of lead, give it a squirt of WD-40 inside to keep the damp out, then push it onto the plug - it should click positively into place. Run the lead across the engine, and onto the right location on the distributor - this is where you'll get confused if you don't do the leads one by one.

It's essential those leads are pinned in place and separated, both so they work properly, and to look their best, of course. The old clips fitted by Mr Honda ain't no good for our chunky new Nology leads, so they get unbolted . . .

05

. . . while we make up some new brackets (using corner brackets from the local DIY hypermarket) to mount on the new, heavier-duty lead separator clips.

06

Place the bottom half of the separator onto its new mounting bracket, then clamp the leads using the top half, and secure with the through-bolt and nut.

07

The leads came with very trick-looking earth braids - without these, the leads won't deliver the goods, so they must be connected to a good earth point. Those engine cover bolts will do, providing you remember to re-tighten them properly afterwards.

08

Silicon heaven

All Civics with fuel injection have an engine management system with a 'computer' at its heart, known as the ECU, or Electronic Control Unit. The ECU contains several computer chips, at least one of which has programmed onto it the preferred fuel/air mixture and ignition advance setting for any given engine speed or load - this information is known as a computer 'map', and the system refers to it constantly while the car's being driven. Obviously, with the current trend towards fuel economy and reducing harmful exhaust emissions, the values in this 'map' are set, well, conservatively, let's say (read 'boring'). With a little tweaking - like richening-up the mixture, say - the engine can be made to produce more power, or response will be improved, or both. At the expense of the environment. Oh well.

Companies like Superchips offer replacement computer chips which feature a computer map where driveability and performance are given priority over outright economy (although the company claims that, under certain conditions, even fuel economy can be better, with their products). While a chip like this does offer proven power gains on its own, it's obviously best to combine a chip with other enhancements, and to have the whole lot set up at the same time. By the time you've fitted an induction kit, four-branch manifold, big-bore pipe, and maybe even a fast-road cam, adding a chip is the icing on the cake - chipping an already-modified motor will liberate even more horses, or at least combine it with

majorly-improved response. Honda tuning specialists are best placed to advise you on the most effective tuning mods.

Another feature programmed into the ECU is a rev limiter, which cuts the ignition (or fuel) progressively when the pre-set rev limit is reached. Most replacement chips have the rev limiter reset higher, or removed altogether. Not totally sure this is a good thing - if the engine's not maintained properly (low oil level, cambelt changes neglected), removing the rev limiter and running beyond the red line would be a quick way to kill it. But a well-maintained engine with rally cam(s) fitted could rev off the clock, if the ECU would let it, so maybe not a bad thing after all…

Now the bad news

Chipping is often thought of as an easy, 'no-tell' route to increased performance and driveability - after all, the ECU is well-buried inside the car, not on show under the bonnet, so who's gonna know? Needless to say, the insurance companies have been wise to this trick for a long time. A sure way to tell whether any 'performance' product does what it says on the tin is to see what it'll do to your premium - telling them you're fitting a sports ROM chip will cost. Big-time. But, in the event of a claim, if they suspect your car's been 'chipped', rest assured, they will make efforts to find out, because if you haven't told them about it, it means they save on paying out. What's an insurance assessor's salary for one day, compared to the thousands you could be claiming in case of an accident or theft? Do it by all means, but at least be honest.

Engine tuning

So you've done the filter/induction kit and exhaust box - what's next, short of going for a complete engine swap?

If you've got a sports back box, try a performance exhaust manifold up front - or better still, a full 'cat-back' system for the best gains. Your Civic is, of course, being strangled all the time you're driving. By a cat - how embarrassing is that? There's the option of a de-cat pipe, which does away with the power-sapping catalytic converter at a stroke, freeing-up as many as 10 or 15 Honda horses on the way (but remember the car's not MOT-able with one of these fitted, so isn't strictly legal for use on the road).

A new camshaft's often a juicy way to pep up a standard motor, but the standard Civic cams are pretty good, so unless yours is/are knackered, all you'll achieve is moving the power further up the rev range. But - treat your Civic to a skimmed, gas-flowed, big-valve cylinder head (and a fast road cam or two) and it'll really start to percolate.

VTEC controllers

Power's nothing without control. For those of you fortunate enough (or minted enough) to own a VTEC machine, we don't need to tell you how great it feels when the VTEC kicks in at 5500 rpm. But how would you like that same kick at 4000 revs? With a VTEC controller, the theory is you can set the VTEC point wherever you like (the system is electronically-controlled, after all).

The reality seems to be that there's only a small-ish 'window' the VTEC system works best in. The standard car had its ignition timing, cam timing and air/fuel mapping set to work with the standard switch point, so a controller alone won't give you the best gains. But it's fun to play with, and not too pricey. To get the best from a controller, you'd need to heavily mod the rest of the engine (head, valves, cams, chip).

Engine **swaps**

Most young Civic owners wait 'til they've built up some no-claims bonus on their insurance, and go for a bigger Honda engine. Owning any Honda engine is no reason for embarrassment, and why throw shedloads of cash modding a weenie Honda engine, when the same money spent on fitting a new motor buys you monster power? The one everyone wants, and offering serious performance gains over a basic 1.3 or 1.5 lump, is the 1.6 twin-cam B16A engine from the Civic VTi. And that's a standard engine, remember - tune one of these, and your front tyres won't last a week!

If you're gonna change an engine, though, why not make it worthwhile, and get 2.0 litres of Accord/Prelude/Civic Type R power under your bonnet? Not quite such an easy DIY proposition, some 'modification' of the engine bay's needed, as well as custom-made driveshafts - check the internet forums for advice before diving into this kind of project.

And finally tonight - the bad news. Any major engine mods means telling those nice suits who work for your insurance company, and it's likely they'll insist on a full engineer's report (these aren't especially expensive - look one up in the Yellow Pages, under *Garage Services* or *Vehicle Inspection*).

Exhausts

It's gotta be done, hasn't it? Your rusty old exhaust lacks the girth to impress, and doesn't so much growl as miaow. Don't be a wimp and fit an exhaust trim - they'll fool nobody who really knows, and they certainly won't add to your aural pleasure (oo-er). Sort yourself out a decent back box upgrade, and even a timid 1.3 Civic can begin to cut it at the cruise.

What a back box won't do on its own is increase engine power - although it'll certainly sound like it has, provided you choose the right one, and fit it properly. Check when you're buying that it can be fitted to a standard system - you'll probably need something called a reducing sleeve for a decent fit, which is a section of pipe designed to bridge the difference between your small-diameter pipe and the larger-diameter silencer. Try and measure your standard pipe as accurately as possible, or you'll have major problems trying to get a decent seal between the old and new bits - don't assume that exhaust paste will sort everything out, because it won't.

Fashion has even entered the aftermarket exhaust scene, with different rear pipe designs going in and out of style. Everyone's done the upswept twin-pipe 'DTM' style pipes, while currently the trend in single pipes is massive Jap-style round exits, or fat oval (or twin-oval) designs. If you must have the phattest Civic on the block,

Know your enemy - this is what your cat looks like inside. Is it any wonder they restrict gas flow?

you can't beat a twin-exit system (from someone like Powerflow), even though it'll probably mean losing your spare wheel in the fitting process. Well, when was the last time you had a puncture? And what are mobiles and breakdown cover for, anyway?

If you've got a capacity-challenged Civic, you might need to lightly modify even your standard rear bodywork/bumper to accommodate a bigger rear pipe; if you're going for a bodykit later, your back box will have to come off again, so it can be poked through your rear valance/mesh.

You'll see some useful power gains if you go for the complete performance exhaust system, rather than just the back box. Like the factory-fit system, the sports silencer again will only work at its best if combined with the front pipe and manifold it was designed for! Performance four-branch manifolds alone can give very useful power gains. Watch what you buy, though - cheap exhaust manifolds which crack for a pastime are not unknown, and many aftermarket systems need careful fitting and fettling before you'll stop it resonating or banging away underneath. A sports rear box alone shouldn't attract an increased insurance premium, but a full system probably will.

All Civics are lumbered with a catalytic converter (or 'cat'), which acts like a restrictor in the exhaust, inhibiting the gas flow and sapping some engine power (maybe 5 to 10%). Various specialist exhaust companies market replacement sections which do away with the cat (a 'de-cat pipe'), and get you your power back. Unfortunately, by taking off or disabling the cat, your car won't be able to pass the emissions test at MOT time, so you'll have to 're-convert' the car every 12 months. This fact, arguably, means that the car is illegal on the road with a de-cat pipe fitted - you'd have no defence for this, if questions were asked at the roadside, and potentially no insurance if the unthinkable happens. Sorry, but we have to say it…

One other point to consider, if your Civic's been slammed to the floor - will your big new sports system be leaving behind a trail of sparks as it scrapes along the deck? Shouldn't do, if it's been properly fitted, but will the local multi-storey be out-of-bounds for your Civic, from now on? And - pub trivia moment - you can actually be done for causing damage to the highway, if your exhaust's dragging. Well, great.

You probably couldn't give a stuff if your loud system's a very loud major public nuisance, but will that loud pipe start interfering with your sound system? If you rack up many motorway miles, you might find the constant drone of a loud pipe gets to be a real pain on a long trip, too…

Fitting a twin-exit system

There are loads of manufacturers that supply ready-to-fit back boxes, cat by-passes to full exhaust systems. But what if you want something with a custom feel, perhaps different tail pipes or relocated exits? If you do, then Powerflow have the answer! We popped down to our local dealers, Sargents of Yeovil, to find out more about the seemingly-endless possibilities for creating that custom exhaust. Speak to Mike at Sargents to find out more about exhausts as well as the other car goodies they stock, or visit their website. We chose a very sexy twin, twin exit cat-back system in stainless steel with carbon fibre tips – nice.

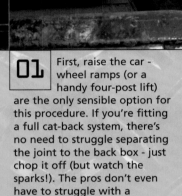
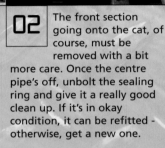

01 First, raise the car - wheel ramps (or a handy four-post lift) are the only sensible option for this procedure. If you're fitting a full cat-back system, there's no need to struggle separating the joint to the back box - just chop it off (but watch the sparks!). The pros don't even have to struggle with a hacksaw - easy life.

02 The front section going onto the cat, of course, must be removed with a bit more care. Once the centre pipe's off, unbolt the sealing ring and give it a really good clean up. If it's in okay condition, it can be refitted - otherwise, get a new one.

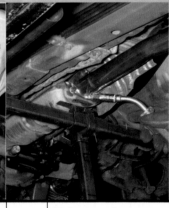

03 Now starts the fun part. Firstly, a length of phat stainless steel tube was cut to size (the same length as the centre section of the existing exhaust pipe) . . .

04 . . . and taken over to this wicked bending machine, where after much time and careful twisting of pipe, we find ourselves with a carbon-copy of the original centre pipe. These guys are so experienced they do it by sight, which is really clever because it has to be identical – nice one lads!

05 Chop off the existing mounting flange, and weld the old flange onto the new section of pipe.

06 Make sure the new centre pipe fits into the floor pan and then weld into position, remembering to support the other end of the pipe - which, until the back boxes are on, will hang down.

07 Then select a suitable back box. Obviously, the smaller the silencer box, the louder the sound – that's right mate – nice and small please!

08 Next, weld your chosen tips to the back box, wrapping the tips up to protect them from weld sparks.

09 We now come to the tricky job of cutting recesses into each side of the rear bumper to fit the new exhaust tips. This takes lots of time, measuring and patience to get it right.

10 When the exhaust is positioned correctly, a Y-sleeve is added to the end of the centre pipe and welded into place. The first of the two back boxes is then welded into place.

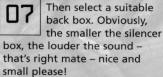

11 In the same way as before, another length of pipe is cut and bent to feed across to the opposite side of the car, where the other back box will sit.

12 After the bumper has been correctly cut to incorporate the second back box and everything is aligned, the second can then be welded into place.

13 The full system is then supported in place whilst brackets are made to hold the boxes firmly in place. The final job of checking that the measurements are all ok is done now, so that any adjustment needed can be done.

14 The exhaust brackets are then tightened and all seals checked to ensure everything's welded properly. The very last thing to be done is a quick coat of black heat-resistant paint to the flat edges of both back boxes, and the pipe joining them. This means they won't be seen from behind, and creates a much neater finish. Hey presto – one very sexy custom-fit exhaust. And does it ever bark!

14 Safety and tools

Safety

We all know that working on your car can be dangerous - and we're not talking about the danger of losing your street cred by fitting naff alloys or furry dice! Okay, so you'd be hard-pushed to injure yourself fitting some cool floor mats or a tax disc holder, but tackle more-serious mods, and you could be treading dangerous ground. Let's be honest - we have to put this safety section in to cover ourselves, but now it's in, it would be nice if you read it...

Burning/scalding

The only way you'll really burn yourself is if your car's just been running - avoid this, and you won't get burned. Easy, eh? Otherwise, you risk burns from any hot parts of the engine (and especially the exhaust - if you've got one, the cat runs very hot), or from spilling hot coolant if you undo the radiator hoses or filler cap, as you might when you're braiding hoses.

Fire

Sadly, there's several ways your car could catch fire, when you think about it. You've got a big tank full of fuel (and other flammable liquids about, like brake fluid), together with electrics - some of which run to very high voltages. If you smoke too, this could be even worse for your health than you thought.

a Liquid fuel is flammable. Fuel vapour can explode - don't smoke, or create any kind of spark, if there's fuel vapour (fuel smell) about.

b Letting fuel spill onto a hot engine is dangerous, but brake fluid spills go up even more readily. Respect is due with brake fluid, which also attacks paintwork and plastics - wash off with water.

c Fires can also be started by careless modding involving the electrical system. It's possible to overload (and overheat) existing wiring by tapping off too many times for new live feeds. Not insulating bare wires or connections can lead to short-circuits, and the sparks or overheated wiring which results can start a fire. Always investigate any newly-wired-in kit which stops working, or which keeps blowing fuses - those wires could already be smouldering…

Crushing

Having your car land on top of you is no laughing matter, and it's a nasty accident waiting to happen if you risk using dodgy old jacks, bricks, and other means of lifting/supporting your car. Please don't.

Your standard vehicle jack is for emergency roadside use only - a proper trolley jack and a set of axle stands won't break the overdraft, and might save broken bones. Don't buy a cheap trolley jack, and don't expect a well-used secondhand one to be perfect, either - when the hydraulic seals start to fail, a trolley jack will drop very fast; this is why you should always have decent stands in place under the car as well.

Steering, suspension & brakes

Screwing up any one of these on your car, through badly-fitted mods, could land you and others in hospital or worse. Nuff said? It's always worth getting a mate, or a friendly garage, to check over what you've just fitted (or even what you've just had fitted, in some cases - not all "pro" fitters are perfect!). Pay attention to tightening vital nuts and bolts properly - buy or borrow a torque wrench.

To be absolutely sure, take your newly-modded machine to a friendly MOT tester (if there is such a thing) - this man's your ultimate authority on safety, after all. Even if he's normally a pain once a year, he could save your life. Think it over.

Even properly-fitted mods can radically alter the car's handling - and not always for the better. Take a few days getting used to how the car feels before showing off.

Wheels

Don't take liberties fitting wheels. Make sure the wheels have the right stud/bolt hole pattern for your car, and that the wheel nuts/bolts are doing their job. Bolts which are too long might catch on your brakes (especially rear drums) - too short, and, well, the wheels are just waiting to fall off. Not nice. Also pay attention to the bolt heads or wheel nuts - some are supposed to have large tapered washers fitted, to locate properly in the wheel. If the nuts/bolts "pull through" the wheel when tightened, the wheel's gonna fall off, isn't it?

Asbestos

Only likely to be a major worry when working on, or near, your brakes. That black dust that gets all over your alloys comes from your brake pads, and it may contain asbestos. Breathing in asbestos dust can lead to a disease called asbestosis (inflammation of the lungs - very nasty indeed), so try not to inhale brake dust when you're changing your pads or discs.

Airbags

Unless you run into something at high speed, the only time an airbag will enter your life is when you change your steering wheel for something more sexy, and have to disable the airbag in the process. Pay attention to all the precautionary advice given in our text, and you'll have no problems.

One more thing - don't tap into the airbag wiring to run any extra electrical kit. Any mods to the airbag circuit could set it off unexpectedly.

Exhaust gases

Even on cars with cats, exhaust fumes are still potentially lethal. Don't work in an unventilated garage with the engine running. When fitting new exhaust bits, be sure that there's no gas leakage from the joints. When modifying in the tailgate area, note that exhaust gas can get sucked into the car through badly-fitting tailgate seals/joints (or even through your rear arches, if they've been trimmed so much there's holes into the car).

Tools

In writing this book, we've assumed you already have a selection of basic tools - screwdrivers, socket set, spanners, hammer, sharp knife, power drill. Any unusual extra tools you might need are mentioned in the relevant text. Torx and Allen screws are often found on trim panels, so a set of keys of each type is a wise purchase.

From a safety angle, always buy the best tools you can afford - or if you must use cheap ones, remember that they can break under stress or unusual usage (and we've all got the busted screwdrivers to prove it!).

DO Wear goggles when using power tools.

DO Keep loose clothing/long hair away from moving engine parts.

DO Take off watches and jewellery when working on electrics.

DO Keep the work area tidy - stops accidents and losing parts.

DON'T Rush a job, or take stupid short-cuts.

DON'T Use the wrong tools for the job, or ones which don't fit.

DON'T Let kids or pets play around your car when you're working.

DON'T Work entirely alone under a car that's been jacked up.

Legal modding?
No such thing!!

The harsh & painful truth

The minute you start down the road to a modified motor, you stand a good chance of being in trouble with the Man. It seems like there's almost nothing worthwhile you can do to your car, without breaking some sort of law. So the answer's not to do it at all, then? Well, no, but let's keep it real.

There's this bunch of vehicle-related regulations called Construction & Use. It's a huge set of books, used by the car manufacturers and the Department of Transport among others, and it sets out in black and white all the legal issues that could land you in trouble. It's the ultimate authority for modifying, in theory. But few people (and even fewer policemen) know all of it inside-out, and it's forever being updated and revised, so it's not often enforced to the letter at the roadside - just in court. Despite the existence of C & U, in trying to put together any guide to the law and modifying, it quickly becomes clear that almost everything's a "grey area", with no-one prepared to go on record and say what is okay to modify and what's not. Well, brilliant. So if there's no fixed rules (in the real world), how are you meant to live by them? In the circumstances, all we can promise to do is help to make sense of nonsense…

Avoiding roadside interviews

Why do some people get pulled all the time, and others hardly ever? It's often all about attitude. We'd all like to be free to drive around "in yer face", windows down, system full up, loud exhaust bellowing, sparks striking, tyres squealing - but - nothing is a bigger "come-on" to the boys in blue than "irresponsible" driving like this. Rest assured, if your motor's anywhere near fully sorted, the coppers will find something they can nick you for, when they pull you over - it's a dead cert. Trying not to wind them up too much before this happens (and certainly not once you're stopped) will make for an easier life. There's showing off, and then there's taking the pee. Save it for the next cruise.

The worst thing from your point of view is that, once you've been stopped, it's down to that particular copper's judgement as to whether your car's illegal. If he/she's having a bad day anyway, smart-mouthing-off isn't gonna help your case at all. If you can persuade him/her that you're at least taking on board what's being said, you might be let off with a warning. If it goes further, you'll be reported for an offence - while this doesn't mean you'll end up being prosecuted for it, it ain't good. Some defects (like worn tyres) will result in a so-called "seven-day wonder", which usually means you have to fix whatever's deemed wrong, maybe get the car inspected, and present yourself with the proof at a police station, inside seven days, or face prosecution.

If you can manage to drive reasonably sensibly when the law's about, and can ideally show that you've tried to keep your car legal when you get questioned, you stand a much better chance of enjoying your relationship with your modded beast. This guide is intended to help you steer clear of the more obvious things you could get pulled for. By reading it, you might even be able to have an informed, well-mannered discussion about things legal with the next officer of the law you meet at the side of the road. As in: "Oh really, officer? I was not aware of that. Thank you for pointing it out." Just don't argue with them, that's all…

Documents

The first thing you'll be asked to produce. If you're driving around without tax, MOT or insurance, we might as well stop now, as you won't be doing much more driving of anything after just one pull.

Okay, so you don't normally carry all your car-related documents with you - for safety, you've got them stashed carefully at home, haven't you? But carrying photocopies of your licence, MOT and insurance certificate is a good idea. While they're not legally-binding absolute proof, producing these in a roadside check might mean you don't have to produce the real things at a copshop later in the week. Shows a certain responsibility, and confidence in your own legality on the road, too. In some parts of the country, it's even said to be a good idea to carry copies of any receipts for your stereo gear - if there's any suspicion about it being stolen (surely not), some coppers have been known to confiscate it (or the car it's in) on the spot!

Number plates

One of the simplest mods, and one of the easiest to spot (and prove) if you're a copper. Nowadays, any changes made to the standard approved character font (such as italics or fancy type), spacing, or size of the plate constitutes an offence. Remember too that if you've moved the rear plate from its original spot (like from the tailgate recess, during smoothing) it still has to be properly lit at night. You're unlikely to even buy an illegal plate now, as the companies making them are also liable for prosecution if you get stopped. It's all just something else to blame on speed cameras - plates have to be easy for them to shoot, and modding yours suggests you're trying to escape a speeding conviction (well, who isn't?).

Getting pulled for an illegal plate is for suckers - you're making it too easy for them. While this offence only entails a small fine and confiscation of the plates, you're drawing unwelcome police attention to the rest of your car. Not smart. At all.

Sunstrips and tints

The sunstrip is now an essential item for any modded motor, but telling Mr Plod you had to fit one is no defence if you've gone a bit too far. The sunstrip should not be so low down the screen that it interferes with your ability to see out. Is this obvious? Apparently not. As a guide, if the strip's so low your wiper(s) touch it, it's too low. Don't try fitting short wiper blades to get round this - the police aren't as stupid as that, and you could get done for wipers that don't clear a sufficient area of the screen. Push it so far, and no further!

Window tinting is a trickier area. It seems you can have up to a 25% tint on a windscreen, and up to 30% on all other glass - but how do you measure this? Er. And what do you do if your glass is tinted to start with? Er, probably nothing. Of course you can buy window film in various "darknesses", from not-very-dark to "ambulance-black", but being able to buy it does not make it legal for road use (most companies cover themselves by saying "for show use only"). Go for just a light smoke on the side and rear glass, and you'd have to be unlucky to get done for it. If you must fit really dark tints, you're safest doing the rear side windows only.

Some forces now have a light meter to test light transmission through glass at the roadside - fail this, and it's a big on-the-spot fine.

Single wiper conversion

Not usually a problem, and certainly not worth a pull on its own, but combine a big sunstrip with a short wiper blade, and you're just asking for trouble. Insufficient view of the road ahead. There's also the question of whether it's legal to have the arm parking vertically, in the centre of the screen, as it obscures your vision. Probably not legal, then - even if it looks cool. Unfortunately, the Man doesn't do cool.

Lights

Lights of all kinds have to be one of the single biggest problem areas in modifying, and the police are depressingly well-informed. Most people make light mods a priority, whether it's Morette conversions for headlights or Lexus-style rear clusters. If they fit alright, and work, what's the problem?

First off, don't bother with any lights which aren't fully UK-legal - it's just too much hassle. Being "E-marked" only makes them legal in Europe, and most of our Euro-chums drive on the right. One of our project cars ended up with left-hand-drive rear clusters, and as a result, had no rear reflectors and a rear foglight on the wrong side (should be on the right). Getting stopped for not having rear reflectors would be a bit harsh, but why risk it, even to save a few quid?

Once you've had any headlight mods done (other than light brows) always have the beam alignment checked - it's part of the MOT, after all. The same applies to any front fogs or spots you've fitted (the various points of law involved here are too many to mention - light colour, height, spacing, operation with main/dipped headlights - ask at an MOT centre before fitting, and have them checked out after fitting).

If Plod's really having a bad day, he might even question the legality of your new blue headlight bulbs - are they too powerful? Keeping the bulb packaging in the glovebox might be a neat solution here (60/55W max).

Many modders favour spraying rear light clusters to make them look trick, as opposed to replacing them - but there's trouble in store here, too. One of the greyest of grey areas is - how much light tinting is too much? The much-talked-about but not-often-seen "common sense" comes into play here. Making your lights so dim that they're reduced to a feeble red/orange glow is pretty dim itself. If you're spraying, only use proper light-tinting spray, and not too many coats of that. Colour-coding lights with ordinary spray paint is best left to a pro sprayer or bodyshop (it can be done by mixing lots of lacquer with not much paint, for instance). Tinted lights are actually more of a problem in daylight than at night, so check yours while the sun's out.

Lastly, two words about neons. Oh, dear. It seems that neons of all kinds have now been deemed illegal for road use (and that's

interior ones as well as exteriors, which have pretty much always been a no-no). If you fit neons inside, make sure you rig in a switch so you can easily turn them off when the law arrives - or don't drive around with them on (save it for when you're parked up). Distracts other road users, apparently.

ICE

Jungle massive, or massive public nuisance? The two sides of the ICE argument in a nutshell. If you've been around the modding scene for any length of time, you'll already know stories of people who've been done for playing car stereos too loud. Seems some local authorities now have by-laws concerning "music audible from outside a vehicle", and hefty fines if you're caught. Even where this isn't the case, and assuming a dB meter isn't on hand to prove the offence of "excessive noise", the police can still prosecute for "disturbing the peace" - on the basis of one officer's judgement of the noise level. If a case is proved, you could lose your gear. Whoops. Seems we're back to "do it - but don't over-do it" again. If you really want to demo your system, pick somewhere a bit less public (like a quiet trading estate, after dark) or go for safety in numbers (at a cruise).

Big alloys/tyres

One of the first things to go on any lad's car, sexy alloys are right at the heart of car modifying. So what'll interest the law?

Well, the first thing every copper's going to wonder is - are the wheels nicked? He'd need a good reason to accuse you, but this is another instance where having copies of receipts might prove useful.

Otherwise, the wheels mustn't rub on, or stick out from, the arches - either of these will prove to be a problem if you get stopped. And you don't need to drive a modded motor to get done for having bald tyres…

Lowered suspension

Of course you have to lower your car, to have any hope of street cred. But did you know it's actually an offence to cause damage to the road surface, if your car's so low (or your mates so lardy) that it grounds out? Apparently so! Never mind what damage it might be doing to your exhaust, or the brake/fuel lines under the car - you can actually get done for risking damage to the road. Well, great. What's the answer? Once you've lowered the car, load it up with your biggest mates, and test it over roads you normally use - or else find a route into town that avoids all speed bumps. If you've got coilovers, you'll have an easier time tuning out the scraping noises.

Remember that your new big-bore exhaust or backbox must be hung up well enough that it doesn't hit the deck, even if you haven't absolutely slammed your car on the floor. At night, leaving a trail of sparks behind is a bit of a giveaway…

Exhausts

One of the easiest-to-fit performance upgrades, and another essential item if you want to be taken seriously on the street. Unless your chosen pipe/system is just too damn loud, you'd be very unlucky to get stopped for it, but if you will draw attention this way, you could be kicking yourself later.

For instance - have you in fact fitted a home-made straight-through pipe, to a car which used to have a "cat"? By drawing Plod's attention with that extra-loud system, he could then ask you to get the car's emissions tested - worse, you could get pulled for a "random" roadside emissions check. Fail this (and you surely will), and you could be right in the brown stuff. Even if you re-convert the car back to stock for the MOT, you'll be illegal on the road (and therefore without insurance) whenever your loud pipe's on. Still sound like fun, or would you be happier with just a back box?

It's also worth mentioning that your tailpipe mustn't stick out beyond the very back of the car, or in any other way which might be dangerous to pedestrians. Come on - you were a ped once!

Bodykits

The popular bodykits for the UK market have all passed the relevant tests, and are fully-approved for use on the specific vehicles they're intended for. As long as you haven't messed up fitting a standard kit, you should be fine, legally-speaking. The trouble starts when you do your own little mods and tweaks, such as bodging on that huge whale-tail spoiler or front air dam/splitter - it can be argued in some cases that these aren't appropriate on safety grounds, and you can get prosecuted. If any bodywork is fitted so it obscured your lights, or so badly attached that a strong breeze might blow it off, you can see their point. At least there's no such thing as Style Police. Not yet, anyway.

Seats and harnesses

Have to meet the UK safety standards, and must be securely bolted in. That's about it. It should be possible to fasten and release any seat belt or harness with one hand. Given that seat belts are pretty important safety features, it's understandable then that the police don't like to see flimsy alloy rear strut braces used as seat harness mounting points. Any other signs of bodging will also spell trouble. It's unlikely they'd bother with a full safety inspection at the roadside, but they could insist on a full MOT test/engineer's report inside 7 days. It's your life.

While we're on the subject of crash safety, the police also don't like to see sub boxes and amps just lying on the carpet, where the back seat used to be - if it's not anchored down, where are these items gonna end up, in a big shunt? Embedded in you, possibly?

Other mods

We'll never cover everything else here, and the law's always changing anyway, so we're fighting a losing battle in a book like this, but here goes with some other legalistic points we've noted on the way:

a It's illegal to remove side repeaters from front wings, even to create the ultimate smoothed/flushed motor. Sorry.

b All except the most prehistoric cars must have at least one rear foglight. If there's only one, it must be fitted on the right. We've never heard of anyone getting stopped for it, but you must also have a pair of rear reflectors. If your rear clusters ain't got 'em, can you get trendy ones? Er, no.

c Fuel filler caps have to be fitted so there's no danger of fuel spillage, or of excess fumes leaking from the top of the filler neck. This means using an appropriate petrol-resistant sealer (should be supplied in the kit). Oh, and not bodging the job in general seems a good idea. Unlikely to attract a pull, though.

d Front doors have to retain a manual means of opening from outside, even if they've been de-locked for remote locking. This means you can't take off the front door handles, usually. It seems that rear door handles can be removed if you like.

e Tailgates have to have some means of opening, even if it's only from inside, once the lock/handle's been removed. We think it's another safety thing - means of escape in a crash, and all that.

f You have to have at least one exterior mirror, and it must be capable of being adjusted somehow.

g If you fit new fog and spotlights, they actually have to work. No-one fits new lights just for show (or do they?), but if they stop working later when a fuse blows, relay packs up, or the wiring connectors rust up, you'd better fix 'em or remove 'em.

h Pedal extensions must have rubbers fitted on the brake and clutch pedals, and must be spaced sufficiently so there's no chance of hitting two pedals at once. This last bit sounds obvious, but lots of extension sets out there are so hard to fit that achieving this can be rather difficult. Don't get caught out.

i On cars with airbags, if you fit a sports wheel and disconnect the airbag in the process, the airbag warning light will be on permanently. Apart from being annoying, this is also illegal.

j Pace-car strobe lights (or any other flashing lights, apart from indicators) are illegal for road use. Of course.

k Anything else we didn't think of - is probably illegal too. Sorry.

Any questions? Try the MOT Helpline (0845 6005977). Yes, really.

Thanks to Andrew Dare of the Vehicle Inspectorate, Exeter, for his help in steering us through this minefield!

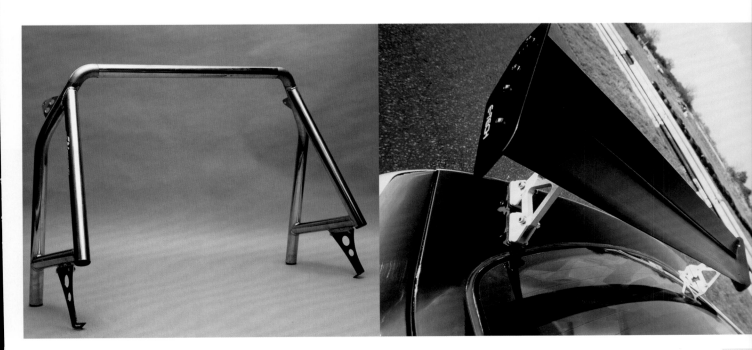

Thanks to:

We gratefully acknowledge all the help and advice offered from the following suppliers, without whom, etc, etc. Many of those credited below went way beyond the call of duty to help us produce this book - you know who you are. Cheers, guys! Roll the credits...

ABC Design Autostyling Ltd (AutoArt & MHW)
www.abcdesignltd.com

Auto Inparts Ltd
01525 382713

Avon Custom Engineering
01934 876250
www.avoncustom.co.uk

Brown & Geeson
(Momo)
01268 764411
www.brownandgeeson.com

Cooper Avon Tyres
01225 703101
www.coopertire.com

Demon Tweeks
(accessories)
01978 664466
www.demon-tweeks.co.uk

Draper Tools
(tools)
023 8026 6355
www.draper.co.uk

Eibach UK
(B&M short shift kit)
01455 286524

Eurostyling
(Folia tec)
01908 324950
www.eurostyling.com

Halfords
08457 626 625

House of Kolor
(paint)
01302 341788
www.houseofkolor.com

Invo Auto Ltd
020 7607 1677
www.invoauto.co.uk

Motorsport International
(Wings West)
08702 412382
www.msionline.co.uk

Pipercross
(induction systems)
01604 494945
www.pipercross.com

L.A & R.W Piper
(car trimming)
01963 441431
www.trimmers.fsnet.co.uk

Red Dot Racing
(brake discs & pads)
020 8888 2354
www.reddotracing.co.uk

Richbrook
(sport auto accessories)
020 8543 7111
www.richbrook.co.uk

Ripspeed at Halfords
0845 609 1259

Sargents Performance Centre
(Powerflow exhaust systems)
01935 427554
www.philipsargent.co.uk

South Coast Wheels
023 8063 7972

SPAX
01869 244771
www.spaxperformance.com

Wolfrace Wheels (UK) Ltd
01621 843770
www.wolfrace.co.uk

A special thank you to:
Bryn Musselwhite

Editorial Director	Matthew Minter
Designer	Simon Larkin
Page Build	James Robertson
Workshop	Paul Buckland
	Pete Trott
Editor	Ian Barnes
Project Co-ordinator	Carole Turk
Production Control	Kevin Heals

Haynes Car Manuals

* = Classic Reprints

Haynes Manuals

Haynes Car Service and Repair Manuals are available from car accessory retailers.
For further information or to find your nearest stockist, call
01963 442030 or visit
www.haynes.co.uk